DATE DUE

~~06 3 04~~			
~~MY 12'00~~			

DEMCO 38-296

Winning the Peace:

America and World Order in the New Era

The Twentieth Century Fund sponsors and supervises timely analyses of economic policy, foreign affairs, and domestic political issues. Not-for-profit and nonpartisan, the Fund was founded in 1919 and endowed by Edward A. Filene.

Winning the Peace:
America and World Order in the New Era

John Gerard Ruggie

A TWENTIETH CENTURY FUND BOOK

Columbia University Press
NEW YORK

Columbia University Press

New York   Chichester, West Sussex

Publishers since 1893

Copyright © 1996 The Twentieth Century Fund

All rights reserved

Library of Congress Cataloging-in-Publication Data

Ruggie, John Gerard,

    Winning the peace : America and world order in the new era /
John Gerard Ruggie.

        p. cm.

    "A Twentieth Century Fund book."

    Includes bibliographical references and index.

    ISBN 0-231-10426-X

    1. United States—Foreign relations—1989– 2. United States—Foreign relations—
1945–1989. 3. World politics—1989– I. Title.E840.R78 1996

        327.73—dc20   96–7385

                                                                             CIP

Casebound editions of Columbia University Press books are printed on permanent and durable
acid-free paper.

Printed in the United States of America

c 10 9 8 7 6 5 4 3 2 1

For my son Andreas and his young friends everywhere;
they are the answer to What has the future done for us lately?

Contents

Foreword   *ix*

Preface   *xiii*

Introduction: Third Try at World Order?   *1*

1. An American Dilemma   7

2. The Postwar Compromises   28

3. Competitive Security   50

4. Cooperative Security   77

5. Economic Stabilization   107

6. Economic Transformation   135

7. Polarity, Plurality, and the Future   157

Notes   *175*

Index   *223*

Foreword

By historical standards, we have barely emerged from the cold war era and are beginning to move into the phase of awkward adjustment to new, developing realities. Students of international affairs, statesmen, and journalists still are wrestling with ways to understand and explain what global politics will encompass during the few years remaining of this century; most are far from ready to predict the architecture of relations among states in the next one. Among scholars, there is even considerable debate about how to describe the basics of the present situation: for example, does the current preponderance of American military force define a unipolar world, or, rather, does the rapid and vast economic growth of nations such as Japan and Germany indicate that we are at the beginning of a new multipolar balance of power? And in terms of diplomatic activity, the most fundamental uncertainty may concern the shape and significance of multilateral institutions.

Multilateralism, as a guiding principle of international relations, is a relatively recent development. Having germinated during the nineteenth century, it emerged full-blown in the aftermath of World War I with the establishment of the League of Nations. Then in the 1930s, it receded as economic nationalism and the growing hostility between the democracies and the totalitarian states held sway. Then it was born anew following World War II, with the United States leading the way. The cold war version of multilateralism, of course, was of a very special sort. Those international institutions that could not be used as vehicles for furthering the interests of the grand Western alliance against communism were often seen more as irritants than as building blocks of policy. And even today, with the Iron Curtain swept away, American policy and public opinion about multilateralism is often confused and inconsistent. One point in the so-called Contract with America, for example, prohibits the use of American forces in any venture not commanded overall by a U.S. military officer. And the United States remains more than $1 billion behind on its dues and other financial obligations to the United Nations.

John Gerard Ruggie, professor of political science at Columbia University and longtime analyst of international affairs, has spent the last several years thinking and writing about these central questions of foreign policy. Given the tumultuous events in the former Soviet Union and elsewhere during that time, it is a measure of Professor Ruggie's knowledge, experience, and surefootedness that he has been able to produce so cogent and provocative a work of scholarship.

The world will not wait for us to catch on to its new way of spinning. Policymakers must decide now about how to react to crises and how to avoid dangers. In this environment, the highest calling of the "expert" is to answer the need for relevant information and advice. The greatest virtue of Ruggie's book—and there are many—is that it will provide practical help to those who must shape America's response to the transformation of global politics. That accomplishment is especially gratifying to those of us at the Twentieth Century Fund. For our mission is to provide thoughtful work that is of real utility in public affairs.

Winning the Peace joins a substantial list of other recent Fund studies of foreign policy after the cold war, including Richard Ullman's *Securing Europe*, Jonathan Dean's *Ending Europe's Wars*, Rosemary Righter's *Utopia Lost*, and Tony Smith's *America's Mission*. During the next year or two, we also expect to publish Stephen Burg's look at nationalism—particularly the resurgence of ethnic conflicts—in post-cold war Europe; Michael Mandelbaum's study of NATO; David Calleo's examination of Europe's future; and Robert Art's analysis of America's future foreign policy strategies.

As Ruggie points out, the apparent overwhelming importance of economic affairs in international relations should not be seen as preempting all the other important components of national interest and the goals that should shape the course of diplomatic and national security affairs. His richly historic perspective helps to clarify the past, present, and possible future course of policy while elaborating on the complexity of democratic politics. Perhaps the greatest strength of this solid work of scholarship is its strong roots in the enduring realities of American policy: the fact that our actions abroad are never totally divorced from our perception of ourselves and our sense of our proper role in the world.

On behalf of the Trustees of the Twentieth Century Fund, I congratulate Professor Ruggie on his accomplishment.

Richard C. Leone, President
The Twentieth Century Fund
January 1996

Preface

This is the story of a great power that was historically reluctant to accept sustained involvement in the political and security affairs of the world, a country that finally assumed international leadership but only on the premise that it would change the traditional conduct of those affairs, which then undertook and won an epochal struggle vis-à-vis an adversary that was its mirror image, but was left, by that very victory, without anchor or compass. It is, in short, the story of America and world order in the twentieth century, with an eye toward how to continue a constructive relationship after the cold war, in the new era of global and domestic realignment. In contrast to most other such efforts, this study draws on the ideas and strategies for accomplishing that goal articulated by the last generation of American leaders before the cold war froze firmly in place and its rigidities became accepted routine.

I developed an interest in the subject of America and world order early in life. On a gray winter's day, at the age of seven if memory serves me correctly, I first encountered what was then the other superpower. This took place on a train journey from my hometown of Graz, Austria, to visit family friends in Vienna. The train stopped at the Semmering Pass, marking the perimeter of the Soviet occupation zone. Russian soldiers boarded to check documents. I recall their bulky uniforms, karakul hats, high boots and rifles slung over their shoulders. The adults around me became nervous, so I did too—a recurrent experience for years thereafter whenever I approached a frontier crossing.

A short while later I met the other superpower. It introduced itself with a knock on the door of our one-room cold-water flat. We found ourselves the unexpected but happy recipients of a package of provisions—with blue-stencilled outstretched hands and the letters "USA" on its wrapping. The package contained canned meat, flour, sugar, powdered milk, cocoa, an unidentified (and quickly discarded) substance that we learned only after the fact was powdered eggs—and Hershey bars. Some people follow the yellow brick road; I followed the Hershey bars. Eventually, they led me to the issues raised in this book.

A consistent theme that runs throughout this study is the relationship between interests and identity in the making of foreign policy. This is the subject of, at one and the same time, the oldest debate about America's role in the world—the question of American "exceptionalism"—and one of the newest concerns in the academic study of international affairs. Drawing on insights from the latter in the hope of illuminating the former, I conclude that who we are as a nation, and what we wish to become, has been and remains central to how we define our interests at home and abroad.

One of the (few) academic advantages of being a dean is that requests for comments on draft chapters (usually) elicit quick and helpful responses. I am immensely grateful to the following friends and colleagues who have made this a better book by doing so: Richard Betts, Jagdish Bhagwati, Richard Clarida, Sam Cross, Hans Decker, Merit Janow, Robert Jervis, Geir Lundestad, Edward Mansfield, Dani Rodrik, Tony Smith, Anders Stephanson, Steve Weber, Robert Wolfe, and Mark Zacher.

I want also to acknowledge my graduate school mentor, Ernst B. Haas, who first introduced me to the systematic study of international relations, and who has served ever since as a role model of imaginative yet rigorous scholarship. Robert Keohane has been a tough but supportive intellectual critic for a quarter century, and Branislav Gosovic for an equal duration has challenged my views on political grounds.

To my wife, Mary Ruggie, my date since high school, I owe, quite simply, everything.

I dedicate this book to our son, Andreas—skiing partner, scuba buddy, and constant source of joy, pride, and inspiration.

John Gerard Ruggie
Bronxville, New York
May 1996

Winning the Peace:
America and World Order in the New Era

Introduction: Third Try at World Order?

"**W**e have learned a terrible lesson," President Franklin D. Roosevelt mused in a radio address to the American people just two days after Japan's surprise attack on Pearl Harbor in December 1941. Reflecting on the public's isolationist sentiment during the interwar years, the president declared: "we cannot measure our safety in terms of miles on any map." Alluding to the Senate's rejection of U.S. membership in the League of Nations at the end of World War I, the president added: this time "we are going to win the war and we are going to win the peace that follows."[1] Winning the peace, Roosevelt believed, would require sustained American involvement to help create and maintain a stable international order. The State Department was instructed to proceed almost immediately with planning for a postwar United Nations—the name was Roosevelt's invention—and, along with Treasury, for the multilateral organization of postwar monetary and trade relations.

Not long after victory had been achieved in World War II, the cold war confrontation began. President Harry S Truman set a course that he believed would ultimately prevail, starting with the doctrine that bears his name—promising "to support free peoples who are resisting attempted subjugation by armed minorities or by outside pressures"—and including the Marshall Plan, North Atlantic Treaty Organization (NATO), and support for European unification; the Berlin airlift and defense of South Korea; the reconstruction of Japan and its integration into the liberal world economy.

"There will have to come a time of change in the Soviet world," Truman predicted confidently in his January 1953 farewell address to the nation. "Nobody can say for sure when that is going to be, or exactly how it will come about, whether by revolution, or trouble in the satellite states, or by a change inside the Kremlin. . . . With patience and courage, we shall some day move on into a new era."[2]

That new era is now. Today, America's leaders are called upon once again to refashion this nation's foreign policy for yet another postwar world, to try to win yet another postwar peace. But without the Soviet military threat and anticommunist ideological fervor as driving impulses, the policymaking community has become confused and deeply divided by disagreements about how best to frame the calculation of U.S. interests and about how most effectively to pursue them. Indeed, these disagreements echo debates about America's role in the world that have erupted previously on comparable occasions since the United States became a major power.

The first two post-cold war presidents, George Bush and Bill Clinton, articulated visions of the new era that may be characterized as broadly Wilsonian in rhetoric and aspiration.[3] President Bush heralded the promise of a "new world order," in which self-determination, cooperative deterrence and joint action against aggression would hold greater sway; President Clinton vowed to enlarge "the family of free-market democracies" and consolidate "the democratic peace." George Bush mobilized the United Nations to orchestrate a winning coalition in the Gulf War and to secure humanitarian relief for Somalia; the Clinton national security team came into office committed to "assertive multilateralism" through UN peacekeeping and peacemaking operations. In the economic realm, the Bush administration redoubled America's long-standing commitment to liberalizing international trade by launching the Uruguay Round of the General Agreement on Tariffs and Trade (GATT) as well as negotiations to create a North American Free Trade Agreement (NAFTA) with Canada and Mexico; the Clinton administration successfully concluded both and also led the transformation of GATT into the more comprehensive and potentially more robust World Trade Organization (WTO). Finally, by means of NATO's Partnership for Peace, the United States has sought to extend, in President Clinton's words, "the fabric of transatlantic prosperity and security" into Central and Eastern Europe, as well as parts of the former Soviet Union.[4]

By the mid-1990s, however, a very different orientation toward the post-cold war world had gained prominence, reminiscent not of Wilson but of his adversaries in 1919—and which the other side promptly portrayed as "the new isolationism."[5] Among the militia movement fringe of American politics the United Nations and the "new world order" loomed so large as to trigger fears of tyrannical world government. For presidential aspirants in the Republican primaries, attacks on the UN emerged as a visceral issue eliciting foot-stomping approval,[6] while the newly elected Republican Congressional majority adopted legislation intended to severely restrict U.S. participation in UN peace operations.[7] At the same time, Congressionally mandated budget cuts forced the State Department to shut down overseas posts even as the number of new countries increased, and the United States dropped to last place among all industrialized countries in its share of gross national product devoted to foreign aid.[8] Though more subtle in effect, the realignment between the public sector and the private, as well as between the federal government and the states, underway for some time but picking up rapid momentum after the 1994 midterm elections, seemed similarly to entail a diminished role for the United States government in related fields of world affairs, such as environmental protection, for example, or certain areas of social policy. Economic nationalism initially entered the electoral politics of the 1990s through organized labor's influence within the Democratic party; in 1992 it found additional expression in the populist third-party candidacy of Ross Perot; and by mid-decade Pat Buchanan had won for it representation in the conservative wing of the Republican party.[9] Lastly, the landslide victory of Proposition 187 in California, denying educational, health care, and social services to illegal immigrants, together with proposals to ban certain federal benefits to legal resident aliens, appeared to many observers to usher in a new wave of anti-immigrant nativism in American politics.

Yet a third orientation to the post-cold war world draws on the doctrine of *realpolitik* or power politics. Realism commands considerable attention among foreign-policy commentarors—more than is warranted, we shall have occasions to note, by its practical efficacy. The realist tradition in American foreign policy, exemplified in recent decades by Henry Kissinger, traces its ancestry back to Theodore Roosevelt who, at the turn of the century, worked indefatigably for the United States to assume the role of a great power.[10] Realists today stress the need for America to articulate a new set of interests that are deemed vital and sufficiently compelling to mobilize the country behind sustained foreign-policy efforts, an objective with which few would disagree. However, short of repelling external threats to the United States itself, realists appear to have a much easier time arguing persuasively that purported interests are *not* vital than they are affirming any.[11] In fact, Teddy Roosevelt had discovered as much back in 1914, when he urged, unsuccessfully, American military preparedness on balance-of-power grounds. "I have no influence whatever in shaping public action," he confessed to the British foreign secretary, "very little influence indeed in shaping public opinion."[12] And today Kissinger concludes, ruefully, that without the Soviet threat realism, by itself, does not suffice to frame U.S. foreign policy, that it must be coupled with an animating "vision," a sense of "hope and possibility that are, in their essence, conjectural"—and for which he, the master practitioner of the realist craft, now looks to the American "idealism" that he spent his career mocking.[13]

So where are we today? America's leaders after World War II provided a coherent answer to the question "of what the United States ought to be and ought to do" in the world.[14] How will the current generation respond? Will it go the way of 1945? Or 1919? For now, U.S. foreign policy seems adrift, lost in a fog of befuddlement, "buffeted by winds of emotion and twisted by media agendas and pressure groups."[15]

This book is intended to clarify one key architectural element in the foundational choices before us: the relationship between the United States and the multilateral world order and institutions it has helped to create. At three defining moments in this century, at the end of the two world wars and the cold war, this has emerged as a signal issue. Why? What is at stake? And do these prior experiences embody any lessons for the future?

Our first task is to clear up the rhetorical obfuscation that results from the use of such terms as "internationalism," "isolationism," and "idealism" in the current policy debate. None means quite what its protagonists claim. There are few outright isolationists in mainstream America today, and most political leaders claim the internationalist creed. Nevertheless, significant differences exist among various forms of internationalism and their consequences. Moreover, idealism is equally compatible with a robust military posture, as Ronald Reagan proved, and pacifism, as exemplified by interwar religiously based or socialist peace movements. Indeed, to this day no American president used force more often to meddle in the domestic affairs of other countries than Woodrow Wilson, everyone's archetype of liberal internationalist idealism. At best, therefore, the terms are imprecise and their predictive value indeterminate. Historically, the key difference, as we shall see in chapter 1, has been between policy preferences for an international order in which the United States seeks to institute and live by certain mildly communitarian organizing principles, and one in which it avoids entanglement in any serious institutionalized commitments. These positions are defined as "multilateralism" and "unilateralism," respectively. Contrary to frequently heard refrains, the multilateral impulse, on the whole, has not been based in idealism but in a geopolitical assessment that, given America's geographic isolation, size, wealth, power, and multi-ethnic make-up, unilateralism in practice would slip into and encourage isolationism. In contrast, the record of the 1930s suggests that a belief in the viability of unfettered unilateralism, which may have made sense before the United States emerged as a world power, ultimately came to rest on little more than wishful thinking.

Our second task is to better understand the world order designs of "the generation that changed America's role in the world"—David Fromkin's depiction of American leaders from FDR to Dwight Eisenhower.[16] Above all else, they sought to learn from Wilson's failure in 1919, and to avoid the horrendously costly consequences of American isolationism which followed in its wake. Like Wilson, they appreciated that balance-of-power-politics was an inadequate platform from which to launch and sustain American engagement in world affairs, and from Wilson, therefore, they inherited a reformist agenda for refashioning the international order. Unlike Wilson, however, they were well versed in power-political realities and not in the least averse to dealing with them. Combining the two strands, this remarkable group devised an ideational bridge between America's sense of exceptionalism, on the one hand, and, on the other, what Americans had traditionally regarded as the inferior international political machinations of the old world. In addition, they saw that extensive American commercial and cultural ties with the rest of the world in the interwar years had failed to compensate for lack of sustained political involvement, so they developed a political economy of statecraft in which those elements became mutually supportive. Along the way, they were obliged to battle not only the remnants of prewar isolationism but also postwar realists, who consistently viewed their reformist agenda, especially in security relations, to be both unnecessary and undesirable. An overview of their world order designs is presented in chapter 2, with greater detail about some of the institutional arrangements for security and economic relations in chapters 3 and 5, respectively.

Third, we want to examine the institutional legacy that this generation has left us. Clearly, winning the post-cold war peace requires a fundamental rethinking of the premises and modalities of U.S. foreign policy—and so, too, in the economic realm do the forces of globalization. But this effort cannot and should not proceed as though there were no prior history. In addition to, and in the process of, containing the Soviet Union the United States made extensive institutional investments to reshape the interna-

tional security order after World War II. Similarly, the United States created institutional arrangements to achieve the twin goals of domestic and
international economic stability. Are there still benefits to be had from
these investments? Is it not worth knowing which institutional arrangements still work, which don't, and why? Chapter 4 addresses those questions for the major postwar U.S. multilateral initiatives in security relations, and chapter 6 does the same for the organization of international
economic relations. A lurking danger in security affairs is that the recrudescence of realist unilateralism may lead us to miss opportunities that will
not come around again, while in economic affairs the revival of neo-
laissez-faire may cause us to ignore the fragile domestic basis of the international economic order.

Finally, what of the future? The core problem American leaders faced in
1919 and 1945 once again has become pressing: devising a coherent rationale to ensure continuous and active international engagement by the
United States in support of a stable international order. A la carte interest
calculations are unlikely to suffice, as Kissinger now agrees. But what are
the grander alternatives? Fears of a Russia gone mad? Threats posed by
rogue states? The clash of civilizations? The doctrine of enlargement? Jobs,
jobs, jobs? No overarching framework equivalent to the cold war is likely
to reappear in the foreseeable future, we conclude in chapter 7, and
attempts to define one in the abstract are destined to prove futile. In this
ambiguous context, it is less of a stretch than it first appears to go back and
reflect upon the animating ideas America's leaders had in mind for the
postwar era, before the advent, and during the early days, of bipolarity.
Many of the remaining modalities they devised have outlived their purpose. But on both domestic and international grounds, their underlying
rationale still—or perhaps one should say again—has surprising relevance
today. A central task for American foreign policy analysts and practitioners, then, is to adapt this ideational and institutional legacy to the new,
post-cold war international landscape.

1 | An American Dilemma

The historically minded observer of American foreign policy debates was apt to feel a certain sense of *déjà vu* in the mid-1990s. In its "Contract with America," a common platform adopted for the 1994 midterm elections, the Congressional wing of the Republican party claimed that "the Clinton administration appears to salute the day when American men and women will fight, and die, 'in the service' of the United Nations."[1] The document, which apart from defense spending addressed no other foreign policy issue, went on to detail steps a Republican majority would—and later did—take not to let that happen. Out on the presidential hustings, Senator Phil Gramm vowed: "I will NEVER send Americans into combat under U.N. command"—reportedly to "roof-raising shouts" of approval at the California Republican convention and similar "pandemonium repeated at Republican campaign events across the country."[2] And back in Washington, the newly Republican-controlled House Budget Committee, in cutting President Clinton's funding requests for peacekeeping and foreign aid, criticized the administration for "subordinating US interests in favor of ill-defined goals and policies established by international civil servants and foreign nations."[3]

At that time, it should be noted, there were sixteen ongoing UN missions deploying over 64,000 troops—of which 3,300 were American, none in combat situations. Of the 3,300 total, 2,400 served in Haiti—under U.S. command, in what had begun as an American operation in pursuit of U.S.

interests. And of all the ongoing missions that included U.S. troops, only two had been established since the Clinton administration took office.[4] In short, this was not the kind of searing foreign policy crisis, like an unpopular war or the seizing of hostages, that forces its way onto the congressional electoral agenda once in a generation or so, and into a presidential race with barely greater frequency. Instead, it was designed to be, in the words of a Republican pollster, a "damn-right" issue: "As soon as someone hears a politician talk about it, they say, 'Damn right!'"[5]

The Clinton administration played its part in the unfolding drama by responding with charges of "isolationism."[6] The term may retain rhetorical utility, but it did not quite capture the Republican position. For the same "Contract with America" that portrayed President Clinton as an agent of the UN also promised to increase defense spending. The same legislation that set strict limits on the president's ability to commit U.S. troops to multinational operations also sought to repeal the War Powers Act of 1973, intended, in the wake of Vietnam, to constrain the president's ability to introduce U.S. forces unilaterally into hostilities abroad without congressional authorization.

What the country was witnessing, a half-decade after the collapse of the Soviet Union, was not a clash between internationalism and isolationism so much as between two sets of policy positions which could both claim to be internationalist in orientation: multilateralism vs. unilateralism.[7] Indeed, a similar struggle took place at the end of the two world wars. Isolationism enters the picture because it has been, historically, a consequence of unfettered unilateralism. Whether it could be again today is a question we suspend until the final chapter. Here, we take a closer look at the terms of the discourse, and how they have been shaped by the American experience.

The Dilemma

As a nation, America was not only born free, Harvard political scientist Robert Keohane has remarked, it was also "born lucky."[8] Far removed from the constant jostling of European power politics, heavily self-sufficient, able to grow into continental scale, protected by vast oceans on either side and adjoined by relatively weak and usually friendly neighbors to the north and south, and a magnet attracting a constant inflow of newcomers eager to make a fresh start, the United States, for much of its history before the turn of this century, luxuriated in the posture, described by John Quincy Adams, of being "the well-wisher to the freedom and independence of all . . . the champion and vindicator only of her own."[9] Thus, America's traditional aversion to "entangling alliances," first expressed in Washington's farewell address, flowed naturally from its geopolitical constitution.[10] By 1823, the United States felt sure enough of itself for President Monroe to enunciate the doctrine that the U.S. would view as "an unfriendly disposition" any European intervention in the Americas, though until the end of the nineteenth century the British navy, for reasons of its own, undoubtedly played a greater role in safeguarding the Monroe Doctrine than did the United States itself.

By the turn of this century, however, the world was closing in on the United States. On September 5, 1901, President McKinley delivered a major address on America's new role in the world, at the new century's first world's fair, in Buffalo, New York. "God and men have linked nations together," he said. "No nation can longer be indifferent to any other."[11] The very next day, at the same place, McKinley was assassinated, making Theodore Roosevelt, or TR as he came to be known, the nation's president. TR picked up on McKinley's theme and carried it a step further a few months later in his State of the Union message. "The increasing interdependence and complexity of international political and economic relations," he declared, "render it incumbent on all civilized and orderly powers to insist on the proper policing of the world."[12] The dilemma was how to interest an unconcerned country—the Congress as well as the public—in that mission.

For the Republican McKinley and Roosevelt administrations the issue initially was unproblematic: the United States would simply have to become a great power, like the European great powers, and for the same reason: the United States, as were the European powers, was affected by the global balance of power. And so the United States went on a brief imperialist fling following the Spanish-American war of 1898, annexing Hawaii and the Philippines while making a protectorate of Cuba; it instigated the creation of the state of Panama and built the isthmus canal; TR issued the Roosevelt corollary to the Monroe Doctrine, whereby the United States claimed the right to intervene in the affairs of its southern neighbors; and he sent the American fleet—sixteen battleships strong—on a symbolic around-the-world cruise. But the "fever of imperialism," as David Fromkin describes it,[13] died down quickly, stymied by Congressional purse strings and declining public interest, though interventions in Central America continued in response to real and imagined threats to the security of the canal and the sanctity of American investments.

As for balance-of-power politics, Robert Dallek reports that "most Americans in Roosevelt's day were unprepared to accept his realism as a guideline for current and future actions abroad."[14] Accordingly, Roosevelt, with equal enthusiasm, invoked a mixture of piety, patriotism, and jingoism to mobilize the nation for its world challenge—so much so that, in Cooper's biography of Roosevelt and Wilson, it is a toss-up who ends up "the priest" and who "the warrior."[15] Yet nothing sufficed when TR, no longer president, sought to warn America, first about its lack of military readiness, and then about the need to intervene, after world war broke out—producing TR's darkest and most erratic moments, which he often acted out by attacking the Democrat who was president, Woodrow Wilson, and who hoped to bind the United States to a larger world role by means of the postwar settlement.[16]

Indeed, McKinley and Roosevelt had already discovered the need for unorthodox foreign policy instruments when routine ways were unavailable. Finding no domestic support for joining Europe in a scramble to partition China at the turn of the century, the McKinley administration instead called on the powers to adopt a nondiscriminatory "open door" commercial policy in China and to preserve China's territorial and administrative integrity. In 1905, TR, who privately ridiculed international arbitration as "that noxious form of silliness which always accompanies the sentimental refusal to look facts in the face," successfully mediated the Russo-Japanese war, for which he won the Nobel peace prize.[17] And it is little remembered that TR was the first American leader to propose a league of nations: a "World League for the Peace of Righteousness," he called it in an October 1914 article, which should function as "a posse comitatus of powerful and civilized nations."[18]

Roosevelt never resolved the dilemma of how to get the United States to act as a normal great power because the country simply did not see itself as one. With his posse analogy, he tried to enlist a distinctly American experience in the cause, the old West before law and order were instituted, but to no avail. Woodrow Wilson, when everything else is stripped away, took a similar tack, though invoking different terms of reference. When Wilson finally took the United States into the war, he reminded the nation of its unique political birth and promised to predicate American involvement in the war itself and, to him more importantly, in the peace beyond, on corresponding principles. Success, he explained, would lessen the need for future American sacrifice.

With election day, 1916, approaching, and with the United States still a nonbelligerent, Wilson decried the European balance-of-power system in a major campaign speech: "Now, revive that after the war is over, and, sooner or later, you will have just such another war. And this is the last war of the kind, or of any kind that involves the world, that the United States can keep out of." Since neutrality could no longer protect the United States, and with the balance-of-power doomed to failure, Wilson concluded, "We must have a society of nations."[19] He elaborated these ideas in his January 1917 "Peace without Victory" address to the Senate, proposing a postwar league of nations as the institutional expression, not of a balance of power, but "a community of power."[20]

When Wilson asked Congress, on April 2, 1917, to declare war on imperial Germany, he stated solemnly that if Americans must shed blood, it would be "for the things which we have always carried nearest our hearts—for democracy, for the right of those who submit to authority to have a voice in their own governments, for the rights and liberties of small nations, for a universal dominion of right by such a concert of free peoples as shall bring peace and safety to all nations and make the world itself at last free."[21] Finally, his famous Fourteen Points, proclaimed a year later, incorporated Wilson's previous proposals into a comprehensive agenda for postwar peace: sovereign equality and national self-determination, mutual guarantees of political independence and territorial integrity, free trade, freedom of the seas, transparent diplomacy, and the spread of democracy to autocratic—and for Wilson, therefore, militaristic—governments, coupled with a reduction of armaments and the institution of collective security.

Let us elaborate briefly Wilson's proposals for international political and economic relations, respectively, which were revived, albeit in substantially amended form, after World War II. The centerpiece of his international political agenda was the League of Nations. Open to all states willing to adhere to its terms, the League would offer mechanisms for arbitration and conciliation. Under its auspices, arms were to be reduced to levels that, in the long run, precluded wars of conquest. Instances of armed aggression would be deemed acts of war against the entire community of nations, a move which in itself was expected to serve as the chief deterrent against aggression. If that deterrence failed, the League could employ sanctions, ranging from the imposition of diplomatic isolation, severing commercial ties, and ultimately the collective use of force. By these means, Wilson hoped, future shots, such as the ones in Sarajevo in June 1914 that ignited the great war, would be muffled before they had a chance to reverberate around the world.

Wilson declined to be much more specific about how the system would work because he believed that the League's covenant should largely express general principles, and that concrete modalities should be established only gradually. In a letter to Colonel Edward House, his principal aide, written in March 1918, Wilson stated: "My own conviction, as you know, is that the administrative constitution of the League must *grow* and not be made; that we must *begin* with solemn covenants . . . but that the methods of carrying those mutual pledges out should be left to develop of itself, case by case."[22] And even at the Paris peace conference, Wilson remarked to the President of Switzerland "that only the essential lines could be immediately traced and that the rest will be the fruit of long labor and repeated experiences."[23] This, the onetime government professor held, was how constitutions in common law systems evolved.

In response to America's traditional aversion to "entangling alliances" Wilson retorted: "There is no entangling alliance in a concert of power. When all unite to act in the same purpose all act in the common interest and are free to live their own lives under a common protection."[24] In response to the objection that the League would involve the United States militarily in all manner of disputes abroad in which it had no vital interests, Wilson stressed the deterrent effect of moral commitments, public opinion, common desires for peace on the part of democratic states, reduced armaments, as well as diplomatic and economic sanctions—all of which, he believed, would make military enforcement only a remote necessity. Indeed, Wilson rejected the concept of an international military force, as he did putting American troops at the League's disposal—a position which, ironically, put him at odds with Roosevelt's 1914 proposal, as well as with the conservative League to Enforce Peace, headed by former Republican President William Howard Taft, though theirs would have been a big power club, not a universal body.[25] Finally, whereas Roosevelt had complained about his lack of influence on public opinion, Wilson basked in it until very late in the day. The highly regarded Wilson scholar, Lawrence Gelfand, summarizes prevailing views: "Existing evidence, essentially the considered judgment of seasoned politicians and journalists in the fall of 1918 and well into the spring of 1919, pointed toward solid public support for American membership in the League of Nations."[26]

By mid-1919, however, domestic opposition to the League began to mount. Wilson lost support on the left because, as the Versailles negotiations went on, he was unable to prevent the gutting of his Fourteen Points from the overall peace settlement, in which the League was embedded, which came to feature: French occupation of the Rhineland, imposition of excessive war reparations on Germany, excluding Germany and the Soviet Union from the League at the outset, limiting national self-determination to the war's losers and their colonial possessions, and the territorial aggrandizement of Italy and Japan. "THIS IS NOT PEACE," blared the *New*

Republic's banner headline in May 1919. Its editors described the League as "not powerful enough to redeem the treaty," but the treaty as "vicious enough to incriminate the League."[27] Wilson's adversaries to the right found his concessions at Versailles agreeable enough but they remained implacable regarding his concept of the League, successfully raising fears about American boys repeatedly being sent overseas to fight for the League—as Roosevelt put it on one occasion, "every time a Jugoslav wishes to slap a Czechoslav in the face."[28]

In the more prosaic domain of international economic relations, free trade had been among Wilson's Fourteen Points—for, as Fromkin puts it, "With no internal frontiers or bars to trade, [Americans] prospered, and saw in this a lesson for the rest of the world."[29] But Congress would not yet hear of it. Thus, Wilson began to move toward greater economic openness by reconfiguring domestic arrangements that stood in the way of that objective. In 1913, the Underwood-Simmons bill resulted in the first overall downward revision of the tariff since the Civil War. And in 1916, Wilson created the U.S. Tariff Commission, appointing Professor Frank Taussig, the leading historian of the American tariff, as its first chair. The Commission immediately began a review of the peculiar practice by the United States of insisting on a conditional form of the most-favored-nation (MFN) provision in its commercial treaties, which in effect negated its multilateral benefits. "A policy of special arrangements, such as the United States has followed in recent decades, leads to troublesome complications," the Commission wrote in 1919. "The separate and individual treatment of each case tends to create misunderstanding and friction with [third] countries which, though supposed to be not concerned, yet are in reality much concerned." In its place, the Commission recommended a policy of equality of treatment, which is to say, unconditional MFN. "Equality of treatment should mean that the United States treat all countries on the same terms, and in return require equal treatment from every other country."[30] The United States finally abandoned its idiosyncratic unilateralist commercial form and adopted unconditional MFN in 1923—but by then tariffs had begun to soar again.

In the end, of course, Wilson lost the treaty fight in the Senate, which had shifted to Republican control in the 1918 midterm elections, as a result of which the United States never joined the League. Two folk myths have been handed down the generations about that fight, which obfuscate rather than elucidate its historic meaning. One depicts the jousts between Roosevelt and Wilson as a titanic clash between realism and idealism in which sophisticated realism tried to leaven naive idealism but failed.

Henry Kissinger repeats this myth in his recent magnum opus—indeed, he makes it the central organizing device of the book.[31] The characterizations, however, don't fully match the characters. According to John Milton Cooper, author of a joint biography, "categorizing Roosevelt as a realist and Wilson as an idealist is a half-truth. In domestic affairs the two men professed to reverse these positions; in foreign affairs, they were by no means polar opposites. In both realms Roosevelt continually proclaimed himself an idealist, appealed in even more exalted terms than Wilson to transcendent values, and scorned Wilson as the opposite of idealistic—as narrow, timid, and selfish. In both realms Wilson extolled what he called 'expediency,' argued for patience and caution, and rejected Roosevelt's approach as wrong-headedly and excessively idealistic—as quixotic and deluded."[32]

Even more importantly, the characterizations obscure the common core in Roosevelt's and Wilson's projects: both were trying to get a reluctant nation to assume a greater role in world affairs, which both believed to be in the nation's best interests—and which Wilson, at least until the end, evidently did with greater success.

The second myth, perpetrated by the liberal end of the philosophical spectrum, is that the treaty fight was a titanic clash between internationalism and isolationism in which the forces of darkness prevailed over the forces of light. That's not quite right either. There were barely more than a dozen hard-core irreconcilables in the Senate—opposed to American membership in a League of any form. Henry Cabot Lodge (R-Mass), Chairman of the Foreign Relations Committee, was prepared to vote for the League and deliver enough Republican votes to ratify the treaty—provided that Wilson accepted Lodge's "reservations." Fourteen in number (like Wilson's Fourteen Points), they covered much ground. But in essence it came down to this nonnegotiable issue: in Lodge's words, to "release us from obligations which might not be kept, and to preserve rights which ought not to be infringed."[33] In other words, Lodge feared that the League might pressure—it could not require—the United States to take measures the United States might not wish to take, and pose a hindrance when it did wish to act. This was not isolationism, however; it was unilateralism.

In view of the evolutionary nature Wilson intended for the League, it is far from certain that the reservations would have done irreparable harm. But Wilson, for a variety of reasons too complex to take up here, would not or could not compromise. The finale was bizarre. Republican irreconcilables voted *with* the Democrats to defeat the various Republican reservations. On a straight up-or-down vote, the irreconcilables then rejoined the Republican majority against the treaty. "Irreconcilables had feared that

Democrats would eventually approve reservations, possibly even Lodge's, as a way of saving the treaty. Instead of pursuing that course, Democratic senators enabled the irreconcilables to achieve their goal of keeping the United States out of the League."[34] Compounding that irony, Lodge, like his protégé TR, had worked assiduously throughout his career to have the United States play a larger role in world affairs. And yet at the decisive moment, by insisting on strictly unilateralist means, he, too, undermined his own objective and helped usher in an era of isolationism. For Lodge, it was in part a principled issue; but indications are that he also tried to make it a "damn-right" issue.[35]

Isolationism

When the Senate turned its back on the League, America turned its back on the political affairs of the world. Dallek has put it poignantly: "In its nostalgia, [the nation] turned instead to Warren G. Harding, who promised 'not heroism, but healing, not nostrums but normalcy.'"[36] With the modest exception of the 1922 naval arms limitation treaties, the United States was content during the interwar years to limit itself largely to symbolic gestures in international political cooperation, such as the 1928 treaty outlawing war and the 1932–34 League-sponsored disarmament conference. Until the 1929 crash, American private-sector financial institutions were extensively involved in postwar European reconstruction, and there was considerable cooperation among the central banks of the major economic powers, including the United States. But not being required, by virtue of any institutionalized commitment or undertaking, to assume any practical stand regarding the forces pushing the world toward war again in the 1930s, the United States took none. If anything, the growing threat of war intensified American isolationist sentiments.

There was no single, coherent isolationist creed, as Manfred Jonas has shown in his classic study.[37] The movement encompassed socialist and religious pacifists, who had followed Wilson, as well as political descendents of the Republican party's imperialist faction under McKinley and Roosevelt. It was geographically diverse and had a broad ethnic base. Among its leaders were "irreconcilable" Senators William E. Borah of Idaho and Hiram W. Johnson of California who, though Republicans, were rooted in trust-busting, reform-oriented progressive politics; their followers, however, included decidedly anti-progressive elements that were suspicious of government while nativist and xenophobic in orientation, such as the Ku Klux Klan. The vast majority of Americans who embraced isolationism wanted little more than to get on with their lives, especially once the economic crisis of the great depression began to take its toll.

Despite this enormous diversity, it is possible analytically to reconstruct a threefold isolationist program. The key—or perhaps we should call it the hinge on which the American door toward the world swung shut—was unilateralism. It was the one tenet uniting isolationists of all kinds. And it was the tenet that linked postwar isolationism to the prewar posture of Roosevelt and Lodge, thereby permitting the political mainstream to slip away from their lifelong objective and into the isolationist fold.

Senator William Borah, one of the few isolationist leaders seriously interested in foreign affairs, believed that Americans should freely interact with the rest of the world in matters of trade and commerce, finance, as well as humanitarian and cultural endeavors. Nevertheless, in words reminiscent of Lodge's objection to the League, quoted above, Borah insisted that the United States "does propose . . . to determine for itself when civilization is threatened, when there may be a breach of human rights and human liberty sufficient to warrant action, and it proposes also to determine for itself when to act and in what manner it shall discharge the obligation which time and circumstances impose."[38] Looking back on the postwar experience in 1934, Borah elaborated on the last point at the internationalist Council on Foreign Relations: "in all matters political, in all commitments of any nature or kind, which encroach in the slightest upon the free and unembarrassed action of our people, or which circumscribe their discretion and judgment, we have been free, we have been independent, we have been isolationist."[39] Strict unilateralism, then, was the first component of the isolationist program.

The second was a very high threshold for agreeing when it would be appropriate for the United States to involve itself in some world crisis. The 1930s offered ample opportunities to say, here and now. But none passed the "vital interest" test which isolationists adapted from realist prescriptions for the conduct of foreign policy. "The American people," the Philadelphia *Record* asserted after Japan invaded Manchuria, "don't give two hoots in a rain barrel who controls North China"[40]—nor did they when Italy invaded Ethiopia, or when Germany reoccupied the Rhineland, annexed Austria, and moved into the Sudetenland. Two isolationist arguments always proved persuasive: foreign crises reflect endemic rivalries that the United States cannot resolve; and America has enough problems at home without going to look for more abroad. "Even when the activities of other nations posed a potential threat to the security of the United States, they were regarded by many as distractions diverting the [government] from the country's 'real' problems."[41] In Dallek's words, only the direct attack on Pearl Harbor, twenty-seven months into World War II, "broke this emotional deadlock."[42]

The third component of the isolationist program consisted of domestic legislation intended to insulate the United States from undesirable international currents. Too numerous to recount here, only a few of the most egregious are noted. In 1924, Congress passed the National Origins Act, banning "oriental" immigration and limiting the entry of alpine, mediterranean, and semitic peoples.[43] The Smoot-Hawley tariff, enacted in 1930 on the promise of protecting domestic employment, brought U.S. tariff levels to their highest in history and triggered mutually destructive retaliation around the world.[44] And the neutrality laws of 1935–37, adopted as fascist aggression was gaining momentum on three continents, made it impossible for the United States government to treat differentially the perpetrators and victims of attack.[45] As late as October 1937, Franklin Roosevelt felt obliged to use the metaphor of a "quarantine" to arouse interest at home about growing threats from abroad.

Throughout, there was also a strong idealist streak in isolationism. Senator Borah, for instance, "did more than any other man to bring about approval of the Kellogg-Briand Pact by the Senate in 1929," a treaty which promised, implausibly, to outlaw war.[46] Those who still clung to isolationist views at the end of the 1930s were living in a world defined almost entirely by creed, immune to world events and to America's role in them.

The obvious lesson that was later drawn from the nation's isolationist posture was about the folly and high cost of leaving the most fundamental decisions concerning war and peace in the hands of others, often one's adversaries. As FDR said in his radio address two days after Pearl Harbor, the nation was determined not to repeat that mistake. There were also more subtle lessons, which still bear consideration even today.

One concerned the inability of the rest of the world to insulate itself from American actions. Even under strict neutrality laws, by virtue of its size and power the United States simply could not avoid influencing crises in faraway places.[47] For example, after Italy invaded Ethiopia, the Roosevelt administration was required to issue a declaration of neutrality and impose an arms embargo on both belligerents. Those actions, however, did not affect the two alike. Italy had no need to import munitions from the United States, being largely self-sufficient in their production; Ethiopia, in contrast, lacked any indigenous capacity. At the same time, Italy was dependent on the United States for the import of strategic raw materials, but these were not covered by the embargo. On both counts, therefore, the

United States was inadvertently supporting Mussolini's aggression. An appeal by Secretary of State Cordell Hull to rectify this imbalance with a "moral" embargo of certain strategic materials, applied equally to both parties, brought immediate protests of "unneutrality" from Italy, which would have been more heavily affected. Then, once the League of Nations moved to impose economic sanctions on Italy, the United States found itself in the awkward position of having to choose either continuing all trade with Italy and undermining, thereby, the League's sanctions against a declared aggressor, or going along with the League and undermining, thereby, its own rationale for unilateralism. Like it or not, the United States seemed fated to affect major world crises; its only choice was between acts of commission or omission.

Moreover, it proved impossible for Americans, including isolationist leaders, not to have or develop strong preferences about a particular aggressor or victim. For example, the Spanish civil war caused considerable agony among America's left-of-center isolationists, who naturally favored the duly elected socialist government of Spain over the fascist insurgency. The government was short of strategic supplies; the insurgents were supplied by Hitler and Mussolini. Treating both sides equally helped the fascists. This, most American liberal and socialist isolationists were loath to do, but it was required by legislated neutrality which was a centerpiece of the isolationist program. The quest for particular exceptions whittled away at the credibility of principled objections to intervention.

Finally, the interwar experience suggests that it was not necessary to be a political isolationist, or to harbor such objectives, in order to contribute to the isolationist outcome. Among political leaders, it was enough initially to favor unfettered unilateralism; among the public at large it sufficed initially to give tacit approval "as long as domestic problems were pressing and it seemed easier to put off serious consideration of foreign affairs."[48] Americans often worry about the slippery slope of foreign involvements; the 1930s demonstrated dramatically that the course of foreign policy can slope in the opposite direction as well.

Multilateralism

With America drawn into world war for the second time in a generation, and having done little either time to arrest the downward spiral spinning toward calamity, Franklin Delano Roosevelt began almost at once to plan a postwar order to which America would be solidly anchored and in which the likelihood of future collapse would be greatly reduced. As Wilson's

Assistant Secretary of the Navy, Roosevelt had witnessed first hand the clash between Wilson and TR, FDR's distant cousin, whom he saw often and admired much.[49] Better than most of their contemporaries or later commentators, FDR understood that Wilson and TR had sought the same end of binding the United States to sustained international involvement, to which he, too, was committed. He also appreciated how and why their preferred means differed. With the experience of isolationism as interlude, there was no doubt in FDR's mind about which tack to take: the multilateralism of Wilson, not the unilateralism of TR.

Thus, though FDR initially favored a "four policemen" scheme for the organization of postwar security relations, he explained to British Foreign Minister Anthony Eden in the spring of 1943 that "the only appeal which would be likely to carry weight with the United States public . . . would be one based upon a world-wide conception."[50] And so he proposed a universal United Nations, in which the major powers would play a special role. In the economic sphere, FDR, like Wilson, sought a global version of the "open door," implying the end of empire and other forms of economic discrimination together with reduced levels of tariffs. It fell to Harry Truman to devise an appropriate American response to the newly emerged Soviet threat in Europe. Signs of Wilson's desire to remake European power politics could be seen in Truman's program as well, first in the Marshall Plan's deliberate impetus to European economic unity, and then in the indivisible security commitments embodied in the North Atlantic Treaty Organization (NATO).

Most of these endeavors enjoyed broad bipartisan support even before anticommunist fervor cemented a cold war consensus. Republican backers of the UN included Thomas E. Dewey, the party's 1944 presidential nominee, and prewar isolationist Senator Arthur H. Vandenberg, ranking minority member on the Foreign Relations committee—who crafted a key article of the UN charter at its 1945 San Francisco founding conference and later, as committee chair, facilitated the creation of NATO. Dwight Eisenhower was a leading advocate of a European defense community, and, at the global level, helped inaugurate UN nuclear nonproliferation and peacekeeping.

We take up these arrangements' specific designs in the next chapter. Two preliminary tasks remain for the present. First, we must define more precisely the meaning of multilateralism as an American vision of world order up to the half-century mark. Second, we need to understand more clearly why Wilson and his post-World War II successors gravitated toward this set of ideas, and not some other, when the shape of the international order, and America's role in it, have been at stake.

What is Multilateralism?

The term multilateral has a simple dictionary definition, denoting relations among three or more parties.[51] That definition suffices for most uses.
When it comes to depicting an entire order of international relations, however—a vision or plan for how overall relations among nations should be
organized—this numerical feature encompasses only the necessary but not
the sufficient condition of multilateralism. The sufficient condition concerns the principles on the basis of which the relations among parties are
organized. In its pure form, a multilateral world order would embody rules
of conduct that are commonly applicable to all countries, as opposed to discriminating among them based on situational exigencies or particularistic
preferences. Such an order also would exhibit a greater degree of indivisibility among the interests of countries than do its alternative forms.
Greater indivisibility, in principle, entails two further effects: it increases
the incentive to pursue interests via joint action, and permits each country to calculate its gains and losses from international transactions in the
aggregate, across the full array of relations and partners, as opposed to
requiring case-by-case bilateral reciprocity.

These substantive organizing principles are more decisive than the
question of mere numbers, not only definitionally, but in practice as well.
For example, economic historians consider the bilateral trade agreements
reached by United States Secretary of State Cordell Hull in the 1930s to
have differed significantly from those of Hjalmar Schacht, the architect of
Nazi Germany's economic order. The Hullean kind were intended to produce an expansion of open and largely nondiscriminatory trade relations,
and hence are deemed to have been compatible with multilateralism. In
contrast, Schacht sought to create exclusive and discriminatory trading
blocs, built up from bilateral deals none of which held for any other party
or under any other circumstances except those for which they were negotiated or on which they were imposed. The Schachtian scheme, therefore,
was antithetical to multilateralism.[52] Similarly, Bismarck's League of the
Three Emperors of 1873 was a traditional alliance, unrelated to multilateral organizing principles, despite having had three members. But Roosevelt's concept for the postwar security order may be termed multilateral
because, as historian Warren Kimball notes, FDR wished to avoid "old-
fashioned, exclusive spheres-of-influence/power-politics relationships, by
which he meant both Metternichian coalitions against change and geopolitical Bismarckian alliances."[53]

In its pure form, a multilateral security order would provide equal protection under a common security umbrella—an arrangement typically

called collective security. Sir Arthur Salter over a half-century ago described collective security as a potential universal alliance "against the *unknown* enemy"[54]—and, he should have added, in behalf of the *unknown* victim.[55] The counterpart principle in international economic relations prescribes an economic order in which exclusive blocs or differential treatment of trading partners and currencies are forbidden, and in which point-of-entry barriers to economic transactions are minimized. Self-determination, and state behavior constrained by universal human rights, round out the multilateral vision. Keep in mind that, in this pure form, multilateralism expresses a set of abstract principles. No American leader, not even Wilson, has ever proposed to institute these principles in their pure form—though Wilson hoped, through the League, "to plant a system which will slowly but surely ripen into fruition."[56] America's post-World War II planners drew on multilateral principles, not as blueprint, but as animating ideas concerning the organization of the international order they were constructing.

The conjunction of America and multilateralism is potentially subject to two sources of confusion. One is that the concept of multilateralism can refer not only to the overall order of relations among countries, in the manner described above, but also to specific institutions that exist within any such order—and U.S. policy preferences have been quite different for these two spheres of multilateralism. The United States helped establish numerous multilateral institutions throughout this century. Membership in them, by definition, constrains unilateral degrees of freedom in some measure and over some range of issues. But rarely if ever has it been American policy to endow multilateral institutions with significant independent powers. Thus, the United States insisted on a veto in the UN Security Council every bit as much as the Soviets did. Voting in the International Monetary Fund and World Bank was and remains weighted, with the United States still having the largest single share. At American insistence, the General Agreement on Tariffs and Trade barely existed as a formal organization, though it has now been folded into an institutionally stronger World Trade Organization. And the "O" in NATO refers to a policy forum, secretariat, and largely American-dominated military command structure, not an autonomous body providing security to its members. Specific administrations have differed on this issue, to be sure, yet not even Wilson sought to deviate dramatically from this general American posture. Nor should this posture cause surprise. Smaller and weaker countries are far more likely than the large and strong to identify the core feature of multilateralism with creating and adhering to independent multilateral institutions.

A second source of confusion is that the term multilateralism has never commanded appeal in American political circles to describe security relations—the problem does not affect the less delicate domain of international economics. From 1945 into the Eisenhower years "collective security" was the preferred locution—though it always denoted arrangements far looser than formal collective security systems, and by the time it was invoked by John Foster Dulles to express the "pactomania" of the 1950s it had become nothing more than verbal window-dressing. The Clinton administration was unusual by entering office as self-proclaimed multilateralists even in security affairs. But after bruising Republican charges of "subcontracting" American foreign policy to the United Nations, its UN ambassador quickly jettisoned the term: "Multilateralism is a word for policy wonks," she declared, "so let's not use it anymore." Instead, she suggested, "let's call it burden sharing."[57]

In short, the American multilateral vision of world order has included a desire to avoid the bilateral alliance systems on which countries have relied historically in favor of more comprehensive and institutionalized security arrangements; an "open door" world economy comprising uniform rules governing trade and monetary relations together with minimal state-imposed barriers to the flow of international economic transactions; anti-imperialism grounded in self-determination; and anti-statism grounded in human rights. Juxtaposed against traditional European-style balance-of-power politics or its McKinley-Roosevelt-Lodge unilateralist corollary, it is a mildly communitarian world order vision. The Wilsonian variant was the most far-reaching but failed. The post-1945 version, as we shall see in the next chapter, was more realistic—which is to say that its transformational aspirations, while not abandoned, were informed by a far greater appreciation of the realities of power politics—and also more successful.

Why Multilateralism?

One precursory consideration remains: why this set of ideas, as opposed to some other?

Realists have been partial to two answers. One, typically proffered by realist policy practitioners, has to do with the alleged naiveté of the American people: Kissinger calls it "idealism," which the cosmopolitan realist is obliged to enlist in the subtle game of power-balancing;[58] George Kennan, originator of the postwar doctrine of "containing" the Soviet Union, is more dismissive, reproaching Americans for viewing tough foreign policy choices through "legalistic-moralistic" lenses and complicating, thereby, the straightforward pursuit of the national interest.[59]

There may well be some truth in this contention, but ultimately it fails to satisfy. For there is no indication that America acted against its self-interest in advocating multilateral world order ideas, or that the pursuit of its interests was hindered by those ideas. The problem stems from the realist tendency to confuse *ideas* with *idealism* as their basis. Whereas idealism and interests may comprise polarities, as Kissinger and Kennan believe, ideas and interests do not. The great sociologist Max Weber put it well long ago when he wrote: "very frequently the 'world images' that have been created by 'ideas' have, like switchmen, determined the tracks along which action has been pushed by the dynamic of interest."[60]

A second realist answer, more likely to be advanced by academics, has to do with the cynicism of leaders, especially leaders of leading powers. As a renowned realist theorist, Kenneth Waltz, has written, "England claimed to bear the white man's burden; France spoke of her *mission civilisatrice*. In like spirit, we [the United States] say that we act to make and maintain world order. . . . For countries at the top, this is predictable behavior."[61] This treats the multilateral world order vision as a set of ideas, to be sure, but one which serves merely as a source of rhetoric designed to legitimate the pursuit of great power interests abroad and generate support for those actions at home.

At some level this answer, too, has merit. Without a preponderance of power the United States would have had neither the inclination nor the capability to try to reshape the international order in this or any other fashion. But to the extent it is possible to know such things, other great powers would have done it differently, so that the rhetoric is not *mere* rhetoric, but expresses differential policy preferences with real consequences.

For example, had either Nazi Germany or the Soviet Union ended up as the country "at the top" after World War II, there is no indication that their intentions included creating anything remotely like the international order that came to prevail. Politically, Germany's "new order" consisted of an imperial design. Economically, the Nazi scheme of bilateralist, tributary, and state-controlled trade pacts and monetary clearing arrangements presumably would have been expanded to complement its political objectives. The Soviet Union would have extended political control through a restored Comintern, while instituting centrally administered economic relations among its subject economies. Indeed, even if Britain had ended up at the top things would have differed in key respects. Colonialism would have continued longer. And while monetary relations probably would have been organized similarly, though based on sterling instead of the dollar, British imperial preferences would have remained a central feature in

international trade, possibly forcing other countries to carve out discriminatory trading blocs for themselves. Finally, Europe certainly would have
been "integrated" by a German or a Soviet imperium—but in a very different manner than exists via the European Union today. Under a British-run
system, Europe most probably would have returned to prewar multipolarity
and the continued existence of separate national economies. Hence, this
realist response, far from answering the question, only leads to its recapitulation: why *this* set of ideas?

Closer to the mark is the view that America's reform agenda abroad has
been a natural byproduct of corresponding endeavors at home. The internal roots of Woodrow Wilson's international program have long been
explored by historians. The more conventional rendition stresses Wilson's
scholarly and practical concerns with constitutionalism and public administration, leading him to advocate a program of legal/institutional reforms
in domestic and international affairs alike.[62] Other interpretations are
more explicitly interest-based, attributing Wilson's "new diplomacy" to a
desire to strengthen domestic social democracy,[63] and many of FDR's international initiatives to the socioeconomic objectives as well as administrative and legal instruments of the New Deal.[64]

This account seems persuasive for certain economic and social policy
realms where, indeed, its efficacy is reinforced by changes in the structure
of the American economy. After the turn of the century, the United States
was fast becoming the world's leading economy. And New York's financial
sector, as well as some manufacturing sectors in the Northeast and Mid-
west, were becoming increasingly internationally oriented, as the cotton-
exporting South had long been. Accordingly, sociopolitical coalitional
possibilities changed, creating both pressures and opportunities for new
foreign policy initiatives.[65]

But it is unclear how this account helps explain American multilateral
initiatives in the security sphere. Why would a system of bilateral alliances
have been incompatible with Wilson's domestic social democratic politics?
Why would the desire to create an international economic and social context that was consistent with the New Deal have led FDR to abandon the
regional "four policemen" scheme that he initially favored? Wilson was
ideologically predisposed against the power-political system of bilateral
alliances, favoring collective security intrinsically, but that was not true of
FDR, who had no such personal predilections.

We have to dig deeper and look for a more inclusive rationale. Recall
the contexts and tasks Wilson and FDR faced. Wilson had witnessed Teddy
Roosevelt's failure to rally public support for joining the other great powers

in a campaign for "the proper policing of the world," while FDR took office amid the nation's isolationist trauma which, it seemed, nothing could shake. On instrumental grounds alone, therefore, neither would have needed much convincing that framing American world order policy within the traditional balance-of-power calculus and the principles of *raison d'é-tat*, invented for the more densely configured European international system wherein external threats were ever-present, had little resonance with the American people. But the reason was not "idealism" or "legalistic-moralistic" beliefs. It was simple geopolitical fact. Americans refused to see their country as a "normal" great power because it wasn't one. In geopolitical terms alone, there had never been a great power like it. Realists either have not understood or not accepted this geopolitically rooted American sense of self—which is ironic insofar as geopolitics is their special forte. Instead, from Teddy Roosevelt on down they have tried to "normalize" America in the hope of securing its international involvement. In contrast, Wilson and FDR, far from denying American exceptionalism, sought to anchor the nation's international involvement in it.

A multilateral vision of world order is singularly compatible with America's collective self-concept as a nation. Indeed, the vision taps into the very *idea* of America. "Americans have always thought that their founding was special," the political philosopher Tracy Strong reminds us, "and central to being an American."[66] The word *nation* stems from the Latin *nascor*, "I am born." Thus, to be British, French, or Japanese typically has been considered a matter of birth, not choice, and of belonging to a collectivity embodying an "organic specificity," as David Rieff puts it.[67] But in principle anyone can become an American. America has viewed itself as a willful community, an elective community—"making a new nation out of literally any old nation that comes along," G. K. Chesterton remarked.[68] That is made possible, in turn, only because the American concept of political community rests on, not the exclusive organic specificities of traditional nations but, in Strong's words, "a universal or general foundation open in principle to everyone."[69]

America's multilateralist vision reflects an analogous idea: the willed formation of an international order premised on "a universal or general foundation open in principle to everyone." For Wilson and FDR alike, multilateral world order principles provided the evocative vocabulary, the justificatory ideas, and the aspirational program without which they found it difficult to imagine that the United States, a continental and largely self-sufficient power, and the haven to which millions flocked to escape the ways of the old world, would engage in any international efforts beyond those commercial and humanitarian in nature. International political involvement in pursuit of principles that the United States itself was constituted to embody offered a viable solution.

On a practical plane, the pursuit of multilateral principles abroad also had direct appeal to the domestic politics of ethnicity in America. As an astute political scientist notes, "multilateralism favored everybody's homeland."[70] Before the United States entered the first world war, the British ambassador in Washington reported to London Wilson's fear that taking sides in the war might unleash severe ethnic clashes in America.[71] Wilson's "Peace Without Victory" speech, and his desire for a postwar security system based on the defense of general principles, might have reflected this concern. Similar fears were raised throughout the interwar period.[72] Multilateralism proved very useful in this context after World War II, when the United States dispensed substantial economic and security assistance abroad, especially in Europe. The ethnic politics of country-by-country allocations of aid and security guarantees at best would have been exceedingly complex, and at worst highly divisive. As it was, a multilateral approach through the Marshall Plan and NATO made it possible to assist Europe as a whole—except where the Soviets would not permit it. That had the effect of transforming the domestic politics of particularistic ethnic preferences into more of a median voter issue, thereby avoiding interethnic rivalry and enhancing bipartisan support for the policy.

The close link between the foundational principle of America's sense of community and America's multilateral approach to world order also helps account for the depths of the ideological antipathy and competition between the United States and the Soviet Union during the cold war. This was no mere geopolitical conflict conducted in accord with the prudential dictates of power balancing. The Soviet Union challenged not only American interests, but also America's collective sense of self. The Soviet Union no less than the United States claimed to embody universal rights. But the two views of rights were, of course, mutually exclusive, as were the world order designs they entailed. The contest had begun in 1919. The Communist International was formed just before the Versailles peace conference, which was to draft the Covenant of the League of Nations, got under way. Adopting a manifesto addressed "To the Proletarians of the Whole World," the Bolshevik gathering denounced bourgeois democracy and parliamentarianism, defended the dictatorship of the proletariat and, perhaps most importantly, constituted itself as the institutional vehicle of what Lenin described as "the international republic of Soviets"—the Soviet version of world order.[73] Little came of this challenge in the interwar period because the Soviet Union lacked the power to project its vision abroad. By 1947, however, the challenge, even if exaggerated, was real enough.[74]

The outbreak of the cold war fundamentally altered the foreign policy dilemma America's leaders had struggled with since the turn of this century. Now a direct external threat existed that the nation acknowledged as such and was prepared to deal with. The Truman Doctrine, *Newsweek* wrote at the time, "had clearly put America into power politics to stay."[75] The cold war even led to "entangling" American security commitments in Europe. And yet, that involvement in European security affairs continued to evidence signs of the ideational framework that reached back, through FDR, to Wilson. It was not the traditional system of bilateral alliances, but an imagined and indivisible North Atlantic security community in which an attack on one was to be considered an attack on all—which, of course, is the core element of collective security.

These achievements by America's postwar leaders, beginning with Roosevelt, were monumental. They laid down the tracks, in Weber's metaphor, along which action was then pushed by the dynamic of interest. The tracks were defined by ideas. And the ideas expressed America's identity, its sense of self.

Perhaps no requiem for the cold war was more poignant, therefore, than the embrace of neo-Wilsonian notions by the last Soviet President, Mikhail Gorbachev. Speaking at Stanford University in May 1990, he appeared to paraphrase Wilson's "Peace without Victory" speech:

> I'm convinced that we stand on the threshold of revising the concept of alliance building. Until now, alliances have been built on a selective, and in fact discriminatory, basis. They were based on setting countries against each other. . . . But we are approaching a time when the very principle of alliance-building should become different. It should mean unity to create conditions for a life worthy of a human being.[76]

This was an especially graceful concession speech, signaling not merely a détente, nor a tactical retreat in the cold war, but its end, because it endorsed the adversary's aspirational principles as a common vision of world order.

2 | The Postwar Compromises

By the summer of 1944, well before the war was won, Franklin Delano Roosevelt's administration had convened the Bretton Woods conference to design the postwar monetary order, and the Dumbarton Oaks conference at which the allies hammered out the most important political and military provisions of the United Nations charter. The Republican Party lined up in support of postwar multilateralism behind such figures as Wendell Willkie, author of a best-selling tract entitled *One World*, who campaigned for its presidential nomination; John Foster Dulles, Wall Street lawyer and the party's leading foreign-policy voice; and New York Governor Thomas E. Dewey, the party's eventual nominee.[1] "What is the job before us in 1944?" Roosevelt asked the Democratic party convention renominating him for an unprecedented fourth term. "First, to win the war—to win the war fast, to win it overpoweringly. Second, to form worldwide international organizations, and to arrange to use the armed forces of the sovereign nations of the world to make another war impossible."[2]

When Harry S Truman unexpectedly found himself the 33rd President of the United States on April 12, 1945 his very first decision, he reminded the nation in his farewell address nearly eight years later, was to go forward with the United Nations. On July 2, he urged the Senate to ratify the charter: "It comes from the reality of experience," he testified, "in a world where one generation has twice failed to keep the peace."[3] Negotiations to create an International Trade Organization eventually yielded a more modest

General Agreement on Tariffs and Trade (GATT). The need for a Truman Doctrine, Marshall Plan, and North Atlantic Treaty Organization (NATO) was not yet anticipated, but in the event they did not so much abandon as adapt to a radically different geopolitical setting, some of the same organizing principles.

There was much talk at the time about the country having learned powerful lessons. Virtually every mistake that observers attributed to Woodrow Wilson, FDR sought to avoid: he separated planning for the postwar world from prosecuting the war or settling the peace; he courted Republicans; he prepared public opinion; and far from being rigid, he gleefully described himself as "the juggler."[4] Isolationism and protectionism were construed as public "bads," never to be repeated. The same was true of the League of Nations: "so fully was the league perceived to have failed . . . that its main role in planning for the [Dumbarton Oaks] conference . . . was to serve as an example of what the new organization ought not to do."[5] Finally, and on a more symbolic plane, thanks largely to social healing effects of the New Deal, the country again felt confident about itself. Robert Dallek has put it well: "More than at any time since the late nineteenth century Americans had a sense of membership in a national community, a sense of belonging and participation in something larger than themselves."[6]

America was poised to win the peace. Here we examine the organizational features of its mission.

FDR and 1945

Professional students of international relations typically view the post-World War II international order through the lens of strategic bipolarity: two opposing blocs, each highly militarized, ready to strike back if attacked and eager to seek any advantage over the other. The model becomes useful once bipolarity existed as, and was understood to be, a geopolitical fact. But Roosevelt, like William Fox, who introduced the term "the superpowers" into the political lexicon in 1944,[7] foresaw a strategic world that had, at minimum, three major players—personified in the triumvirate he comprised along with Churchill and Stalin. The Soviets participated in the 1944 Bretton Woods monetary conference and in efforts to draft a world trade charter, and they performed a lead role at Dumbarton Oaks and San Francisco in devising the UN charter. Bipolarity, in short, was not a factor shaping initial American plans for the organization of the postwar world. Multilateralism was, in security and economic relations alike—inspired by the Wilsonian vision but also tempered by its failure, grounded in the American experience but also in tune with the ways of power politics.

The Security Order

Historians have found it exceedingly difficult to capture accurately Roosevelt's views about the United Nations he helped to create. Some have depicted him as a closet Wilsonian, others as pursuing traditional power politics in liberal internationalist guise.[8] Neither interpretation does him justice. Here as elsewhere, Roosevelt was a tinkerer—"the juggler." He sought to construct a mechanism that would achieve the objectives of helping to keep the United States and the Soviet Union jointly engaged in the task of creating and maintaining a stable postwar security order, and one that would prove viable in the domestic political context. The UN that emerged in 1945 reflected these objectives about as well as could be expected.

Although the State Department began planning for the United Nations in 1942, "FDR, like Wilson, was for the most part his own secretary of state and developed plans of his own on important matters."[9] So it was in this case. From an American vantage, Roosevelt above all else saw in the United Nations an institutional tripwire, as it were, forcing American policymakers to take a position on potential threats to international peace— before it was too late and the United States faced a far more difficult situation or, even worse, was dragged yet again into a major war that it had done little to prevent. Needless to say, the origins of World War II were uppermost in his mind. But from the start, Roosevelt made it clear that he could not, as he told Soviet Foreign Minister Vyacheslav Molotov as early as 1942, "visualize another League of Nations."[10] It had not worked in practice, and could not work in principle.

Concerned about Germany, Churchill and Stalin were keen to establish some form of European council, provided the United States belonged. Roosevelt's initial impulse had also run along regional lines, though his was a "four policemen" scheme, China being added to the beat. But he soon concluded that the American people would find regional spheres-of-influence schemes too cynical, and he feared that Congress might use them as an excuse to shirk involvement in the postwar stabilization of Europe and Asia. Only a universal framework, he determined, would ensure American support.[11] The allies readily accepted the move toward universalism so as to accommodate the United States. Roosevelt's idea of the "four policemen" was not abandoned entirely, however; it became the basis for the permanent members of the UN Security Council.[12]

Roosevelt believed that a stable postwar security order also required, in the words of John Lewis Gaddis, "offering Moscow a prominent place in it; by making it, so to speak, a member of the club."[13] Gaddis calls this the strategy of "containment by integration"—in contrast to the subsequent American strategy of containing the Soviets by exclusion and exhaustion. But this strategy required a club to which both Washington and Moscow belonged. Roosevelt hoped that the UN Security Council would perform that function. In holding this position, William Widenor notes, Roosevelt "assumed not that the Big Four would maintain their unity [after the war] but that the U.N. plan would work if, and only if, they did."[14] If it did not work other means would have to be fashioned, but until such a time the pursuit of concerted behavior remained a core objective.

Finally, Roosevelt believed that the United Nations had to have "teeth" and be able to enforce its decisions by military means if others failed. Without teeth, it would neither provide deterrent value vis-à-vis potential aggressors nor would it possess the credibility required for the geopolitical objectives of engaging the United States while constraining the Soviet Union. The allies explored the possibility of establishing an international force—the United States and the Soviet Union at one point considered an international air corps. In the end, Roosevelt assured the American people that "we are not thinking of a superstate with its own police force and other paraphernalia of coercive power." Instead, the United States and the other major powers, he said, planned to devise a mechanism for "joint action" by national forces.[15] These forces would be made available to the UN Security Council "on its call," coordinated by a Military Staff Committee comprised of representatives of the permanent members' national chiefs of staff.

Roosevelt, Churchill, and Stalin fully intended a dominant role, but also special responsibilities, for the great powers in the UN. The allies would determine the peace settlement and future fate of the Axis countries, not the UN. Each permanent member would enjoy a veto in the Security Council. And Article 106 of the charter permitted "joint action" among the permanent members, "on behalf of the Organization," until enough military forces were made available to the Council so that, in its *own* opinion, it was able to follow the prescribed modalities for military enforcement.[16] Those military forces were expected to come, moreover, primarily from permanent members. What these countries could not do on their own was to affirm that a threat to international peace had occurred warranting UN action; that required concurrence of smaller countries which would join the Council on a rotating basis.

Over Stalin's objections, Roosevelt succeeded in getting China added to the ranks of Security Council permanent members, as a counterweight to the Soviet Union in East Asia; and with an eye on Germany, France was added at the urging of Great Britain, despite Stalin's observation that France, after the war, would be "charming but weak."[17]

In keeping with America's traditional anti-imperialist sentiment, and no doubt with economic and military interests also in mind, Roosevelt conducted an "unceasing public and private campaign aimed at eliminating European empires and setting the colonial world on the road toward independence."[18] He seized every opportunity to include references to self-determination in official allied declarations, starting with the August 1941 Anglo-American Atlantic Charter; he criticized British and French colonialism openly and sought to negotiate its termination behind closed doors; and he hoped that his own commitment to immediate Philippine independence once the island was cleared of Japanese troops would send an unmistakable message to the European colonial powers. At the same time, Roosevelt wished to avoid weakening Great Britain or undermining its resolve in the war, and to ensure both British and French postwar cooperation. The eventual compromise took the form of a trusteeship system that included existing League mandates, ex-enemy dependent territories, and territories that might be placed voluntarily under United Nations control. But Roosevelt successfully insisted on the international accountability of trusteeship holders, among them the United States, which planned to install military bases in several Pacific locations.

Roosevelt paid relatively little attention to what the rest of the United Nations would be or do. That was the province of State Department experts, led by Secretary Hull's assistant, Leo Pasvolsky; and of internationalists inside the government and beyond. It was they who concerned themselves with charter provisions for the peaceful resolution of disputes (disarmament being mentioned only in passing), the Economic and Social Council, the role of the Secretary General, the World Court, and so on. Indeed, Roosevelt thought of the UN less as an entity in its own right than as a collectivity of member countries. For example, in a Cabinet discussion of his trusteeship idea shortly after Yalta, Roosevelt stated that "sovereignty would be vested in *all* of the United Nations [but] we would be requested by *them* to exercise . . . trusteeship."[19] He correspondingly discounted the role of whatever organizational expression the UN would come to have. As he put it at an October 1944 press conference, "Well, what you want on that is to get an office building—have an office building—I don't care where, particularly—and make that the place where they keep all their records, and have a lot of papers of all kinds, and maps, and so forth and so on. Then, when you decide where the assembly is going to meet the next time, then come with the necessary documents."[20]

Thus, ambiguities that may exist about Roosevelt's concept for the United Nations in security relations begin to resolve themselves once it is understood that he deliberately envisioned a hybrid design: he sought to base a universal security organization in concert of power.[21] In effect, and perhaps consciously, FDR tried to reconcile the leagues of Wilson and TR—as we saw in the previous chapter, the one a universal organization of formal equals, the other a big power club.[22] Doubts about whether FDR fashioned "a truly internationalist organization," then, simply miss the crux of his achievement.[23] His position is contrasted, of course, with Wilson's. But the contrast overlooks the central similarity between the two: both sought to create a universal framework that would bind the United States to the maintenance of international order. Their critical difference was in means. Wilson, the committed liberal internationalist, rejected power politics as a legitimate instrument within a collective security scheme. Roosevelt, "the juggler," grafted a collective security scheme onto a concert of power. That move circumscribed the scope of the UN's collective security mechanisms, to be sure. But it offered the only plausible basis for the success of any collective security mechanism, while also potentially moderating the functioning of the concert in the long run. Ironically, Wilson, the paragon of internationalism, opposed provisions in the covenant that would have put American forces at the disposal of the League; Roosevelt devised an arrangement that made possible United States military participation in UN efforts to keep the peace.

What was the American public thinking about these matters? Few were familiar with the details. But by the time the war in Europe was drawing to a close, and just before the San Francisco conference, a Gallup poll reported that 81 percent of Americans favored U.S. entry into a "world organization with police power to maintain world peace;" of those responding affirmatively, 83 percent described entry as "very important." A confidential poll taken for the State Department yielded similar results: eight of ten surveyed supported the commitment of American forces to the United Nations to help keep peace.[24]

It had not always been so. In 1942 Roosevelt feared a replay of the 1918 midterm elections.[25] Once plans for the postwar security organization began to crystallize, he worked assiduously with Congress to ensure its support.[26] In 1944 Undersecretary of State Edward Stettinius began a major campaign of public education, which continued on through to the Senate vote on the UN charter and employed every medium imaginable, from high-level briefings to films and comic books. The 1944 Congressional elections produced favorable results: virtually all isolationists in both parties lost their seats. By 1945, in terms of partisan politics, "all [the Republicans] could do was to accept the nonpartisan role that [Secretary of State Cordell] Hull had prepared for them and ratify the administration's plans for peace."[27]

Did these views concerning America's second try at world order reflect mere naiveté—"the triumph of hope over experience," as Dr. Johnson said about second marriages? It seems not. The same opinion polls also revealed that nearly 40 percent of the public believed that the United States would find itself involved in another war within a quarter century.[28] In his final State of the Union address, in January 1945, Roosevelt expressed this measured mood. Denouncing isolationism, power politics, and imperialism, he warned even more sternly against perfectionism: "In our disillusionment after the last war," he reminded Congress, "we gave up the hope of gradually achieving a better peace because we had not the courage to fulfill our responsibilities in an admittedly imperfect world. . . . We must not let that happen again."[29]

Congress obliged. When the UN charter came to a vote in the Senate Foreign Relations Committee it carried 21–1; California's Republican Hiram Johnson, an "irreconcilables" leader in 1919 and irreconcilable still, was the lone dissenter. The full Senate approved by a vote of 89–2. Perhaps even more astonishingly, Congress decided in December 1945 that once it had ratified the basic forces agreement with the United Nations, making U.S. troops available to the UN on call, the president would require no additional Congressional authorization to commit them to specific UN missions.[30]

When all was said and done, the only sustained opposition the multilateral approach to postwar security organization aroused was among realist practitioners and commentators, including, Tony Smith reminds us, "some of the most influential thinkers in this country on the proper conduct of American foreign policy—Walter Lippmann, George Kennan, Hans Morgenthau, and Reinhold Niebuhr."[31] Kennan, serving in the Moscow embassy, urged "burying" the Dumbarton Oaks UN proposals. "We are badly enmeshed in our own unsound slogans," he admonished Washington in an unsolicited cable.[32] But the main object of realist vitriol and even contempt was Woodrow Wilson, dead for a quarter century but whose idealist folly was presumed to linger on.[33] Wherever it may have been lingering, it was not in the heterodox thinking of FDR.

The Economic Order

Negotiations on the postwar economic order lacked the high drama of world leaders traveling halfway around the globe—as in Churchill's doggerel, "No more let us falter! From Malta to Yalta! Let nobody alter!"—deciding on burning issues of war and peace, with public attention riveted on their every pronouncement. The economic talks were conducted at more technical levels and in greater obscurity. Nonetheless, the multilateral agenda we saw in the security realm had its counterpart in economic relations.

The United States brought to these negotiations a global version of the "open door"—a concept, as we saw in the previous chapter, the McKinley administration introduced to secure nondiscriminatory access to China at the turn of this century. Now for the entire world economy discriminatory trade barriers and currency practices, which had proliferated in the interwar period, were to be dismantled; tariff levels, which had become prohibitive, in no small measure due to America's own Smoot-Hawley act of 1930, were to be progressively reduced; and currency convertibility and stability restored.

Discrimination evoked particular animus on the part of the United States. The exclusive trade and monetary blocs of the interwar period in effect shut out nonparticipants, thereby limiting American economic opportunities abroad. American officials also believed that exclusive economic blocs inevitably triggered economic conflicts, which readily spilled over into the security realm. "Nations which act as enemies in the marketplace cannot long be friends at the council table," warned Assistant Secretary of State for Economic Affairs William L. Clayton, echoing a favorite refrain of his boss, Cordell Hull.[34] Winthrop Aldrich, Chairman of the Chase National Bank and a frequent government adviser, was more succinct: "Bilateralism is the road to war; multilateralism is the highway to peace."[35]

Before the United States entered the war, the Nazis' "new international economic order" and Japan's similarly structured East Asian Co-Prosperity Sphere were the primary focal points of American antipathy. Nazi Germany had negotiated with and/or imposed on its trading partners a series of trade and monetary clearing arrangements. Each was specific to a particular trading partner, who often became locked into dependence on Germany. This was achieved by, for example, Germany importing more from its trading partners than it exported to them, but requiring them to liquidate their claims on Germany through reinvestment there or by purchasing deliberately overpriced German goods.[36] Japan's scarcity of raw materi-

als and need for export markets naturally drove it toward the Asian mainland. But American policymakers took great exception to the means
Tokyo's leaders had selected: "military force, the establishment of puppet
regimes, and the attempted creation of an exclusive sphere of influence."[37]
Negotiations to construct the postwar economic order, which began well
before the war was won, were premised on the assumption that Germany
and Japan would be defeated and that their noxious international economic systems, therefore, would collapse and be replaced by global multilateralism.

The place of the Soviet Union in these negotiations was anomalous.
The world economy that was being reconstructed was a capitalist one, and
the Soviet Union was not about to abandon its own economic system. Yet
the Soviets participated at the Bretton Woods conference, which designed
the postwar monetary regime, and in the Havana postwar trade negotiations. Attempts were made to draft provisions accommodating centrally
planned economies and state-trading nations. But these could go only so
far.[38] The Soviets apparently chose to participate so as to keep open the
possibility of immediate financial assistance, future credits, and access to
world markets, while determining what the costs of permanent involvement would be as measured in required domestic economic changes. The
costs were likely to be steep and the benefits, especially an oft-promised
American loan, were questionable. In the end, it appears that Stalin
decided personally to drop out of the Bretton Woods monetary regime, driven by his obsession with the secrecy of economic information and the
desire to safeguard Soviet autarchy.[39]

The effective absence from these negotiations of fundamentally different economic systems left the United States to direct most of its energies
toward the more benign but still vexing British posture. There was little
disagreement in principle with Britain about future monetary relations.
But there was plenty concerning trade. The Tories were committed to
imperial preferences, and Labour to controls on foreign economic transactions as part of its program of national economic planning.[40] Both were
inherently discriminatory: preferences because they imposed differential
tariffs, and economic planning because it undoubtedly would have had to
include numerical trade targets and quotas.

Thus, the primary objective of the United States was to achieve greater
openness in, nondiscriminatory treatment of, and lower barriers to the flow
of international economic transactions. But nowhere in the capitalist
world would domestic politics permit a mere return to the laissez faire of
unrestricted trade and the gold standard, wherein the level of domestic

economic activity was governed by the balance of payments.[41] Harry Dexter White, who drafted the American plan for the postwar monetary regime, dismissed them as "harmful hangovers from a nineteenth century creed."[42] And Jacob Viner wrote, just prior to the adoption of GATT, "there are few free traders in the present-day world, no one pays any attention to their views, and no person in authority anywhere advocates free trade."[43] Even for the United States, where domestic stabilization measures remained the least comprehensive and the most contested, the international edifice of the open door had to accommodate the domestic interventionism of the New Deal.

Secretary Hull's 1934 Reciprocal Trade Agreement Act typically is cited as heralding the liberalizing thrust of America's postwar international economic policy. But, as Stephan Haggard reminds us, Roosevelt put off its submission to Congress until domestic legislation was in place shielding business and agriculture from external disruption and extending new guarantees to labor. And even then it contained escape clauses permitting temporary protection of industries injured by liberalizing concessions.[44] What had been politically expedient in the United States in 1934 reached the status of political first principle for the capitalist world a decade later: no international liberalization without domestic safeguards.

As it had done in creating the United Nations, the Roosevelt administration succeeded in juggling twin—and previously contradictory—policy objectives into a hybrid institutional design: economic regimes permitting the simultaneous pursuit of international openness and substantial domestic policy autonomy. Wall Street Republicans derided it as "New Deal gimmickry." Elsewhere, I have called it the compromise of "embedded liberalism."[45] Unlike the economic nationalism of the thirties, the international economic order would be multilateral in character. But unlike the laissez-faire liberalism of the gold standard and free trade, its multilateralism would be predicated on the interventionist character of the modern capitalist state.

Accordingly, the Bretton Woods monetary agreement provided for free and stable currency exchanges—but coupled with a "double screen," in Richard Cooper's suggestive words, to cushion the domestic economy against the strictures of the balance of payments.[46] Free exchanges would be assured by the abolition of all forms of exchange controls and restrictions on current (as opposed to capital) account transactions. Stable exchanges would be secured by setting and maintaining official par values for currencies, expressed in terms of gold. The double screen would include short-term assistance to finance current account payments deficits, made available by an International Monetary Fund (IMF), and, so as to correct any "fundamental disequilibrium," the ability to change exchange rates with IMF concurrence. Governments were permitted to maintain controls over capital transfers.

The United States Senate never ratified the charter of the proposed International Trade Organization, it being too intrusive for some domestic interests and not activist enough for others. As a result, a smaller domain of commercial relations was institutionalized within a General Agreement on Tariffs and Trade.[47] But it exhibited a similar balance of external and internal objectives. The GATT made obligatory the most-favored-nation or equality-of-treatment rule.[48] Quantitative import restrictions, such as quotas, were prohibited, yet they were deemed suitable measures for temporarily safeguarding the balance of payments—explicitly including payments difficulties that resulted from domestic full employment policies. The substantial reduction of tariffs and other barriers to trade was called for, but it, too, was coupled with specified emergency actions, permitted if domestic producers were threatened with injury from imports attributable to past tariff concessions.

In both cases, the measures adopted to effect domestic cushioning were expected to be limited in duration, commensurate with the extent of the external disruption, and compatible with the long-term expansion of international economic transactions.

The Roosevelt administration was responsible for numerous other multilateral initiatives in areas that ranged from agricultural assistance to human rights and educational, scientific, and cultural cooperation: as many domestic constituencies as possible were to have an international stake. But none was as central to FDR's objective of binding America to the international order as these arrangements to organize security and economic relations. In designing them, American policy was not yet driven by bipolarity. No overriding Soviet threat was yet perceived to exist. Indeed, it was a major objective of American policy to integrate the Soviet Union into the postwar security order, and at least superficially to try to accommodate the Soviets in the economic order.

Roosevelt's efforts exhibited both continuity with and change from Wilson's. The element of continuity lies in Roosevelt's pursuit of a universal security system and an open-door world economy. The major difference is that FDR and his team saw the need, on international and domestic grounds alike, to devise more heterodox means. Hence, they constructed institutional arrangements that coupled the universal security system with a concert of power, and the international open door with domestic intervention. These carefully crafted compromises soon confronted the radically different geopolitical environment of the cold war.

Harry Truman and Bipolarity

If bipolarity was lacking from FDR's political vocabulary, events soon enough compelled Harry Truman, his successor, to grapple with and devise appropriate responses to its emergence. It was not easy at first. Truman carried on with FDR's international economic program and hoped to make a go of the UN. But "the year and a half between the close of World War II and Truman's Doctrine in March 1947," Dallek observes, "was one of the most difficult and confusing periods in U.S. diplomatic history. Reflecting swiftly changing domestic and foreign currents, Americans gyrated between hopes of peaceful cooperation and fears of all-out strife."[49] George Kennan, as head of Policy Planning in the State Department, may have been the first American official to use the new geopolitical term: "It should be a cardinal point of our policy," he wrote in a private memo, dated October 1947, "to see to it that other elements of independent power are developed on the Eurasian land mass as rapidly as possible in order to take off our shoulders some of the burden of 'bi-polarity.'"[50] By the following winter, little doubt remained about the redirection of American foreign policy.

One of the decisive turning points had come in early 1947, when Britain found itself unable to cope with growing instability in the Eastern Mediterranean. Secretary of State George C. Marshall, in a February 1947 White House meeting with Congressional leaders, presented a detailed technical survey of the problems in the region, and of what aid was required from the United States. The audience remained unmoved. "My distinguished chief," Dean Acheson, the Undersecretary of State, later wrote, "flubbed his opening statement. In desperation I whispered to him a request to speak." In an exchange that has been repeated frequently by historians, Acheson spoke of apples in a barrel infected by one that was rotten—of how "the corruption of Greece would infect Iran and all to the East. It would also carry infection to Africa through Asia Minor and Egypt, and to Europe through Italy and France, already threatened by the strongest domestic Communist parties in Western Europe. The Soviet Union," Acheson summed up, "was playing one of the greatest gambles in history at minimal cost." After a long silence, Arthur H. Vandenberg, Chairman of the Republican-controlled Senate Foreign Relations Committee, turned to Truman and responded solemnly: "Mr. President, if you will say that to the Congress and the country, I will support you and I believe that most of its members will do the same."[51] The lesson was not lost on the administration, which responded with the Truman Doctrine. Nor was it lost on its successors.

From this moment on, the conventional wisdom among international relations specialists and cold war historians is framed almost entirely in realist terms: containing the Soviet Union became the animating force of U.S. foreign policy; balance-of-power logic and traditional alliance formation prevailed; the "discourse of national security," as Emily Rosenberg calls it, supplied the language of policy debates;[52] the public was swept along by anticommunist ideology; and the multilateral world order agenda, if it ever meant anything at all, was swept aside.

The conventional wisdom got a great many things right about bipolarity and its effects. Cold war America pursued its interests and sought to manage the changing balance of power. Moreover, the Soviet military threat together with anticommunism significantly attenuated the foreign policy dilemma that America's leaders had faced throughout the century. But FDR's immediate successors did not simply abandon the earlier multilateral agenda; they adapted some of its parts to very different geopolitical circumstances. Thus, it is, of course, the case that the Soviet threat drove the United States to assist Europe. But when it did, Truman and Eisenhower agreed to involve the United States militarily in the defense of Europe *only* within institutional frameworks that embodied certain multilateral principles, and which to them held out the promise, thereby, of transforming an intra-European security order that had produced world war twice in the life of one generation. These were objectives Wilson would have happily endorsed—and which realists at the time often dismissed or opposed. Because of the perspective from which the cold war story is usually told, demonstrating a role for multilateralism in its formative period requires a bit of political/institutional excavation, sifting through the sands of history for fragments of evidence.

Few observers question seriously that multilateralism continued to influence trade and monetary relations, so let's begin there. It is not always appreciated, however, that it did so in a complex and circuitous manner. The West European countries were unable to assume their full obligations under the global regimes for trade and money until the late 1950s. Nor could those global arrangements provide Europe the assistance it needed. That had to come from the United States.[53] By 1947, even though the United States had granted Europe nearly $9 billion in bilateral aid, Europe was in worse shape than ever: its gold and dollar reserves were depleted; it suffered from shortages of manpower, coal, steel, and other basic resources;

and its agricultural and industrial production still lagged behind prewar levels. Attempting to cope with these problems, the West European countries, with American acquiescence, constructed a network of more than two hundred bilateral trade and payments agreements among themselves, exactly of the sort the GATT and IMF were intended to eliminate. But still fear of social turmoil and economic collapse continued. Hence, during 1947–48 the United States changed course. Bilateral economic assistance to Europe gave way to the more comprehensive approach of the Marshall Plan. In return for an additional $12 billion aid commitment the United States required the West Europeans to devise multilateral, not merely country-by-country, plans for their reconstruction. The Committee—later the Organization—on European Economic Cooperation (OEEC) was established to orchestrate the process.[54] A European Payments Union was created in 1950, backed by $350 million in Marshall Plan assistance, as an intra-OEEC soft currency preference zone. By deliberately discriminating against the dollar, the scheme facilitated increased trade, trade liberalization, and movement toward currency convertibility among its members.

In short, in the face of bipolarity, and given the near-term deficiencies of the global economic regimes, the United States pushed economic multilateralism in Western Europe down to the regional level and supported it directly. The year 1947 also marked the beginning of an American campaign to encourage the even more ambitious aim of European unity. The idea had strong support in media and political circles. Senator J. William Fulbright and Representative Hale Boggs introduced concurrent resolutions into the Congress asking it to endorse "the creation of a United States of Europe within the framework of the United Nations."[55] The bills were passed overwhelmingly.

But what about security relations? Is not the cold war conventional wisdom bound to be correct here—its core explanatory domain? The answer is yes, but with a blind spot: in some respects, the institutional pattern exhibited in the security field is similar to that in economic relations.

Believing that the Soviet threat to Europe was subversive more than military the United States initially adopted what Pollard describes as a strategy of "economic security"—that is to say, to bolster confidence through economic recovery.[56] The strategy did not suffice, but the United States resisted bilateral alliances with its European friends. Britain and France signed a treaty of "alliance and mutual assistance" in March 1947— the Dunkirk Treaty, still aimed largely at Germany. Following Soviet noncooperation at the London Foreign Ministers Conference in late 1947, and by then increasingly concerned with a potential Soviet threat, Britain and

France sought to extend the Dunkirk model into a network of West European bilateral agreements which, they hoped, the United States would back with military guarantees. Led by Kennan, the State Department discouraged the notion on the grounds that Congress would oppose such a departure from America's traditional aversion to entangling alliances— indeed, Kennan still believed that American military commitments of any kind were unnecessary. Belgian Premier Paul-Henri Spaak was prompted by a Washington visit to hope that the United States would respond positively if the West Europeans established a collective effort of their own. And so the "Brussels Pact" of mutual assistance was born in 1948. President Truman endorsed it, but the United States refused to join or extend it military guarantees.[57]

European security needs kept pressing. Notwithstanding the verbal assurances of the Truman Doctrine, *"la grande peur"* of 1948 convinced European leaders that there was no alternative to having "some measure of military 'reassurance' " from the United States.[58] Their problem, however, remained: how to get the United States committed? The impasse was broken by the Vandenberg Resolution of June 11, 1948, approved by the Republican-controlled Senate, inviting the Truman administration to pursue a collective self-defense arrangement under Article 51 of the United Nations charter. The resolution led directly to negotiations of the North Atlantic Treaty.

Let's pause here for a moment and review the situation. Faced with a Soviet military threat of which the West Europeans, understandably, felt more certain than the United States,[59] the Truman administration had five options. The United States could: turn its back on Europe, as it had done after World War I; extend a unilateral security guarantee to some or all of Western Europe on the model of the Monroe Doctrine, though backed by firmer commitments; enter into bilateral alliances with the European countries most directly threatened; adopt a "dumbbell" model, as it was known, whereby Western Europe would organize a defense pact, the United States and Canada would do the same, with the two sides of the Atlantic linked by guarantees or treaty obligations; or, finally, institute indivisible security commitments for some collectivity of nations. European security needs vis-à-vis the Soviets could have been met by four of these five options—all except the first. Their Brussels treaty would have been compatible with a unilateral American security guarantee, or it could have formed the basis of a dumbbell arrangement. They would have settled for a series of bilateral alliances with the United States or U.S. backing for an extended Dunkirk model. And, of course, they were pleased with a multilateral security arrangement.

Complicating the calculus, the other West Europeans also had concerns about a possible future threat posed by Germany, particularly if, as was becoming apparent, Western Germany had to regain industrial and perhaps military strength to help contain the Soviet Union. From what we know, the Europeans were likely to have deemed credible American assurances in the form of strategically targeted bilateral alliances, though these would have stigmatized Germany; either a unilateral security guaranty to the Brussels pact backed by firm obligations or the dumbbell model, both of which could have included Germany; and the indivisible security commitments of NATO.

In short, the choice was America's to make. And America selected the last option, historically unprecedented, not only for the United States, but for the world.

The views of George Kennan on this issue are illuminating. Author of the containment doctrine and a serious realist practitioner, Kennan was serving as director of policy planning in the State Department. As noted, he initially believed that no U.S. military commitments to Western Europe were necessary. But if they had to be made, Kennan preferred what he called a "particularized" rather than a "legalistic-moralistic" form: such commitments should be specific in nature, limited in time, and contingent on discrete exigencies.[60] For Kennan, NATO represented anything but those attributes. Even though Kennan eventually acquiesced in the creation of NATO, he continued to protest its "legalistic commitments," which he viewed to be barely better than the UN in this regard. In a word, Kennan protested multilateralism in NATO.

Multilateralism was implicated in NATO in two respects. The first was the happenstance of its creation; the second was—and remains—the design of its security commitments. We take up each in turn.

By 1948, numerous proposals had been made in the U.S. Congress calling for UN charter amendments to limit, circumvent, or eliminate the permanent-member veto, of which the Soviets had availed themselves frequently. But the administration resisted, believing that attempts to abolish the veto would end up destroying the organization. Instead, Europeanists and multilateralists in the State Department (like John D. Hickerson, Director of the Office of European Affairs, they were often one and the same) worked feverishly, while Kennan was on an extended Asian trip, to help Senator Vandenberg draft the resolution that bears his name. Undersecretary of State Robert Lovett, who had little use for Kennan, directed the effort.[61] The Senator was pleased to oblige. At the San Francisco conference, Vandenberg, prewar isolationist and Republican from Michigan, had coauthored Article 51 of the UN charter, which endorsed collective self-defense arrangements in the first place.[62] Creating such an arrangement now, the Senator said, would allow the United States to act "within the Charter, but outside the [Soviet] veto."[63] Besides, Vandenberg was reported to have asked, "Why should a Democratic President get all the kudos in an election year?"[64]

The British did their part by defining an imagined security complex from Scandinavia to the Mediterranean and, with Canadian help, stretching it across to the Western hemisphere. British Foreign Secretary Ernest Bevin is given credit for proposing the concept of a single North Atlantic security system.[65] This was not by tradition a geopolitical construct that had delimited the organization of security relations. But it evoked a sense of historical and cultural community which helped tie the knot.

The North Atlantic Treaty was signed in April 1949—the first peacetime military alliance in U.S. history and, for Harry Truman, "with the Marshall Plan, one of the proudest achievements of his presidency."[66] Bevin described NATO approvingly as a step toward "the United Nations as it should have been had the Soviets cooperated."[67]

Multilateralism is also reflected in the type of security commitments NATO embodied. "The signing of the NATO Alliance," Michael Howard has written, "provided a sense that now at last all were for one and one was for all"[68]—the core attribute of collective security. NATO promised its members equal and unqualified protection under a common security umbrella. At the same time, all members pledged to undertake those measures, including the use of armed force, that they deemed necessary to maintain or restore the security of the collectivity. Article 5 of the North Atlantic Treaty, in which these pledges are enshrined, is a direct descendant of Articles 10 and 16 of the League covenant, on which Lodge had skewered Wilson.[69] After the Korean war, an integrated command structure was established in NATO to help execute the pledges.

The cold war conventional wisdom no doubt would raise objections to this rendering of the story. NATO, it would hold, is not a collective security organization, simply the bipolar version of a traditional alliance; the rest is rhetoric and window dressing, designed to generate political support in the United States. The initial premise of the rejoinder is correct: NATO was and is a collective defense scheme, not a collective security system, as Arnold Wolfers pointed out in an influential essay more than a generation ago.[70] It does not follow, however, that there are no principled differences between NATO's form of collective defense and old-fashioned alliances, as cold war security specialists have tended to believe.[71] NATO is a collective defense arrangement that exhibits elements of collective security in the form of its security commitments, far more generalized and indivisible than any mere alliance.

Indeed, those in the United States who objected to the form of NATO's security commitments did so precisely because they were concerned with these differences and their anticipated consequences. Kennan, for instance, feared that a security arrangement based on the indivisibility of peace among its members rather than on discrete and contingent commitments entailed an inherent tendency toward expansion, a prospect he feared the United States could ill afford. Equally telling were the views of Senator Robert A. Taft (R-Ohio)—"the most powerful single legislator of his day," a towering intellect, ardent anticommunist, but also isolationist by predilection.[72] He lobbied and voted against the North Atlantic Treaty. But he would have been prepared for his isolationism to be overruled by his antipathy toward the Soviets, he claimed, for bilateral security ties to specific European countries or a unilateral Monroe Doctrine-like guarantee to all of Western Europe. NATO he found too much to swallow, even in the cause of anticommunism. Why? As Taft explained, "I do not like the obligation written into the pact which binds us for twenty years to come to the defense of any country, no matter by whom it is attacked and even though the aggressor may be another member of the pact."[73] Taft, the isolationist, like Kennan, the realist, understood well the difference between NATO and a traditional alliance, and it was that difference which troubled both.

The Truman administration judged, evidently correctly, that the multilateral approach was the surest route to achieving sustained American involvement in the defense of Europe: indivisible security commitments, within an institutional framework that was compatible with the collective self-defense provision of the UN charter besides. The Senate ratified the North Atlantic Treaty by 82 to 13, suggesting "that a national consensus had been reached."[74]

Thus, multilateralism did not simply vanish in the early Truman years when U.S. foreign policy ran head-on into the emerging realities of bipolar power politics. In Western Europe, multilateralism was pushed down to the regional level. The genius of the Marshall Plan, NATO, and strong American support for European unification was that they simultaneously balanced Soviet power *and* began the process of transforming the West European international order along multilateral lines. The Eisenhower administration, in its support for a European Defense Community, reinforced this process, as we shall see in the next chapter. At the global level, the obvious difference between the economic and security spheres is that the restoration of global (minus the Soviet bloc) economic multilateralism could be achieved without the cooperation of the Soviet Union, and was in place by 1960. With the modest exceptions of peacekeeping and nuclear nonproliferation, initiated by the Eisenhower administration in the 1950s, prospects for multilateralism in global security relations had to await the end of the cold war.

Finally, the institutional differences between America's containment strategy in Western Europe and East Asia are striking and revealing. In East Asia, where the United States had relatively little choice, its approach was far more consistent with what we have called the cold war conventional wisdom than in Western Europe, where it did have a choice. Congressman Jacob K. Javits (R-NY) proposed legislation to create an Asian counterpart to NATO as early as 1950.[75] But multilateralism in security relations could not be exported to that part of the world.[76] The Nationalist Chinese regime was disintegrating under the impact of civil war against communist forces. The Truman administration was appalled by the insatiable greed and corruption of the Kuomintang, and lacked the desire and, it felt, the resources to intervene. Japan had colonized, imposed puppet regimes on, and otherwise exploited its neighbors in some cases for a half century, making reconciliation difficult to imagine. France and Britain retained colonial claims in Indochina and Hong Kong, respectively. That left the United States with a Korean foothold on the Asian mainland, from which it quickly withdrew its troops, together with its occupation of Japan.

Until 1948, the United States occupation authority in Japan, headed by General Douglas MacArthur, sought nothing less than to remake that country. The United States attempted to implement extensive social reforms, establish a Western-style constitution, dismantle the highly concentrated industrial and financial combines that had controlled the prewar Japanese economy, root out militarism, and preclude the future ability of Japan to project force abroad. Japan, in MacArthur's quaint depiction, was to become the "Switzerland of Asia."[77] By 1948, with fear of communist inroads in Japan high and the "loss" of China imminent, the "reverse course" policy was instituted. Japan now became America's bulwark against Asian communism, many of the domestic social and economic reforms became subordinated to that objective, and every effort was made to incorporate Japan quickly into the global economy. In short, first occupation and then sets of traditional alliances together with global economic multilateralism served as the cornerstones of U.S. East Asian strategy.

In addition to generating very different patterns of long-term regional evolution, American multilateral security commitments in the Atlantic and bilateral ties in East Asia also may have had a differential impact on the perceptions and misperceptions by America's adversaries in the short run. In the case of Korea, ambiguity about the "indivisibility" of the U.S. East Asian defense perimeter—about which, thanks to NATO, there was never a question in Europe—is usually assigned some role, albeit of undetermined magnitude, in explaining the outbreak of the Korean war. Later, Vietnam became a domino that could not be permitted to fall; within the sphere of NATO there were no separate dominoes, only an indivisible whole.

Pax Americana?

Writers on the political left, and also some in the realist tradition, have long alleged certain similarities in the postwar international postures of the United States and the Soviet Union. Both, it has been said, were imperial powers, though America's empire was "invisible" more than territorial.[78] In the early 1980s, the Norwegian diplomatic historian Geir Lundestad coined the phrase "empire by invitation" to express a strong pull-factor, the invitational character, of America's postwar international involvement, especially in Europe.[79] Post-1989 history has not been kind to those who had ascribed a moral or even merely a structural equivalency to the two superpowers and their respective "empires"—that of the Soviets evaporated instantly, while the legacy of America's institutional project, at least for the moment, continues to resonate and retain efficacy. In order to appreciate the future prospects of this legacy it is necessary to go beyond the simple—though critical—fact that the one was imposed by force, the other not. It is necessary also to understand the functioning of multilateral organizing principles.

Several key features of American multilateralism were already evident in its first expression: the "open door" notes issued by the McKinley administration at the turn of this century. George Kennan, in his book *American Foreign Policy*, derided the episode as a cynical and meaningless great-power ploy.[80] A great-power ploy it was, and cynical, too, invoked because Congress would not have supported the administration in a scramble to carve up China. But even so, it was not without significant differences from its alternatives. An open door policy differed in its international effects from colonial annexation or partitioning. It is the difference between "equal access" and "closed sphere": the greater third-party opportunities afforded by an equal-access regime were less likely to produce international rivalry and conflict. The target country, presumably, would have preferred to be left alone. But for it as well the "open door" approach held obvious advantages over annexation or partitioning: economically, it was more likely than a colonial relationship to assure fair prices, as Tony Smith has pointed out; politically, by avoiding discriminatory economic concessions, which inevitably led to direct political control, "weak states could thereby work to protect their autonomy."[81]

What was true for weak nations in the periphery amid an imperialist frenzy surely also held, many times over, for America's postwar relations with other industrialized countries, several of which were great powers in their own right. That the United States acted in its interest is not in question. The Soviet Union had to be contained, and a strong Europe and Japan would help limit the financial drain on the United States. But the United States often had multiple means by which to pursue those interests. Where possible, postwar America chose to frame its interests within a vision of world order that stressed openness, nondiscrimination, and greater prospects for joint gains—not relative gains that accrued disproportionately to the United States. Japan and Germany were defeated unconditionally in the war and occupied by the United States. Yet today, David Fromkin asks, "Is not the world economy at least as much Japan's or Germany's 'empire' as America's?"[82] In short, a multilateral order is more likely to create greater third-party opportunities, and thus a broader sense of ownership, than its bilateralist alternatives.

In addition to these distributive effects, multilateral orders are institutionally more durable in times of fundamental change. The respective fates of NATO and the Warsaw Pact are, of course, easily explained by the latter having been imposed by Moscow. But they also illustrate a core institutional difference: the Soviet Union established an East European security system based on country-by-country dyadic ties to Moscow whereas NATO embodied generalized security commitments. Once the Soviet Union conceded the cold war there would have been nothing left for the East Europeans themselves to build on had they been so inclined whereas NATO holds out the promise of enlarging and deepening a European security community. The main means of adjustment in bilateralist alliances, in short, is to abandon dyadic ties and start again from scratch. Furthermore, because multilateral orders facilitate more complex tradeoffs and bargains across issues and over time they are more likely to induce expectations of "diffuse reciprocity" among their participants.[83] That is to say, they need not satisfy specific quid-pro-quos whereby participants insist on being rewarded equally on every round and with every partner. Nowhere is this feature as prominent today as in the European Union, but it has always been evident in the global trade regime as well.

Ultimately, and in a manner that would not displease Wilson, the multilateral features of America's "empire" broaden its appeal by expressing a set of core communitarian values—originating in America's own sense of elective community based on a universal or general foundation open in principle to everyone. The American quest to remake the politics of the old world has helped establish an international political order that exhibits more of the "universal dominion of rights" invoked by Wilson when he took the United States into war in 1917 than would have existed otherwise, and more than the conventional understanding of international politics apprehends. Indeed, in this respect America's "empire" shares some of the characteristics of what Ronald Dworkin calls "law's empire." The international community is a long way from achieving the rule of law that internationalists have aspired to over the years. And it may never get there, for reasons we know only too well. Nevertheless, multilateral world order principles do embody elements of an "inclusive integrity"—the defining attribute of "law's empire." According to Dworkin, "Law's empire is defined by attitude, not territory or power or process. . . . Law's attitude is constructive: it aims, in the interpretive sense, to lay principle over practice to show the best route to a better future, keeping the right faith with the past. It is, finally, a fraternal attitude, an expression of how we are united in community though divided in project, interest, and conviction."[84]

And so, on the second try, American power coupled with American exceptionalism pulled the United States into the world—in the phrase's dual sense.

3 | Competitive Security

Only days after the United States dropped atomic bombs on Hiroshima and Nagasaki in August 1945, effectively ending World War II, the journalist Theodore H. White was received by General Douglas MacArthur. "White," MacArthur thundered, "White, do you know what this means?" "What, sir?" asked White. "Men like me are obsolete," MacArthur exclaimed. "There will be no more wars, White, no more wars."[1] MacArthur was wrong, of course; in fact, he soon found himself commanding United Nations forces in the Korean war. Since 1945, nearly twenty-five million people have been killed in more than a hundred international conflicts. In addition, over twenty million refugees roam the world today, the unhappy byproducts of wars and civil strife; equal numbers are displaced within their own countries. Most of these victims inhabited what became known as the third world, the battleground on which the cold war's hot outbursts were fought.

MacArthur turned out to be right in another regard, however. Never before in the modern era have the major powers gone so long without a major war. Indeed, after the Cuban missile crisis of 1962, the superpowers avoided any comparable confrontation for a period that was longer, Robert Jervis observes, than great powers in the past usually had gone without war.[2] Scholars will argue for years to come about what factors caused this "long peace," as John Lewis Gaddis dubbed it:[3] the strategic advantages of bipolarity, the effectiveness of nuclear deterrence, the dampening of nationalist fervor, and the normative obsolescence of major-power war, to note only a few. But one factor is not in dispute: the sustained involvement by the United States to create and maintain a stable international security order.

Prior to the advent of the cold war, before bipolarity came to be understood as the core geopolitical feature of postwar security relations, Roosevelt sought to ensure American involvement through a universal security organization based in a concert of power. The outbreak of the cold war rendered his strategy largely irrelevant even as it posed a clearly defined military threat and ideological challenge that increasingly animated U.S. involvement. Nevertheless, the Truman administration, as we have seen, did not simply abandon the earlier multilateral course, but where possible adapted it to the newly emerging strategic context. In several instances, as we shall see below, the Eisenhower administration followed suit.

Our aim in chapters 3 through 6 is to assess the legacy these postwar multilateral efforts have left us. In the present chapter, we flesh out the evolving multilateral dimension in U.S. security policy from Roosevelt through to Eisenhower, by which time the cold war had frozen it in place. What makes the pre- and early cold war experience of more than historical interest today is that the post-cold war world in some respects conforms to Roosevelt's geopolitical expectations more closely than did the intervening years. In the next chapter, we explore the impact of the end of the cold war on this institutional legacy, and ask whether and how the arrangements then constructed can help preserve and possibly expand the scope of the long peace.

From Concert to Cacophony

In Roosevelt's thinking, the United Nations was to serve as an institutional tripwire, obliging the United States to take policy positions on international conflicts before they got out of hand—at the extreme, to avoid repeating such costly errors as having stood aside while Hitler, in Fromkin's words, "made the Germany of 1936, which could have been defeated by practically anybody in Europe, into the Germany of 1939, which could be defeated by practically nobody in Europe."[4] Moreover, the UN Security Council was to be the membership club designed to prevent Soviet defection from the cause of international stability. To credibly pursue these political goals and deter aggression the UN needed, in Roosevelt's view, an enforcement capability.

Creating an international military force in some form was a central concern at the four-power Dumbarton Oaks conference held in the summer of 1944.[5] There were two alternatives: a standing international force or ad hoc arrangements providing national contingents when needed. Initially, almost all postwar planners favored a true international police force. But as time went on they drew away from the idea because of not only such practical difficulties as how to recruit, equip, base, train, transport, and command such an operation but also the realization that ad hoc arrangements were likely to arouse less domestic political opposition. Roosevelt, as we have seen, rejected the notion of "a superstate with its own police force and other paraphernalia of coercive power," favoring instead a mechanism for "joint action" by national forces.[6]

Three UN charter provisions on military enforcement emerged from Dumbarton Oaks, representing a radical departure from previous peacetime experience. The first largely reflected U.S. language. It required that each member undertake to make available to the UN Security Council, "on its call" when needed to maintain international peace and security, armed forces, facilities, and other assistance, including rights of passage, in accordance with special agreements that were to be negotiated as soon as possible (Article 43). The agreements would specify the number and types of forces, as well as the kinds of facilities and other assistance, which each member was prepared to make available, and they were subject to the usual treaty ratification process of each member state.

The second provision reflected American and, even more so, Soviet interest in the special role of air forces. To enable the UN to take "urgent military measures," members that had the capability were asked to designate, on a stand-by basis, air contingents for combined international enforcement action (Article 45). They were to be governed by the same special agreements. The Soviet Union's interest presumably reflected the enormous losses they had suffered at the hands of the invading German army during the war, and the desire to have all the help possible to intercept any future attack before it struck deep into its homeland. On the American side, the major advocate, not surprisingly, was the air force.[7] But there was also great interest on political grounds because the use of air power, U.S. policymakers believed, would reduce the domestic difficulties involved in "sending our boys overseas."[8]

Third, at the suggestion of Britain, it was agreed to establish a Military Staff Committee comprising the national chiefs of staff of the Security Council's five permanent members (Article 47). The British drew on the successful precedent of the Combined Chiefs of Staff system for their joint campaigns with the United States in World War II. The Military Staff

Committee was to advise and assist the Security Council on military matters within its jurisdiction, including the "strategic direction" of any armed forces placed at the Council's disposal. Questions regarding the actual command and control of such forces were left to be worked out subsequently.

In the United States the next move was up to Congress. The Senate ratified the UN charter overwhelmingly. But Congress also needed to resolve the constitutional issue of whether and how American armed forces could be deployed by the UN without prior congressional approval in each instance. During the Dumbarton Oaks discussions, Arthur Vandenberg, then ranking minority member on the Senate Foreign Relations Committee, took the position that an affirmative vote by the United States at the United Nations in support of military action that involved U.S. troops was "tantamount to a declaration of war."[9] This responsibility the Constitution lodged in the Congress, he noted, not the Executive. But Vandenberg also acknowledged the "long-term practice," in his words, whereby the president as commander-in-chief deployed military force abroad in situations short of war and without prior congressional approval. He confessed to being unsure how to reconcile the two. Secretary of State Cordell Hull seized the opportunity to clarify the matter for the senator, dispatching a memorandum to the Foreign Relations Committee. There had been as many as seventy-six instances of such force deployments in prior U.S. history, Hull pointed out. What is more, he contended, disputes among members of an international organization are, in any case, akin to civil conflicts within the same political community, not acts of war as traditionally understood. Vandenberg dropped his objections.

Congress as a whole took up the issue in December 1945, in considering the UN participation act. It was resolved, not by insisting on Congressional prerogative, as one would expect today, but in favor of a strong UN enforcement capability. The act stipulated that once Congress ratified the special agreements with the Security Council that the charter called for, "the President shall not be deemed to require the authorization of the Congress to make available to the Security Council . . . the armed forces, facilities, or assistance provided for therein." Attempts to add reservations and contrary amendments were easily swept aside. Hans Kelsen, a leading postwar international legal scholar, underscored the significance: "according to this Act of Congress the employment by the Security Council of the armed forces made available by the United States is not to be considered as an act of war, the declaration of which requires, under Article 1, Section 8, of the Constitution, an act of Congress."[10]

With Congressional support in place, the focus shifted to the United

Nations. In February 1946, the Security Council directed the Military Staff Committee, as its first task, to devise plans for the force agreements stipulated in Article 43. The committee met some 157 times during the next fifteen months, and reached agreements-in-principle on many issues. But by mid-1947 it became clear that its efforts had fallen victim to the escalating cold war. The negotiations foundered on the most basic issue of all: the overall size of the multinational force and the relative sizes to be contributed by each of the permanent five.[11] It may well be that the final U.S. position was submitted with the expectation that it would be rejected by the Soviet Union, but its order of magnitude is astonishing all the same: it advocated a combined total of 20 ground divisions or around 200,000 men, 1,250 bombers, 2,250 fighters, 3 battleships, 6 carriers, 15 cruisers, 84 destroyers, and 90 submarines. The Soviet Union favored a smaller combined force, consisting of 12 ground divisions, 600 bombers, 300 fighters, 5–6 cruisers, 24 destroyers, and 12 submarines. In addition, and no doubt worried about U.S. dominance over UN enforcement activities, the Soviets divined a "principle of equality" in the charter as to the size and composition of forces—in accord with which each of the permanent five would have been limited to the same type and size of forces, thereby reducing all to the lowest level offered by any one of them. This interpretation was particularly problematical for the air component, because it would have lowered all contributions to the level of China's, which barely had an air force. It seems that, having solidified its control over the buffer states on its western borders, the Soviet Union no longer saw any pressing need for a collective air deterrent. Attempts to form UN forces were formally abandoned in August 1948.

There is no telling what might have happened if these negotiations had gone differently and agreements on standby forces had actually been reached. Even in a best-case scenario, the permanent five soon would have come up against the unresolved issue of command and control. Furthermore, they would have confronted the need to formulate a novel doctrine for joint military operations because even at that time relatively few of the conflicts the UN faced were instances of clear-cut interstate aggression. In other words, the UN would have encountered, some forty years earlier, the problems that afflicted its peace operations once they were unshackled by the end of the cold war.

In its first few years of operation the United Nations had a mixed record. With active U.S. support, the UN successfully mediated between the Dutch government and Indonesian nationalists in the Netherlands East Indies, leading to the creation of an independent republic. That precedent launched the world body on a successful career as an agency facilitating and stabilizing the process of decolonization. This process actually benefited from superpower rivalry, much as America's own independence had bene-fited from rivalry between England and France, because the United States, in its campaign for self-determination, could now also bring to bear on its allies fear of the Soviets exploiting the continued existence of colonialism.

Little success was achieved in other types of conflicts, however. Infiltra-tion from Albania, Bulgaria, and Yugoslavia in support of a Greek leftist insurrection in 1946 was not an external attack of the sort the UN had been designed to resist, and it had cold war implications besides. The UN was able to respond only by dispatching a small observer team. The United States ultimately responded with the Truman Doctrine, foreshadowing the policy of containment. In 1948, Britain shed itself of its troublesome Pales-tine mandate, handing it off to the UN. The first step was relatively easy: Israel was declared a state. But war with its Arab neighbors could not be prevented. At the cessation of hostilities, a UN truce supervision organi-zation was established which remains in place to this day.

The impediment of the Soviet veto in the Security Council was increas-ingly troublesome—as was, for the Truman administration, the ire it aroused in Congress.[12] In 1948, Senator Homer Ferguson (R-Michigan) introduced the most draconian of many proposals to amend the veto pro-vision of the charter. His resolution, which had bipartisan co-sponsors, called for removal of the veto in cases of aggression, together with the establishment of an armaments ceiling and an international police force, neither of which would be subject to the veto. In the event these propos-als were themselves vetoed, the resolution further called for the creation of a new international organization from which the vetoers would be excluded. The State Department managed to sidetrack this and similar Congressional demands for UN charter revision on the grounds that they were fruitless as well as destructive—and by arguing that Article 51 of the charter already provided for the viable alternative of collective self-defense arrangements. Down that road lay the creation of NATO.

According to many observers at the time, the first real test for the United Nations finally came in June 1950, when North Korea invaded the South. John Holmes, who was acting Canadian UN ambassador, noted an "extraordinary atmosphere of enthusiasm" in UN corridors, stirred by the hope that the organization was about to come into its own.[13] His fellow Canadian, political scientist Denis Stairs, wrote some years later that "the decision to conduct the American response through United Nations machinery was never at any time seriously debated in Washington, and for all practical purposes it was an automatic reaction."[14] However, far from being paradigmatic, Korea turned out to be a singularity. Far from vindicating the enforcement role of the UN, virtually every aspect of the Korean episode showed that the cold war made it impossible for that original design to hold.

The fact that UN action was possible at all was due to a Soviet boycott of the Security Council over the issue of which China should be represented in the UN. The Soviets did not return to the Council until August 1950, by which time all of the initial decisions authorizing a UN force had been made. Once they returned and vetoed further action, American ingenuity but no firm legal basis produced the so-called uniting-for-peace resolution, whereby the General Assembly was empowered to assume consideration of a conflict if the Security Council was deadlocked. Over the strenuous objections of the Soviets as well as Senator Robert A. Taft and other conservatives in the United States,[15] the resolution was adopted and became the basis for subsequent authorization by the General Assembly of enabling measures for the Korean operation. Finally, because no member state had made troops available to the Security Council as required under Article 43 of the charter, the UN could not deploy any; it could only recommend that course to its members. Sixteen joined the United States in responding positively. And with the UN Military Staff Committee moribund, the sixteen agreed to place their contingents under a unified command led by the United States. Unlike its distant descendent, Operation Desert Storm, the Korean force was designated a UN force and flew the UN flag.

The United States supplied some eighty-five percent of the non-Korean elements of the United Nations force. Of the other countries participating, six were founding members of NATO, and two, Greece and Turkey, were hoping for NATO membership and were admitted before the Korean war was over. Two others, Australia and New Zealand, formed the ANZUS alliance with the United States during the Korean war—the Australian Foreign Minister was so eager to achieve that goal "that he rushed in late July [1950] to pledge Australian troops for Korea hours before the British announcement, thereby making his nation the first Commonwealth member to do so."[16] The other participants were developing countries with close ties to the United States.

Clearly, in practice this was a Western more than a United Nations affair. Even so, it bothered the United States to have to seek authorization from and report to the General Assembly, which included many nations that contributed nothing to the Korean war effort. The U.S. military complained bitterly. But it is unimaginable that General Douglas MacArthur, commander of UN forces, paid any attention to the UN when he ignored even his Washington superiors—and ultimately had to be sacked by President Truman for what amounted to insubordination. The burden of dealing with the UN fell to the State Department. In reporting to President Truman on the General Assembly's Korean armistice debate, for example, Secretary of State Dean Acheson bemoaned "the outstanding fact of the Assembly so far," namely "its dominance by the Arab-Asian bloc," whose interests often differed from those of the U.S.[17] Acheson was particularly displeased with the "Menon cabal," his term for a group of critics organized by Krishna Menon, India's Foreign Minister, which signaled the emergence of the nonaligned movement.

In sum, in the immediate postwar period the United States began to implement some of the institutional components of Roosevelt's concert-based collective security system. The emergence of the cold war arrested further movement. By the time of Korea, with Soviet vetoes blocking the Security Council and Third World "cabals" lurking in the General Assembly, the UN was proving to be unhelpful to the United States as an instrument to cope with the most likely source of direct threats to U.S. interests: the Soviet Union and China. Far from serving as a precedent, then, Korea sealed the fate of Roosevelt's design and left the UN without a clear role in the domain of international security relations.

From Concert to Community

Until the Korean war, U.S. policymakers were nearly unanimous in discounting the likelihood of a direct Soviet military attack on Western Europe, but they were becoming increasingly apprehensive about growing Soviet military capabilities.[18] European apprehensions concerned them even more. NATO as a treaty of mutual security guarantees still was not providing the Europeans with sufficient reassurance. A militarily more robust NATO seemed inescapable, involving the return of U.S. ground troops to Europe. The Soviet atomic explosion in 1949 and North Korea's invasion in 1950 hastened the process. NATO's new military organization was established in the early months of 1951 with the creation of Supreme Headquarters Allied Powers Europe (SHAPE), commanded by General Dwight D. Eisenhower. Two other supreme commands were established a year later, one for the Atlantic, the other for the English Channel and North Sea, and SHAPE was subdivided into northern, central, and southern as well as Mediterranean commands. A 1952 Lisbon meeting of the

Council of Ministers established the political structure of NATO, governed by a ministerial-level North Atlantic Council, with permanent representatives to carry on business between Council meetings, served by a secretary general and an international staff.

From the moment NATO became an integrated military-political organization of unprecedented peacetime commitments it was subject to a fundamental dilemma. Because of the enduring disparity between Soviet and NATO ground forces, the strength of NATO's deterrent depended on the credibility of its nuclear strategy. However, the decision whether or not to use nuclear weapons remained a U.S. prerogative. This dependence on America's nuclear arsenal triggered a twin fear among the European allies. Robert Osgood put it well more than a generation ago:

> First, the allies suspect that the United States will *not* resort to massive nuclear retaliation against a less-than-massive aggression in Europe at the staggering cost of a thermonuclear assault upon the United States and that, therefore, America's nuclear striking power is unreliable as a deterrent against contingencies short of a direct attack upon the United States itself. Second, they fear that the United States *will* resort to massive nuclear retaliation against limited aggressions (inside Europe or outside), which NATO cannot effectively counter by less drastic means, and that, therefore, American retaliation will plunge them into a war of annihilation.[19]

NATO's dual-track decision of 1979—to place Cruise and Pershing II missiles on the territories of five NATO nations while simultaneously pursuing arms control and confidence-building measures with the Soviet Union—was merely the latest in a long series of initiatives designed to cope with the problem, and the last before the cold war ended.

This unresolved dilemma occupied some the best minds in security policy and security studies throughout the cold war. It was a good thing that it did because their temporary fixes helped sustain the requirements of allied deterrence and defense. Along the way, however, the experts became so preoccupied with the technical arcana of the dilemma and its corollaries that they very nearly lost track of America's political transformative mission in Western Europe, in which NATO and European unification played central parts. Let us, therefore, briefly reacquaint ourselves with the unfolding of that mission—leaving it to the next chapter to explore its contemporary relevance.

The United States Congress laid the foundation for NATO's first strategic concept. Congress required that U.S. military assistance be used in support of *joint* strategic plans, so as to achieve "an integrated defense."[20] Accordingly, the military plan that was drafted in early 1950, largely in the Pentagon, called for a system of balanced *collective* forces—that is, for an actual division of labor among the national forces of member countries. In addition to its cost-effectiveness, which Congress prized, the proposal's transformative intent was clear. Congress was merely repeating in the military field the requirement it had imposed for European economic reconstruction via the Marshall Plan: that European efforts be multilateralized. Michael Hogan, the historian of the Marshall Plan, documents that the precedent was explicit in the minds of decisionmakers.[21] NATO was never able to implement this strategic concept. One key obstacle was that it would have made it impossible for smaller NATO countries to maintain adequately balanced *national* forces for purely national defense purposes— especially air and naval forces, which under this plan would have become the primary responsibility of the United States and Britain.

America's transformative mission was equally evident on the subject of a European Defense Community (EDC). West Germany was at the heart of this issue. Endowing NATO with a significant conventional military capability and implementing its "forward strategy" of defending Western Europe as far to the east as possible required a rearmed West Germany. The United States and Britain felt unable to expend the resources that would have been necessary to avoid that, while France's potential contribution to European security was limited to begin with and was further constrained by its costly colonial war in Indochina. But France, not surprisingly, was alarmed at the prospect of rearming Germany. It countered with the Pleven plan, named for the French Premier who proposed it. The plan called for the creation of a European Defense Community, complete with a European defense minister, defense budget, and supranational army comprised of divisional units from France, Britain, and the Benelux countries, as well as Germany and Italy.

The EDC was an oddity.[22] Even though France proposed and signed the treaty that called for its establishment, the EDC was widely regarded as a subterfuge by France to prevent German rearmament. The Germans were not keen on it for precisely that reason: it would have left them without national control over any future German forces. Churchill, once again Prime Minister, did not much care for EDC either, describing it as a "sludgy amalgam" and arguing, correctly as it turned out, that a NATO-only framework sufficed to constrain a rearmed Germany.[23] But they all had to contend with EDC's most ardent champion: the United States. General Eisenhower was an early and strong supporter, and he helped persuade President Truman of its desirability. As president, Eisenhower pushed actively for its establishment: "Only in collective security," he wrote to his friend General Alfred Gruenther during discussions of the EDC, is there "any future for the free world."[24] The Joint Chiefs came to accept EDC, as did Congress, which proposed to make military aid to EDC countries conditional on the adoption of the treaty.[25] On behalf of the administration, Secretary of State John Foster Dulles told the North Atlantic Council in 1953 that if Europe failed to ratify EDC "grave doubts" would arise in the United States concerning the future of European security, and America would be obliged to undertake an "agonizing reappraisal" of its role in Europe.

The respected realist analyst Robert Osgood was still disturbed by this affair a decade later: "Both sides of the argument displayed almost total indifference to the strategic military considerations," he noted reprovingly. "Indeed, in the eyes of its principal architects, EDC became as important as an instrument of Franco-German reconciliation as of military security."[26] But that, of course, was the point of U.S. support for EDC, as Osgood knew full well. Franco-German reconciliation was the key to European transformation.

In the end, the idea of integrating French and German armed forces turned out to be too big, and too humiliating, a jump for France itself, EDC's original proponent. The French National Assembly voted the treaty down in 1954. Thereafter, agreement was quickly reached on the contours of the new NATO. German sovereignty would be restored, and the Federal Republic would join NATO, contributing both army divisions and tactical air wings to NATO's forward defense. But this move necessitated strengthening NATO's multilateral mechanisms.[27] At the suggestion of British Foreign Secretary Anthony Eden, the Western Union, the dormant organizational umbrella created by the 1948 Brussels Treaty, was revived and expanded into the Western European Union (WEU), incorporating Germany and Italy. The WEU was linked to NATO and was empowered to fix maximum force levels of its members on the recommendation of NATO's military authorities. In addition, allied forces would continue to be stationed in Germany not only as protection against the Soviet threat, but also to reassure everyone else, especially France and implicitly the Soviet Union, about any possible future German threat. Lastly, the United States and its allies declared that they would regard NATO to be of "indefinite duration."

Even as this frontal thrust toward European unification represented by

EDC was halted, a more indirect route toward the same end had already been opened. French Foreign Minister Robert Schuman proposed a plan to pursue Franco-German rapprochement and European integration through a strategy of economic security: initially pooling the iron and steel sectors of France, Germany, and other interested countries under a supranational authority. The Schuman proposal led to the creation of the six-member European Coal and Steel Community in 1951[28]—the forerunner of the European Common Market/European Community/European Union.

The failure of EDC left Eisenhower undeterred in his determination to include a military security component in the European integration process. Following his 1953 Atoms for Peace speech, he turned his attention to atomic energy as a potential vehicle, advocating the creation of a European Atomic Energy Community (EURATOM). This move reflected several considerations, the primary of which was political: Eisenhower's effort "was ultimately not so much for the creation of EURATOM per se as for a united Europe."[29] He simply did not believe that the momentum generated by the coal and steel community would be sufficient to achieve economic unity. "EURATOM was one step," he later wrote, "then would come the effort toward economic union."[30] In addition, France was well on its way to becoming a nuclear power, which was expected to strain Franco-German relations unless some compensating cooperative venture in the nuclear field was devised. Apart from its connection to security relations, atomic energy was an attractive vehicle to advance the cause of European unity for several other reasons: few vested interests existed in Europe that had to be overcome; atomic energy had a certain cachet then in the popular imagination, symbolizing the harnessing of science to produce economic plenty; and atomic energy, especially amid the Suez crisis, offered a way out of continued dependence on Middle East oil.

EURATOM pooled fissionable materials for peaceful purposes under a supranational authority, subject to safeguards so as to prevent diversion for military purposes. It also enabled the community entity to receive nuclear technology, materials, and information from the United States. EURATOM came into existence in 1957, along with the European Economic Community (EEC). The Eisenhower administration together with EURATOM's European promoters prevailed despite significant obstacles on both sides of the Atlantic: the U.S. Atomic Energy Commission favored the system of bilateral treaties through which it exercised control over the export of fissionable materials; Britain preferred an intergovernmental formula through the Organization for European Economic Cooperation rather than a supranational entity; France feared that EURATOM would adversely affect its independent nuclear weapons program; and German industrialists as well as Franz-Josef Strauss, Minister of Atomic Questions in Konrad Adenauer's government, objected on the ground that EURATOM's common ownership of fissionable materials might promote socialism.

Eisenhower was unsuccessful in a final European endeavor: sharing American nuclear weapons and delivery systems with a European NATO entity. This was perhaps the most astonishing step of all. Yet it fit the pattern of America getting involved in the security of Europe not only to contain the Soviet Union but also, in doing so, to create institutional means that promised to transform the traditional conduct of European international politics. John Steinbruner confirmed some of Eisenhower's weapons-sharing plans in a study published twenty years ago.[31] Steve Weber, on the basis of recent archival materials, argues that Eisenhower "fully intended that [a NATO nuclear] consortium evolve into an integrated and independent nuclear force for the European NATO allies."[32] According to Weber, Eisenhower was close to achieving this aim when his term in office expired. His efforts were repeatedly delayed and ultimately thwarted by the Congressional Joint Committee on Atomic Energy, jealous of its role as guardian of the nation's atomic secrets.

The administration of John F. Kennedy developed a set of nuclear strategies that were very different from Eisenhower's "massive retaliation"—"to blow hell out of them in a hurry if they start anything," as Eisenhower once described it to a group of Congressional leaders.[33] The new doctrine of "flexible response" was more complex and subtle, and it required a far greater centralization of control over nuclear weapons. Kennedy's Secretary of Defense, Robert McNamara, in a famous 1962 Ann Arbor speech—called "McNamara's foolish speech" by British Prime Minister Harold Macmillan[34] —criticized independent nuclear deterrents on the grounds that they were incompatible with fighting a "restrained" nuclear war. But with European expectations having been raised, the Kennedy administration felt the need to offer an alternative, proposing a NATO multilateral nuclear force of surface ships, which satisfied no one and was discarded in due course.[35]

But far more changed with Kennedy's inauguration than nuclear doctrine. Fromkin captures the shift effectively:

> Kennedy's young men took it for granted that the United States was a superpower with global interests and responsibilities, but Eisenhower's generation had not started from any such

assumption; they had been obliged to question and search for themselves . . . as they groped for a definition of the world role their country should play, pursuing the exceptional mission that they believed history had ordained for the United States, while pursued by doubts that they got it right.[36]

In sum, an era in U.S. foreign policy had come to an end. The sustained American involvement that an earlier generation of leaders struggled to attain Kennedy assumed as a given. His administration possessed a confidence, even a certain hubris, about America's willingness and ability to manage the superpower rivalry—whether by gaming nuclear war fighting scenarios, conquering outer space, or sending counterinsurgency forces into jungles across the world. America will pay any price, bear any burden, the youthful president proclaimed, as his predecessor must have looked on in astonishment.

Before that shift, in the 1950s, the Eisenhower administration sought to trade on the success of NATO and "collective security" became the rhetoric of choice as Secretary Dulles justified the "pactomania" of which he was often accused. But conditions were nowhere as conducive as in Europe. By 1953, the deteriorating French position in Indochina and fears of further communist advances produced grave concern in Washington. But America would not act alone. "No Western power can go to Asia militarily," Eisenhower explained, "except as one of a concert of powers, which concert must include local Asiatic peoples."[37] The Southeast Asia Collective Defense Treaty was signed not long after the fall of the French at Dienbienphu. It represented little more than a traditional alliance, however. In case of attack, consultations were prescribed, and SEATO, its institutional expression, embodied none of the multilateral features of NATO. Moreover, there was no indigenous regional unification process for SEATO to intermingle with and reinforce. This was even more true of the Baghdad Pact (CENTO), which the United States, its instigator, never joined, wishing to alienate neither the Arab states, led by Egypt, nor Israel. During the Korean war, the United States had also formed a valuable alliance with Australia and New Zealand (ANZUS). All withered. Mao Zedong viewed SEATO as a paper tiger and treated it accordingly;[38] it was formally dissolved in 1977. CENTO, which had amounted to even less, was terminated in 1979. During the 1980s, ANZUS fell victim to disagreements with New Zealand about the presence of nuclear weapons aboard U.S. naval vessels in New Zealand's harbors and waters.

In short, beyond Europe the multilateralized collective self-defense

route—where multilateral refers to a set of organizing principles, not simply the number of parties involved—offered America no viable and
durable options. Today, Western Europe is the one place in the world where
it is possible to speak of the existence of a community of nations in more
than euphemistic terms.

Two Concertinos

After the Korean war, the UN was left without any consistent and stable
expectations about its role in international security relations. By the mid-
1950s this situation began to change modestly as a result of two developments: decolonization and the emergence of the so-called third world, and
the allure of nuclear power. In reacting to both, the superpowers discovered
enough of a concert of interest to permit modest new UN security roles in
peacekeeping and nuclear nonproliferation. Both came at the initiative of
the Eisenhower administration.

Cold War Peacekeeping

The first innovation in the UN's security role took the form of military
deployments for purposes far short of enforcement, which came to be
known as peacekeeping. The 1956 Suez crisis provided the occasion. In
late October–early November Israel, Britain, and France launched coordinated attacks against Egypt, having plotted the campaign on the outskirts
of Paris.[39] Israel claimed to be responding to *fedayeen* raids initiated from
Egypt, though the *fedayeen* themselves had been organized in retaliation for
Israel's Gaza raids the previous year. Israel was also concerned with the
buildup of Egyptian military capabilities, as Egypt had recently made a
major weapons purchase from Czechoslovakia, which also implied Soviet
approval. Britain and France sought to reassert control of the Suez Canal,
which Egypt had nationalized in retaliation for loss of U.S. and British support of a loan to build the Aswan dam. In addition, Britain resented Egyptian President Gamal Abdel Nasser's vigorous opposition to the Baghdad
Pact, one of Britain's few remaining instruments of influence in the region,
and France sought to punish Nasser for his support of the Algerian independence movement and more generally for the reverberations of his anticolonial rhetoric throughout North Africa.

   The United States had enjoyed good relations with Nasser; since 1953
he had been carrying on running conversations with locally stationed Central Intelligence Agency operatives.[40] But bilateral relations began to
worsen even before the Aswan rift; thereafter both sides felt humiliated. In

return for the promised loan the United States asked Egypt to recognize Israel's existing borders and lead an effort among Arab states to sign a peace treaty with Israel; Egypt refused. The United States then dropped its support for the loan. The Soviet Union entered the fray by offering Egypt a friendship treaty and hinting that it might help finance Aswan; this in turn piqued the United States. Michael Fry has expressed well the administration's sentiment: "In the period from 26 July to 29 October 1956, Eisenhower and Dulles worked to bring Nasser to heel, but not to bring him down."[41] The three allies, however, saw Nasser's overthrow as the solution to their problems.

Israel struck first, sweeping across the Sinai. Within the week France and Britain joined in, as prearranged, ostensibly as a police action to separate the other two combatants and safeguard the canal. The British had expected Eisenhower to make disapproving public noises but to support the venture privately. They misjudged him. Eisenhower, whom the allies had not informed of the action, was furious. "All right," he instructed Dulles, "Foster, you tell 'em, goddamn it, we're going to apply sanctions, we're going to the United Nations, we're going to do everything that there is so we can stop this thing."[42] Eisenhower did all of that, beginning with a U.S.-sponsored Security Council resolution in response to the Israeli invasion, calling for an immediate cease-fire and the withdrawal of Israeli forces. Britain and France vetoed that resolution. A Franco-British counterproposal called for both sides to withdraw to ten miles on either side of the canal, but that would have left the Israeli forces well within Egyptian territory. The Soviet Union, in support of Egypt, vetoed that. A uniting-for-peace resolution brought the matter to the General Assembly which, by the largest majority to date, adopted essentially the same demands Britain and France had vetoed in the Security Council—with one addition, introduced by the United States: to halt movement of all foreign troops into the area. But to no avail. It was then that Britain and France invaded.

The United States stayed the course at the UN. The administration also cut off the supply of intelligence data to its allies. And it permitted a beating of the British pound to take place in international financial markets, while indicating that it would oppose any loan to Britain from the U.S. Export-Import Bank as well as British requests for International Monetary Fund assistance—unless Britain accepted a cease-fire.[43] "We must stop, we must stop," Chancellor of the Exchequer Harold Macmillan agonized, "or we will have no more dollars left by the end of the week."[44]

Eisenhower's motives in opposing America's two oldest and closest allies, and taking the issue to the United Nations at that, have been analyzed extensively. The invasion took place the week before a U.S. presidential election, and Eisenhower, as he had been in 1952, was the candidate of peace. The invasion gave the Soviets a cover behind which to crush the Hungarian uprising, thereby denying the West a propaganda victory. The balance of power in the Middle East potentially was at stake, and the Soviets might benefit from a shift. Finally, the invasion inflamed opinion among the newly independent countries of the third world, which the United States was trying to cultivate. In fact, Eisenhower seemed especially disturbed by the neocolonial hauteur of the British and French invasions. In his inimitable locution he said: "The British were out-of-date in thinking of this as a mode of action." Elsewhere he described it as action "in the Victorian style."[45]

Whatever Eisenhower's motivations, the consequence of his Suez stance was to involve the UN in a new mode of security operation. The UN served as a convenient forum in which to blend these various elements into a policy. With opposition from the United States implacable and the UN demanding a cease-fire, Britain and France searched for a figleaf. Because theirs had been a police action, they intimated, they would be willing to turn over the policing functions to a UN force if one were created. The UN obliged. With active U.S. encouragement, Canadian Foreign Minister Lester Pearson proposed a United Nations Emergency Force (UNEF), comprising troops from ten middle-sized and smaller countries.[46] A cease-fire and withdrawal of the invading forces was arranged. Egypt (but not Israel) agreed to accept UNEF on its territory. UNEF, which reached a strength of 6,000, supervised the cease-fire and foreign troop withdrawals, arranged to clear the Suez Canal of war-related blockage, and monitored the Israeli-Egyptian border until Egypt withdrew its consent for UNEF's presence in 1967, as a prelude to that Mideast war.

Eisenhower's actions drew strong domestic criticism. The press reported a major crisis in NATO: "The Western alliance, which stood firm as long as it was confronted by open Soviet aggression, is unable to agree on means for dealing with the rising spirit of nationalism in Asia and Africa," the New York Times explained.[47] Among the most severe critics, it will come as little surprise, were leading realists. George Kennan, by then a private citizen, was dejected. "In the course of thirty years' experience in American foreign policy," he stated, "I have known many moments of doubt and unhappiness over positions adopted by the Government; but never have I known such perplexity and unhappiness." By opposing its allies at the UN, he charged, the administration had allowed "the very foundations of American policy [to be] swept away, the victim of an empty legalism"[48]—

by which he meant the concept of collective security Eisenhower had invoked on several occasions.[49] Hans Morgenthau, the *paterfamilias* of American postwar academic realists, was appalled. "Regardless of the intrinsic merits of [the allies'] military operation," he opined, "once it was started we had a vital interest in its quick and complete success."[50] Arnold Wolfers supported these views.[51]

UNEF was not an enforcement action. It was termed peacekeeping. Brian Urquhart, who was present at its creation and presided over the activity for many years, has described peacekeeping as follows:

> the use by the United Nations of military personnel and for-
> mations not in a fighting or enforcement role but interposed as
> a mechanism to bring an end to hostilities and as a buffer
> between hostile forces. In effect, it serves as an internationally
> constituted pretext for the parties to a conflict to stop fighting
> and as a mechanism to maintain a cease-fire.[52]

Because peacekeeping has no explicit constitutional basis in the UN charter, any introduction of UN peacekeeping forces into a conflict requires the consent of the parties. Moreover, peacekeeping has typically involved only lightly armed military personnel, whose rules of engagement permit them to use their weapons only in self-defense. Accordingly, convention has characterized peacekeeping as a "chapter six-and-a-half" operation, that is, as residing in spirit somewhere between the peaceful resolution of disputes (chapter 6 of the UN charter) and enforcement (chapter 7).

Canada's Pearson and UN Secretary General Dag Hammarskjold are, rightfully, accorded main authorship of the peacekeeping concept. But it was Eisenhower's posture at Suez that made it possible. The subsequent rationale for peacekeeping was a direct translation of the Suez experience. It rested on the assumption that, not merely despite but because of the cold war and the existence of nuclear weapons, it was in the interest of the superpowers to prevent certain kinds of conflicts, largely in the emerging third world, from escalating beyond their immediate locale and threatening a fragile global stability. As Eisenhower explained to an American television audience during the crisis, "the United Nations represents the soundest hope for peace."[53] Eisenhower was surely not thinking of the entire universe of security issues, but Suez constituted the kind of conflict situation for which the claim might have been true.

Once the concept of peacekeeping was articulated the United Nations discovered that, like Molière's Monsieur Gentilhomme, it had been speaking prose all along. The 1948 UN Palestine truce supervisory organization as well as its observer team stationed on the Kashmir border of India and Pakistan in 1949 came to seen as antecedents. The peacekeeping mechanism was utilized in Lebanon in 1958, when the United States needed a figleaf behind which to withdraw after President Eisenhower had dispatched U.S. marines to prevent what turned out to be nonexistent infiltration of arms and troops from Syria.[54] In Cyprus, the UN provided a viable option when Britain wanted to rid itself of one of its more insoluble imperial burdens, and which was also pitting two NATO allies, Greece and Turkey, against one another. A UN peacekeeping force was put in place in 1964 and has served there ever since.

The largest peacekeeping operation mounted during the cold war was in the former Belgian Congo. It began in 1960 and was in place four years, at an annual cost which, at its peak, exceeded the regular budget of the United Nations, and with UN troops reaching a maximum strength of nearly 20,000. The mission's tasks expanded from keeping public order following the abrupt and spiteful termination by Belgium of its colonial control; to blocking the Belgian- and French-backed secession of mineral-rich Katanga province; to putting the administration and infrastructure of the country back together again when the fighting was over—what in recent years has been called "state-building." Eisenhower wasted little time in turning "the whole sorry mess," as he later described it, over to the United Nations.[55] The operation enjoyed U.S. support throughout but quickly lost that of the Soviet Union, which backed a different central faction with materiel and personnel; and also of France and Belgium, which supported Katanga's secession. In addition, UN full-scale military involvement in what turned into a civil war more broadly eroded the legitimacy of the Congo mission, while Soviet and French refusal to pay their share of its costs created the first major UN fiscal crisis.

In all, between 1945 and 1980, fourteen peacekeeping missions were fielded, eight in the Middle East. But by the end of the 1970s, UN peacekeeping and conflict management more generally had run aground. According to Ernst Haas, a foremost student of this subject, "the fortunes of intergovernmental collective security organizations were at an abysmal low: referrals [to them] of new disputes were at their lowest point since 1945, as was the effectiveness at managing disputes."[56] The job of supervising the implementation the 1979 Camp David accords was assigned to a non-UN ad hoc multinational force, as was monitoring the evacuation of the Palestine Liberation Organization and the withdrawal of Israeli troops from Beirut in 1982.[57]

What accounts for the decline and eventual demise of cold war peace-keeping? What changed over the course of the quarter century from 1956 to 1980? Numerous factors were responsible. One was the steady loss of interest by the United States, which occurred well before the U.S. discovered the UN to be "a dangerous place," as Daniel Patrick Moynihan called it when he was UN ambassador.[58] The proximate cause was Vietnam. It was difficult for the United States to continue utilizing the UN to manage international conflicts, especially in the third world, while at the same time doing its best to keep the UN from involving itself in attempts to resolve the Vietnam conflict.

A second factor, which reinforced the first, was the emergence of the nonaligned countries as the UN's majority. This had several consequences. By the 1970s, nonaligned states, not the major powers, were the leading "non-implementers" of UN resolutions aimed at containing conflicts or settling disputes, so jealously did they guard their newly gained sovereignty.[59] At the same time, assertive UN action to implement resolutions remained blocked by U.S.-Soviet rivalry, expressed in Security Council vetoes. In addition, the nonaligned states soon pursued their own UN agenda altogether, focused on the redistribution of wealth from the industrialized North to the developing South by means of negotiations toward a New International Economic Order. Finally, in 1975 the nonaligned majority, eagerly supported by the Soviet bloc, succeeded in having the General Assembly adopt the infamous "Zionism is racism" resolution. That act, understandably, gutted the UN's utility in the Middle East, where its conflict management efforts had been most extensive. Furthermore, combined with UNESCO's simultaneous assault on the free press through its so-called New International Information Order, it robbed the UN of credibility and legitimacy in the eyes of the American public.

But there was an even deeper factor at work as well. It was anchored in the very rationale of cold war peacekeeping. Eisenhower's UN move at Suez, and Hammarskjold's amplification of that experience, were premised on an assumed concert of interest between the superpowers to prevent conflicts in the third world from escalating and thereby threatening global stability, possibly even producing nuclear confrontation. Studies of UN conflict resolution efforts during the cold war, ranging from diplomacy to peacekeeping, found that initially the escalatory potential of disputes was closely correlated with UN success at moderating or helping to settle them.[60] Historically, the UN experienced the least success in steady, nagging, sometimes bloody, but contained warfare, especially if it involved truly nonaligned states which had no ability to pull in either superpower.

In contrast, the UN enjoyed the most success in disputes that threatened to escalate into wider regional and even global conflicts, especially if a Western-allied country was involved on the wrong side of the anticolonial divide.

This same logic may explain, perversely, why by 1980 the UN had become largely irrelevant to conflict management. The superpowers, it seems, realized that the potential of local conflicts to escalate, contrary to initial fears, was quite limited. Put differently, they learned that "the nuclear fuse is in fact relatively well-insulated from regional conflicts."[61] Indeed, the Reagan administration counted on that fact as it actively kept the Soviets bogged down in their third world adventures. As a result, UN peacekeeping lost its cold war rationale. Continued U.S.-Soviet rivalry, and differences between North and South, precluded any other rationale for UN peace operations until the Gorbachev initiatives of the mid-1980s and the subsequent end of the cold war itself. We pick up the story at that point in the next chapter.

Nuclear Nonproliferation

Not unlike peacekeeping, nuclear nonproliferation efforts were shaped by the presumed threat posed to the global power balance, in this case by the proliferation of nuclear weapons. The UN charter has relatively little to say on the subject of disarmament, a central feature of the League covenant. The Security Council is directed to submit plans to all UN members for "the regulation of armaments." And the Military Staff Committee is instructed to advise and assist the Council on a variety of military matters, including "the regulation of armaments, and possible disarmament." Nothing ever came of either provision. The General Assembly eventually established a Committee on Disarmament, which played a minor role in negotiations leading to the 1963 Limited Test-Ban Treaty (prohibiting nuclear weapons tests in the atmosphere, outer space, and the seabed), and a more pronounced role in the Nuclear Nonproliferation Treaty (NPT), in effect since 1970. The Assembly itself was the locale for drafting several treaties prohibiting nuclear weapons and other weapons of mass destruction from being placed in space, on satellites, celestial bodies, and the seabed, as well as outlawing environmental warfare. The rest of the more than 700 resolutions the General Assembly has adopted on the subject of arms control have amounted to little more than repetitive rhetoric focused overwhelmingly on nuclear weapons, over which the members of the Assembly have little say, while ignoring the proliferation of ever-more sophisticated and deadly conventional weapons to the developing countries that constitute the Assembly's majority.[62]

The UN's hybrid institutional design, as a concert-based universal security organization, accounts for the charter's muted disarmament provisions. When the charter was drafted the major powers were concerned with how to organize collective deterrent and enforcement capabilities, not with limiting or reducing levels of armaments. Moreover, during the cold war the United States and the Soviet Union became the world's leading arms exporters, acquiring and equipping client states. By the same token, it is not surprising that the major exception should have been in an area that could, conceivably, undermine the nuclear balance of power. But when President Eisenhower initiated the nonproliferation regime in 1953 he also had in mind finding new roles for the United Nations in international security affairs.[63]

The issue of establishing international control over atomic energy actually goes back to the Roosevelt administration. Vannevar Bush and James B. Conant, two leading science administrators, made the argument in its favor as early as 1944: attempting to maintain a U.S. monopoly via a policy of secrecy, they argued, would yield only a temporary advantage while impairing long-term relations with the Soviet Union.[64] The opposing side wanted to use the U.S. nuclear advantage as a diplomatic and strategic tool for as long as possible. The Soviets were not informed in advance of America's nuclear test at Alamogordo, though it turned out they had a spy present, the physicist Klaus Fuchs, who reported it to them fully. President Truman made only an oblique reference about the atomic bomb to Stalin, which Stalin ignored, at their July 1945 Potsdam meeting, held just prior to Hiroshima and Nagasaki. In the end, the Truman administration decided against a direct approach to the Soviets concerning atomic control. With Soviet concurrence, the issue was channeled to the UN, where the General Assembly, in its first resolution, created an Atomic Energy Commission.

Bernard Baruch presented the U.S. plan to the Commission; Andrei Gromyko countered with a Soviet plan. The United States proposed that once a system of controls was implemented, and sanctions for cheating were in place, then the production of bombs would cease and existing weapons would be dismantled. The Security Council veto could not be invoked to avoid sanctions. The Soviet Union proposed a treaty that would first have prohibited manufacture, storage, and use of atomic weapons, to be followed by their complete destruction; only then would signatories provide for penalties against violations. Barton Bernstein describes the stalemate in the following terms:

> [The Baruch plan,] widely hailed as magnanimous, was unsat-
> isfactory to the Russians because it protected the American
> nuclear monopoly and threatened Soviet security and indus-
> trial development. The Soviet plan, in turn, was unacceptable
> to the United States because it called for destroying atomic
> bombs and sharing information while delaying inspection until
> later.[65]

There was movement on the Soviet side, but not enough to satisfy the
United States. Baruch pressed on with a vote on the U.S. plan in December 1946, knowing that the Soviets could not accede to it but that they,
therefore, would be held responsible for the failure to establish international controls. Historians have expended much energy in efforts to assign
blame. Their emphasis is misplaced, however, for the episode illustrates
well the core features of a security dilemma: the inability of one state to satisfy its own security needs without threatening another, a situation in
which failure is close to being inherent to the very enterprise.[66]

Moscow detonated an atomic device in August 1949. Britain joined the
nuclear club in October 1952. The United States and the Soviet Union
exploded hydrogen bombs within ten months of each other in 1952–1953.
Prompted by these developments, President Eisenhower offered his "Atoms
for Peace" initiative to the UN General Assembly in December 1953, calling for the creation of an International Atomic Energy Agency (IAEA).
He proposed that the agency act as a depository of nuclear materials, making it available to states that lacked it, for peaceful purposes and under
agency control. The IAEA that came into being in July 1957, with joint
U.S.-Soviet support, differed from Eisenhower's proposal, acting as a clear-
inghouse rather than a depository. But recipient countries were required to
accept IAEA safeguards, including audits of nuclear materials accounting,
a variety of surveillance techniques, and on-site inspection of facilities
established with international assistance.

Still proliferation continued. France became a nuclear power in 1960,
and China in 1964. The United States did not fret about France, but the
question did arise whether Germany would remain satisfied with its non-
nuclear status. Moreover, both superpowers worried deeply about China's
explosion. U.S.-Soviet cooperation continued, producing the NPT. In
effect since 1970, it has become the most widely ratified arms control
agreement in history. The nuclear-weapons states (France and China
became parties to the NPT relatively recently) undertook not to help other
states acquire nuclear explosives through any means. Non-nuclear-

weapons states pledged not to acquire such explosives. Assistance to develop peaceful uses of atomic energy was provided for. So too was international safeguarding of declared nuclear installations in non-nuclear-weapons signatory states, and of nuclear exports by all participating states. Finally, the treaty obligated the nuclear-weapons states to pursue negotiations in good faith to end the nuclear arms race, with nuclear disarmament as the ultimate objective. The NPT, in short, exhibited the hybrid design Roosevelt had intended for the UN as a whole: a universal system based in, and circumscribed by, a concert of power.

The NPT and IAEA safeguards are at the core of the nuclear nonproliferation regime. They are supplemented by regulations adopted by the so-called Nuclear Suppliers Group.[67] It was formed in 1974, again largely at U.S. urgings, following the explosion of a "peaceful" nuclear device by India, and in the wake of the quadrupling of world oil prices which was expected to increase greatly the demand for nuclear energy. The group includes Belgium, Britain, Canada, France, Germany, Italy, Japan, Netherlands, Russia, Sweden, Switzerland, and the United States. In initiating the group, the United States tried to ensure that safeguards not be bargained away in the quest for nuclear export sales. Thus, a "trigger list" of safeguarded items was negotiated and has been expanded over time. The group also agreed to restrict exports of enrichment and reprocessing technology, the means of producing weapons-grade uranium and plutonium.

The NPT has a regional counterpart in Latin America, the Treaty on the Prohibition of Nuclear Weapons in Latin America (Tlatelolco Treaty), establishing a nuclear-free zone for the continent.[68] Parties to the treaty agree not to manufacture, test, or acquire nuclear weapons, nor to accept on their territory nuclear weapons deployed by others. Adherents accept IAEA safeguards of all their nuclear installations, and a separate Latin American investigatory inspection agency is also provided for.

Finally, individual states, including non-NPT states, have adopted national regulatory policies which in some cases mirror and in others exceed those of the multilateral arrangements. For instance, in 1978 the United States adopted the Nuclear Nonproliferation Act, imposing restrictions beyond existing international standards on nuclear fuel-cycle programs abroad which benefit from U.S. assistance. Also in the late 1970s, France and Germany, under considerable pressure from the United States, undertook not to make any further transfers of reprocessing and enrichment technology. Argentina, Brazil, China, and South Africa have joined in requiring safeguards on their nuclear exports.

Assessing the effectiveness of the nuclear nonproliferation regime is a difficult and highly contested matter.[69] Realists have tended to be most dubious because proliferation clearly has not been halted. Some go so far as to claim that these arrangements induce a false sense of security, thereby making the world worse off.[70] Yet, Secretary Dulles—not known as a liberal internationalist—had it right when he appealed for Senate approval of the IAEA statute with these measured words: "We realize that atomic energy materials and know-how will spread, Agency or no Agency. . . . But a rapid and unsupervised development of nuclear power around the world raises the specter of nuclear weapons ultimately becoming quite general, the byproduct of nuclear power plants."[71] Preventing proliferation outright was never in the cards; the avowed aim from the start has been to detect diversion from civilian power programs.

Seen from this baseline, progress has been modest but positive. In the late 1950s and early 1960s, many government officials and private experts predicted that, by the 1980s, some two-dozen nuclear weapons states would exist.[72] The actual and potential members of the nuclear club today total less than half that number. Indeed, in recent years more countries have left the list of problem cases—including Argentina, Brazil, and South Africa—than have joined it. According to two practitioners of the craft, "virtually every nonproliferation initiative has turned out to be much more effective than expected when it was proposed or designed, and nonproliferation success has been cheaper than expected."[73] At the same time, however, a "nuclear netherworld" has also emerged,[74] an underground network of illegal sales and clandestine activities, which can only get worse in the wake of the breakup of the Soviet Union.

Confidence in the nuclear nonproliferation regime was seriously shaken in 1991 by the discovery that Iraq's nuclear weapons program had been far more ambitious and advanced than previously believed. In another case of suspected nuclear materials diversion, North Korea proclaimed its defection from the nonproliferation regime by giving notice of its intention to withdraw from the IAEA; Iraq paid not even that legal nicety any mind. But the failure in Iraq's case was truly "systemic."[75] A network of some 450 firms supplied Iraq for more than a decade, and the transactions were facilitated by technology brokers, banks, and shipping agents throughout the West, including Germany, France, the United States, and Belgium.[76] This massive clandestine activity supposedly went undetected by any of them. Beyond that egregious failure, the Iraqi case shows serious flaws in the design of the nonproliferation regime: but they are almost entirely flaws of deliberate omission from, not commission by, the nonproliferation regime.

As a non-nuclear-weapons state signatory of the NPT, Iraq committed itself not to acquire nuclear weapons by any means. Iraq violated that commitment. But the IAEA is not empowered to safeguard the non-nuclear pledge. As agreed by governments, "safeguards are only designed to detect one step on one of the paths to nuclear weapons—the diversion of nuclear material from declared peaceful activities to nuclear weapons."[77] Iraq did not choose that one path. Iraq produced enriched uranium using a technology of electromagnetic isotope separation that had been abandoned by the United States a half century earlier, is openly described in the scientific literature, and uses component parts that are so common that their trade may be impossible to control.[78] Iraq imported clandestinely the controlled technologies required for the design, simulation, construction, and testing of nuclear weapons, the sale of which did violate international export restraints.

All the while, Iraq's declared nuclear facilities were under international inspection. No diversion of materials from peaceful facilities was detected because there was none. Iraq did not declare its weapons facilities to the IAEA, another violation of the NPT for which the Agency's General Conference condemned Iraq. But even if the IAEA had known about and been suspicious of Iraq's undeclared facilities it could not have done very much to act on its suspicions; the Agency's right of "special inspection" had never been invoked to examine undeclared facilities. Since the defeat of Iraq by U.S.-led coalition forces in 1991, UN teams, acting under a Security Council resolution, have dismantled as much of Iraq's nuclear program as they could locate.

Stronger and more innovative means to control nuclear proliferation are required. But the NPT will continue to be the bedrock of those efforts, as 170 nations agreed in 1995 to extend the treaty in perpetuity.

Counterfactual history is a perilous game. Historians sometimes play it as a default option because neither experimental methods nor statistical inference can be employed to explain "big" or singular events: there are too few of the first and the second, by definition, are one of a kind. Historians, therefore, have long speculated about the "paths not taken" in their attempt to understand the origins and evolution of the cold war.[79] Because the analytical framing of cold war history and international security studies typically is itself rooted in the cold war, however, the multilateral dimension of postwar U.S. security policy has not featured significantly in these exercises. The fact is, we don't know how the cold war would have played out if Roosevelt had not initiated the move to universalism through the UN, if Truman had not adopted the most multilateralized option in creating NATO, if Eisenhower had not pushed EDC and EURATOM, or had not paved the way for the invention of UN peacekeeping and non-proliferation. But we do know that those initiatives have left an institutional legacy in place that has outlasted the cold war. We examine next what use we can make of it in the new era.

4 | Cooperative Security

On May 9, 1947, Jamie L. Whitten, Democrat of Mississippi, voted in the U.S. House of Representatives to support $400 million in aid to Greece and Turkey, the first concrete expression of the Truman Doctrine and the emerging strategy of containment. On August 6, 1992, Representative Whitten was still there to vote for yet another foreign aid bill: this time providing $1.2 billion in U.S. bilateral assistance to Russia and the other former Soviet Republics, together with a $12 billion increase in the lending capacity of the International Monetary Fund, a good portion of which was destined for the former Soviet Union.[1] Congress adopted both the 1947 and the 1992 measures by substantial majorities.

Containment worked—at great expense, and taking far longer than the strategy's authors anticipated, but eventually resulting in the implosion of the Soviet system they had predicted in the early cold war years. Yet with that victory has come uncertainty. Most professional students of international relations believe that major power peace since 1945—the long peace, as it came to be known[2]—ultimately was rooted in the combined effects of bipolarity and nuclear deterrence, that it was a byproduct, in other words, of managing the U.S.-Soviet balance of terror. Accordingly, few foreign policy questions today are more critical than how to sustain the long peace beyond the foundational conditions that have passed into history.[3]

In the 1990s, with the international security order in a state of flux, governments, including Washington, are only slowly finding their feet in the post-cold war international environment. New major-power rivalries may yet emerge and new geopolitical doctrines devised to deal with them. At the same time, the United States, as we have seen, made extensive institutional investments in the domain of international security relations in the process of responding to the postwar Soviet threat, and even before that became U.S. policy. Can these arrangements be built on or adapted today? Can they help facilitate short-term adjustment to the new international context and, beyond that, help sustain the long peace? If so, how? This chapter undertakes that assessment.

Our primary focus is on the practical potential of two cooperative security constructs, with a briefer discussion of a third. First, across the North Atlantic and within Western Europe a "security community" may be said to exist today, an area within which war as a means of resolving disputes is virtually inconceivable.[4] The cold war clearly had a cohesive effect on the emergence of this security community. Does it follow, therefore, that its years, albeit not necessarily days, are numbered now that the cold war has ended? In fact, institutional means exist to consolidate this security community and even expand its scope. The future of NATO is a central, though not the sole, element. But NATO would not have much of a future if, reflecting cold war conventional wisdom, policymakers conceived of it strictly as a traditional alliance that now needs to be adjusted to as-of-yet unspecified new threats while, in the process, keeping an American foothold in Europe. NATO will have a significant role to play in the new era only if policymakers view it as its founders intended: an instrument of deterrence and defense, to be sure, but also of transformation.

Second, the cold war derailed Roosevelt's scheme of a concert-based UN security system. From this fact it might seem to follow that the end of the U.S.-Soviet rivalry should have created conditions favorable to its realization. That inference is only partially correct, however. Quite apart from Soviet vetoes, Roosevelt's scheme, as noted in the previous chapter, would have confronted practical obstacles, which the UN recently encountered in Somalia and Bosnia. These obstacles can be reduced and the UN made to play a useful global role. But the prospects for that eventuality remain slim if even in the eyes of a U.S. administration that is relatively pro-UN, the UN's peace operations are seen merely as "a sometime tool for third-level American interests," as the *Washington Post* characterized a long-awaited Clinton administration UN policy directive.[5] Here, too, future potential hinges on a more expansive view of the UN by policymakers, whether broad geopolitical rationales, such as Roosevelt held, or tactical roles, as Eisenhower envisioned. Above all, U.S. policymakers have not adequately grasped or articulated the utility of an effective concert-based UN, nor the contributions of UN peace operations to regional stability.

Third, and following up on an institutional difference noted in chapter 2, few prospects existed for postwar multilateral security arrangements in East Asia. U.S. bilateral alliances served as the primary vehicle of containment in the region. But if the end of the cold war casts doubt on the future of NATO, it far more so calls into question strictly bilateral U.S. military support for America's most challenging economic competitors. Multilateral groupings in the Asia-Pacific region are slowly beginning to address security concerns, but in the near term they are unlikely to play significant security roles. Opportunities may exist, however, for movement toward a more modest cooperative security construct, in which joint measures are deliberately inserted into competitive balancing relations with the aim of enhancing predictable stability. We shall term such a construct a cooperative balance. It is a generic approach which has applicability beyond East Asia.

The savvy international affairs columnist Flora Lewis has warned that America's institutional investments of the past half-century "risk being eroded and undermined, without anyone actually wanting that to happen."[6] The present chapter indicates some of the ways in which this outcome can be avoided if the United States were so inclined; what America should do in the new era is addressed in the final chapter.

Cooperative Security Constructs

In his January 1917 "Peace without Victory" address to the Senate, Woodrow Wilson spoke with passion about the desirability of replacing "the balance of power" with "a community of power."[7] The chief advantage of a community of power, in Wilson's view, was that any potential aggressor would confront the certain preponderant force of all states united, unlike the situation under a balance-of-power system, whereby the aggressor faces only the contingent and inferior deterrent created by a coalition made up of those states whose immediate interests are threatened. With a community of power in place, Wilson believed, aggression would come to be seen as an irrational act in the instrumental sense of being unable to yield its desired effects except at the risk of self-destruction—and thus cease to be a standard instrument in the repertoire of states.

Wilson never actually used the term "collective security" to describe his proposed arrangement, but that is how it has been known since the 1930s. Wilson did not expect to implement a fully fledged collective security system in 1919, though he hoped the League would evolve toward one in due course. Franklin Roosevelt harbored no such aim for his hybrid UN scheme for the simple reason that he thought pure collective security to be both unattainable and undesirable. Presumably for the same reasons, since the end of the cold war no one in any position of authority anywhere has advo-cated creating a Wilsonian collective security scheme. And yet, just as real-ists in the late 1940s vilified Wilson out of antipathy toward institutional innovations in security relations, so, too, has "the Wilsonian ideal" become the focal point of realist criticism today of cooperative security constructs.[8] Why the Wilsonian ideal? Because proposals leavened by an appreciation of power politics blur the distinction between collective security and tra-ditional balance-of-power theory, one realist scholar asserts, and thus "con-fuses the actual choices."[9] Hybrid designs are especially inadmissible, another insists, because they rest on "incompatible theories [within] which . . . states behave in fundamentally different and contradictory ways."[10]

With all due regard for the desire to be clear analytically, however, it is simply not possible to speak sensibly about cooperative security relations after the cold war only in terms of Wilsonian collective security and in con-trast to classical balance-of-power politics: the real-world field of play lies between those two. At the same time, grand schemes of cooperative secu-rity constructs intended to encompass the entire international security order are also of little practical utility because different complexes of secu-rity relations across the world require different arrangements. Accordingly, this chapter adopts a grounded approach, utilizing concepts that are rooted in the actual experiences of different groups of states.

By cooperative security relations we mean, generically, any joint means by which potential adversaries prevent, resolve, reduce, contain, or counter threats that could lead to war among them.[11] As indicated above, we focus here on the future potential of three cooperative security constructs, or international institutional arrangements within which cooperative means play significant roles: the concept of security community and the future of Europe, a concert-based UN system for certain types of regional conflicts, and movement toward a cooperative balance in East Asia and possibly else-where. In each case, we first define the concept, and then sketch the gen-eral strategic orientation to which its application would lead in a specific domain of post-cold war international security relations.

Security Community

The concept of security community was devised by students of regional integration in the 1950s, at a time when governments were in the process of creating the European Economic Community, and it was based on extensive historical research on the subject of how political communities were formed from previously independent entities. In the original formulation, a security community was defined as comprising any group of political units whose relations exhibit "dependable expectations of peaceful change," that is, the "assurance that members will not fight each other physically, but will settle their disputes in some other way."[12] The observer knows that such a community exists when no one in the group fears war with any other member and does not prepare for it. Two types were differentiated. Amalgamated security communities involve the formal merger of previously independent units (for example, the United States or Switzerland); pluralistic security communities retain the independence of units (as in North America since Canadian Confederation, or the Nordic countries since 1906, when border fortifications between Sweden and Norway were dismantled). Indeed, pluralistic security communities need not have formal machinery of any sort, though at minimum all offer easy access to one another's decisionmaking processes and typically they have means for routine consultation. History also provides instances of amalgamated political units which were not, however, security communities, including the Austro-Hungarian empire sometime after the turn of this century—and presumably the Soviet Union circa 1990.

Expectations of peaceful change within security communities tend to be most dependable, the historical research suggested, the more they reflect a certain "sense of community," a sense "of 'we-feeling,' trust, and mutual consideration."[13] This sense of community, in turn, is facilitated by a number of conditions, the most important of which is "compatibility of the main values" relevant to the prevailing political, economic, and legal institutions and practices within constituent units.[14] The existence of a pluralistic security community is consistent with very different foreign and security policies on the part of its members; among the Nordic countries during the cold war, for example, Finland adopted a passive neutrality, strongly conditioned by the desire not to provoke the Soviet Union; Sweden pursued a more active policy of neutrality; and Denmark and Norway were founding members of NATO. The core common feature of pluralistic security communities is the existence within them of dependable expectations of peaceful change.

Few observers would challenge the proposition that a very tightly coupled pluralistic security community exists today among the nations of the North Atlantic/West European area.[15] No country within it expects war with any other. Apart from Greece and Turkey, none devotes financial or organizational resources to the possibility of war with any other; as far as we know, none even has military contingency plans for such an eventuality. Observers are likely to differ on two issues, however: first, precisely how this security community came about, or the relative causal weights assigned to external threat, trans-Atlantic security ties, regional economic integration, common bonds of civil society, market economy, and constitutional democracy, together with high levels and broad ranges of movement in people and ideas; and second, whether this security community can be sustained, let alone expanded, in the new era. We cannot conclusively answer the first question—the security-community research program did not fully deliver on its promise to explain and predict community formation, while several of its concepts and thresholds remained fuzzy and proved difficult to operationalize even as descriptive indicators.[16] But the future of this security community is subject to influence by its constituent governments. The issue is: what now?

We might remind ourselves at the outset that the aim of transforming what Woodrow Wilson believed were the war-prone ways of the "old world" was uppermost in his mind as he contemplated U.S. entry into the first world war and devised the League of Nations. The risk of being unable to play an effective European role through the "four policemen" scheme was a major factor leading Franklin Roosevelt in a more universalistic direction for the post-1945 world. The desire to move toward a different European order was an explicit component of Truman's NATO strategy and Eisenhower's support for the European Defense Community and EURATOM. It was only with the Kennedy administration that this aim lost prominence.[17] In short, with the existential fact of a North American/West European security community the United States has almost arrived where Wilson and America's post-World War II leaders wanted it to be. The remaining tasks are for the West European pillar of this community to achieve greater indigenous sustainability, and to help stabilize expectations of peaceful change within the larger Europe beyond its confines.

NATO is central to all "what now?" considerations. The attention of policymakers and analysts has focused almost entirely on the issue of NATO expansion into Eastern and Central Europe as "the key security question facing the West."[18] But by the standard logic of strategic analysis, as we shall see momentarily, the case for NATO expansion at best draws a tie with the case against it. As a result, those who favor it have assigned a growing number of tasks to the expansion process that can only be described as security-community–building. A strategy informed directly by the security-community concept, however, would differ from this prevailing approach in at least two respects. First, it would view consolidation as the more important task—put differently, it would not assume that expansion in itself takes care of the need to attend to consolidation. Second, a security-community strategy would configure and sequence the elements of expansion differently. As a result, such a strategy promises greater long-term success, poses fewer risks, and is more consistent with historical American objectives regarding European political transformation. Let us look more closely at how and why this is so.

We begin with the case for NATO expansion, which enjoys broad bipartisan support in Washington and is backed in all allied capitals as well.[19] Three main arguments have been advanced in its favor.[20] The first holds that expansion is necessary to deter any residual threats of Russian aggression in Eastern and Central Europe, and to reassure the countries of the region that they will be defended from it. The region is deemed sufficiently vital to Western security interests to justify this broad extension of NATO's security commitments. The second is to avoid the existence of a security vacuum between Germany and Russia—Henry Kissinger describes it as a strategic "no-man's land"[21]—on the grounds that states, like nature, abhor vacuums and tend to get drawn into them. Possible German-Russian confrontations over either's attempt to exert influence in the region is in no one's interest. Third, it is said that expansion would dampen the resurgence of ethno-nationalism that could lead to intra-regional conflicts, in turn drawing in outside powers, East or West. "These factors combine to fuel an almost desperate search for security in the region, which itself reinforces the trends toward geopolitical competition, proliferation and instability, as the expectation builds that states may soon pursue unilateral attempts to gain real or perceived security."[22]

The rejoinders to these arguments are not insubstantial. Take, first, the issue of a residual Russian threat. Most observers, including those who favor immediate expansion, agree that the threat is now low—but advocates urge the West to hedge, to "buy insurance."[23] Opponents counter that this insurance policy potentially is a self-fulfilling prophecy, bringing about the very situation it is intended to hedge against. By playing into the hands of communists, extreme nationalists, and political opportunists in Russia, prompt expansion "would probably lead to Russian actions in Eastern Europe and in the area of arms control that would weaken, not enhance, European and American security."[24] Besides, opponents continue, the three most likely early admits to NATO—Poland, Hungary, and the Czech Republic—would not be the first to face any resurgent Russian threat; Ukraine and the Baltic states, or even Romania and Bulgaria, have greater reasons to be worried. Indeed, each of the three at the head of the queue has *reduced* its national military capabilities, hardly "the actions of states concerned about military threats."[25]

It is difficult to know how to counter Kissinger's security vacuum argument, not because it is necessarily so compelling but because it rests on a metaphor that has not been put to a systematic test as a universal proposition—though Kissinger, no doubt, has in mind the specific history of Polish partitions. It is of note, however, that Germany, one of the protagonists in this scenario, has not pushed for rapid NATO expansion; it has been decidedly gradualist.[26] Equally awkward for this case, virtually all scenarios for NATO expansion are, in fact, predicated on retaining a different security vacuum: they assign Ukraine the role of "buffer state" between Russia and an expanded NATO.

There are several responses to the argument that NATO expansion is needed to contain possible intraregional ethno-nationalist conflicts. First, by far the strategically most significant ethnic minority in the entire region consists of Russians left behind in the former Soviet Republics—in the Baltics, Belarus, Ukraine, and Moldova. NATO expansion is not intended to relieve their problem but could well exacerbate it by encouraging nationalist factions in Moscow to demand greater protection for ethnic Russians in the "near abroad" as NATO advances toward them. In addition, expressions of virulent ethnic nationalism and anti-Semitism heard often in the region at the outset of the 1990s in most instances have become muted, due to the disciplining incentives of hoped-for European Union privileges or eventual membership, because they are being addressed through other institutional means, such as the Organization for Security and Cooperation in Europe, and perhaps from the Bosnian tragedy's inoculating effect.[27] Finally, the long-standing confrontation between Greece and Turkey over Cyprus suggests that NATO, in any case, lacks well-developed mechanisms to resolve ethnic conflicts.

Perhaps the most delicate question concerning the strategic rationale for NATO expansion is the ultimate credibility of NATO's commitments. No advocate of NATO expansion recommends placing NATO troops on the new front lines because that, clearly, would be too provocative toward Russia. And yet, as Dana Allin reminds us, even with five American divisions on the central front, backed by a panoply of nuclear weapons, NATO witnessed a running debate throughout the cold war about the credibility of the American commitment. "Without this degree of physical coupling, a stark and brutal uncertainty emerges: are America and Western Europe ready to send troops, much less risk nuclear war, to defend Polish independence?"[28]

In short, no matter how they are construed, neither meeting a residual Russian threat nor managing possible East European conflicts requires the most powerful and integrated peacetime alliance in modern history—if not all recorded history. Acknowledging this fact, U.S. policymakers and analysts have come to stress a far broader set of objectives. As President Clinton said in a 1994 Warsaw speech, NATO expansion "will not depend on the appearance of a new threat in Europe. It will be an instrument to advance security and stability for the entire region."[29] In addition to extending security commitments, "projecting stability" has become linked to such tasks as strengthening fragile democracies and economic reforms, instituting civic as opposed to ethnic nationalism, crisis management, and peacekeeping, thereby fostering peaceful change within and among the countries of Eastern and Central Europe.[30] Similarly, for NATO's most likely would-be members, expansion has become less an issue of security than of identity politics, an affirmation that they belong to "the West." Czech President Václav Havel gives eloquent expression to this sentiment: "If we in [the] 'postcommunist countries' call for a new order, if we appeal to the West not to close itself off to us, and if we demand a radical reevaluation of the new situation, then this is not because we are concerned about our own security and stability. . . . We are concerned about the destiny of the values and principles that communism denied, and in whose name we resisted communism and ultimately brought it down . . . . the traditional values of Western civilization."[31]

Thus, the issue of NATO expansion has been pushed squarely into the domain of "security-community–building." It is worth asking, therefore, what a NATO strategy derived directly from the security-community perspective would look like. Indeed, it would not do things in quite the same way.[32]

Historically, the formation of tightly coupled security communities has tended to grow around "core areas" characterized by high potential for economic rewards as well as high and diverse social communication flows. According to Deutsch and his colleagues, in the emergence of such communities security commitments typically follow and reinforce economic and cultural ties. Military alliances have turned out to be "a relatively poor pathway" toward security communities unless they were embedded in a broader process of political, economic, and social integration.[33] Keep in mind that the creation of NATO itself followed the Marshall Plan by a full two years. American policymakers initially pursued a policy of "economic security" for Western Europe, as noted in the previous chapter, in which the Marshall Plan was viewed as the primary vehicle for European reconstruction—its necessary condition, as it were—and only gradually moved toward NATO as a reinforcing security mechanism—the sufficient condition. Furthermore, Spain's admission into NATO in 1982 was meant to complement its entry into the European Economic Community; at that late date, it was hardly driven by international security concerns.

A NATO strategy informed by the security-community concept, then, would concern itself first and foremost with consolidating its "core area." In the 1950s, North America was the core around which the trans-Atlantic security community was constructed. Today, the European Union potentially forms the foundation for a more balanced relationship. Indeed, as François Heisbourg argues, continued success of European unification is *the* critical factor that will determine whether Western Europe remains a functioning security community or reverts to a pre-1914 balance-of-power system. The latter, Heisbourg contends, "would be fragmented, probably inward-looking, and, in the absence of a shared and permanent threat, would not provide a solid basis for the Atlantic Alliance."[34] Consolidating NATO's core area, in short, implies strengthening its European pillar.

In calibrating a new balance of responsibilities within NATO between North America and Europe an indivisible security link remains essential, for reasons Henry Kissinger states eloquently: "Without America, Europe turns into a peninsula at the tip of Eurasia, unable to find equilibrium much less unity. . . . Without Europe, America will become an island off the shores of Eurasia condemned to a kind of pure balance-of-power politics that does not reflect its national genius."[35] In addition, the United States possesses military capabilities that even a united Europe would be hard pressed to match but needs.[36] These considerations suggest a NATO strategic concept whereby the United States provide security guarantees to a European collective self-defense effort within NATO, backed by U.S. strategic systems, lift, logistical, and intelligence support, and limited ground troops.

Such a move would require the institutional link between NATO and the European Union (EU) to become better articulated and made stronger. That link is the Western European Union (WEU), designated in the 1991 Maastricht Treaty as the EU's defense component.[37] Until recently, the United States had grave reservations about the WEU as well as its five-nation, 50,000-strong Eurocorps and other EU military units, fearing that they would undermine NATO.[38] At the January 1994 NATO summit, however, a new consensus was forged—largely reflecting a prior U.S.-French understanding. On the one hand, NATO agreed, in the words of the summit's declaration, "to make collective assets of the Alliance available, on the basis of consultations in the North Atlantic Council, for WEU operations undertaken by the European Allies in pursuit of their Common Foreign and Security Policy." Those assets include command facilities that draw on but are not limited to NATO's integrated command structure, called Combined Joint Task Forces.[39] On the other hand, France agreed that the Eurocorps would be equally available to NATO and the WEU. To work out the modalities of both parts of this bargain France has rejoined NATO military deliberations at the ministerial level for the first time since 1966.[40]

A NATO strategy derived from the security-community concept would also assign a far greater role to the EU in projecting stability eastward. The EU is, in fact, better equipped than NATO to deal with most of the nonmilitary tasks of security-community–building that the United States, in particular, has placed on NATO's shoulders. Prospects of membership or associate status in the EU provide it with far greater day-to-day leverage over states in its orbit to reinforce democratic and economic reforms and encourage the protection of minority rights. Moreover, continued EU integration is by far the most decisive bond in the future Franco-German relationship, and is most likely to prevent EU members from being drawn into opposing sides of ethnic or any other kinds of conflicts on the European periphery.[41] The next step would be for the WEU to become a credible vehicle for some of the newer peacekeeping and humanitarian assistance tasks in Eastern and Central Europe.[42]

Finally, there is the most inclusive of all the "Europes"—the aspiring pluralistic security community stretching eastward from Vancouver to Vladivostok.[43] Its institutional expression is the Organization for Security and Cooperation in Europe (OSCE), which replaced the "Conference" by the same name that launched the Helsinki process in the mid-1970s, intended to moderate East-West tensions. The OSCE remains institutionally weak despite its new status as a permanent organization, and notwithstanding Russia's desire to turn it into a United Nations "regional arrangement" (under chapter 8 of the UN charter) as well as to endow it with a Security Council.[44] But the OSCE does perform several functions conducive to security-community–building and which intersect with the issue of EU/WEU/NATO expansion. For one, the OSCE has become a recognized regional vehicle for promulgating norms of acceptable state behavior, especially with regard to the protection of minority rights. Reflecting agreement among more than fifty member states, OSCE norms can be invoked by other organizations, such as the European Bank for Reconstruction and Development, to condition aid to East and Central European states on their adherence to these norms. In addition, the OSCE has established modest crisis prevention and conflict management mechanisms that can complement the more robust capacities of NATO and potentially the WEU.

To conclude, current plans for NATO expansion have left the standard strategic calculus well behind and have moved squarely into the domain of security-community–building. A strategy derived directly from the security-community concept contains many of the same elements but differs in how they are configured and in the sequencing of their implementation. It would start with consolidating NATO's European pillar. In addition, its expansion agenda would be more Europe-driven, closely tied to EU expansion, while assigning a greater role to NATO's Partnership for Peace and WEU associate membership. Thus, it would pose fewer risks vis-à-vis Russia, especially if it were coupled with a NATO-Russia or U.S.-Russia security treaty.[45] And it would be more consistent with long-standing American objectives in Europe, which have been not to dominate but to transform its international politics.

Concerts of Powers

With no central cleavage dividing the major powers, the post-cold war global geopolitical environment resembles the world of Franklin Roosevelt's expectations more closely than did the intervening period of bipolarity. As a result, a number of observers have suggested that cooperative security relations through concert systems may be appropriate and achievable today, in Europe and at the global level.[46] Advocates of this construct, in essence, generalize from a single historical case. Between the Napoleonic and Crimean wars, from 1815 to 1854, stability in Europe was maintained, in Henry Kissinger's words, by an institutional framework that participants regarded as "legitimate," so that "they sought adjustment within [it] rather than in its overthrow."[47] The five concert powers—Austria, Great Britain, Prussia, Russia, and a French monarchy restored with the aid of the other four—constituted themselves as "an executive body" of the European system of states,[48] convening frequent consultations on matters that could have undermined their precarious balance.[49]

Thus, in a concert system the major powers strive for security not via competitive jostling and the formation of bilateral alliances, but by concerting aspects of their behavior.[50] In the Concert of Europe, Robert Jervis argues, the five "behaved in ways that sharply diverged from normal 'power politics.'"[51] According to Jervis, they refrained from seeking to maximize their relative power positions vis-à-vis one another, instead moderating

their demands and behavior; they avoided exploiting each other's temporary weaknesses and vulnerabilities; and they threatened force sparingly
and used it rarely to resolve differences among themselves—though, as
Kalevi Holsti adds, they "were clearly of the opinion that force could be
used individually or collectively for enforcing certain decisions and for
coercing those who threatened the foundations of the order or the system
of governance."[52] Concert members continued to behave in self-interested
ways, to be sure; but, as Jervis stresses, self-interest was defined in terms
"broader than usual" and "also longer-run than usual," while "statesmen
believed that they would be more secure if the other major powers were
also more secure."[53]

Pure concerts seem far-fetched today, for the simple reason that the vast
majority of states can hardly be expected to favor a scheme in which they
would be the objects, not subjects, of concert behavior. But the end of the
cold war makes it possible to take another look at Roosevelt's hybrid UN
design. Roosevelt, it will be recalled, had in mind grafting elements of a
collective security system, involving a UN with some capability to deploy
force, onto a concert of powers which would determine when, where, and
how force would be used. It assigned a more prominent role to lesser powers than the post-Napoleonic concert while remaining based on the concert form by virtue of the special rights and responsibilities held by the permanent members of the Security Council. It was not intended to replace,
but to supplement and moderate, the traditional conduct of balance-of-
power politics. Nor was it intended to deal with all conflicts, but with that
subset which the permanent members agreed threatened international
peace and security. Reviving or adapting the Rooseveltian design today
would entail a move, in short, from the UN's modest cold war peacekeeping role toward a more robust posture.

A Concert-Based UN Today?

The possibility of a concert-based "new era" for the United Nations was
signaled in a September 1987 Pravda article by Soviet President Mikhail
Gorbachev, titled "Realities and Guarantees for a Secure World." Gorbachev proposed "a comprehensive system of international security" based
on the UN charter. For the next two years, Soviet officials at every turn
elaborated on the ideas contained in Gorbachev's proposal.[54] The Persian
Gulf crisis was an early test: Iraq had been a Soviet client state. In the
event, Iraq's invasion of Kuwait triggered a U.S.-Soviet declaration of
"joint responsibilities for peace and security," which condemned the invasion and characterized it as "a most serious threat to the integrity of the

emerging international system."[55] The Bush administration subsequently made effective use of the United Nations to build international support for Operation Desert Storm.

The UN responded to this shift with an outburst of activity, facilitating the disengagement of troops from conflicts that would have been axiomatically beyond its reach during the cold war: Soviet forces in Afghanistan, Cuban forces in Angola, South African forces in Namibia, the Nicaraguan contras. It helped engineer political transitions in Namibia, Nicaragua, El Salvador, the Western Sahara, Cambodia, and Mozambique. All told, the UN fielded more peacekeeping missions in a five-year span than in its entire prior history. But then, almost as suddenly, talk of the UN's ineffectiveness became pervasive and retrenchment set in, fueled by adverse experiences in Somalia and Bosnia combined with a more general sense of institutional overload. What went wrong, and can the momentum be restored? We take up three sets of issues below: the viability of the very concept of a UN-based concert; problems of strategy and doctrine regarding the collective use of force; and difficulties attending the command and control of collective forces.

The Concept

The minimum consensual requirements of a concert-based UN system have been present throughout the brief post-cold war period. None among the major powers has sought to destabilize or threaten any other, and when they have intervened in an international conflict, more often than not they have acted jointly or in pursuit of joint objectives. Britain and France have played their roles assiduously. Russian rhetoric has become more assertive over time, reflecting its internal economic and political problems as well as its external deprivation of status, but its actions regarding UN peace missions on the whole have remained constructive. China invariably abstains on Security Council resolutions authorizing the use of force, but to date has not blocked any actual operation.[56]

Furthermore, a commitment to concerted action in several cases has actively shaped the major powers' behavior. For example, whatever else can be said about the UN's and NATO's irresolute and inept Bosnian intervention over the course of its first forty months, once war broke out the five major powers most directly involved retained a common position through their "contact group." They avoided, thereby, unilateral interventions on opposing sides, possibly triggering a wider war, typical of a previous age. This holds even for Russia, which has strong ties to the Serbs.[57] In addition, a French scholar has noted, "France has been heavily involved in UN peacekeeping in order to justify her permanent membership on the Security Council."[58] France has had more of its troops serving in UN missions than any other country and commanded UN forces in ex-Yugoslavia; with UN approval but near-universal reluctance to act, France also dispatched troops to Rwanda, helping to stop a torrent of genocidal violence. Germany and Japan, both hoping to become permanent Security Council members, are utilizing the UN effectively to ease into fuller international military roles in ways that are externally nonthreatening and domestically acceptable.[59] German logistical units participated in the UN's Cambodia and Somalia operations; its crew members served on NATO air-patrols of the "no-fly zone" over Bosnia; Germany committed logistical support and combat air cover in the event UN forces were obliged to withdraw from Bosnia; and in July 1995, German Tornado squadrons were deployed in support of the newly constituted European Rapid Reaction Force in Bosnia. Japan contributed substantial police and civilian contingents to Cambodia, as well as civilian personnel to Namibia, the Rwandan refugee camps in Zaire, and the UN's Mozambique operation. Participation in these missions appears to have had the desired domestic effect in both countries without triggering adverse international consequences.[60]

The situation with regard to Russia is trickier.[61] Russian troops in Tajikistan, placed there by agreement with the host government, wore blue armbands and were called a peacekeeping force but had not been authorized by any international body; Russia requested Security Council endorsement of a predominantly Russian force in Georgia; and the OSCE called for (but failed to produce) a 3,000-strong multinational force for Nagorno-Karabakh, the ethnic Armenian enclave in Azerbaijan. Part of the problem lies with the Western countries, which have found it hard to square this circle: on one hand, they have wished to avoid legitimizing unilateral Russian intervention in the newly independent nations along its borders—to endorse a "Monroesky Doctrine," as The Economist has dubbed it;[62] on the other, they have been disinclined to contribute their own troops for these missions or to have them become fully fledged UN operations, which would entail UN financing.[63] As a result, the UN's involvement in Russia's "near abroad" has been limited to monitoring the actions of largely Russian contingents.

In sum, the UN in recent years has provided a basis for orchestrating major-power concertation in several significant areas of regional conflict. But by the same token, many nonpermanent members of the Security Council, especially developing countries, do not much care for a concert-based system on the grounds that it endows the victors of World War II with excessive prerogatives in a radically changed world. Some expansion of the Council is inevitable, therefore. Germany and Japan will almost certainly become new permanent members, as will a small number of developing countries, which in recent years have provided some two-thirds of all peacekeeping forces—once they determine who among them will serve and on what basis. In the meantime, the Security Council has agreed, "as a matter of course," to consult all countries contributing troops whenever the mandate of a mission in which they are participating is at issue or if unforeseen developments occur that may affect the mission.[64]

A concert-based system, by definition, is selective. Only when major-power consensus exists is collective action possible. This, too, has concerned other members, who fear that the collective security mechanism may be hijacked to serve only the permanent members' particularistic interests. But Somalia and Rwanda hardly fit that characterization. And the Clinton administration acted in Haiti only with great reluctance and despite substantial domestic opposition—though an implicit linkage between Russian support for UN authorization of U.S. action in Haiti and U.S. backing for Russian action in Georgia served to reinforce the concern.[65] On balance, a stronger case can be made that the Security Council has been insufficiently selective, swept away by the ease of reaching consensus but often without due regard to the feasibility of its mandates.[66] As Lt. Gen. Francis Briquemont of Belgium complained when he led UN forces in Bosnia: "There is a fantastic gap between the resolutions of the Security Council, the will to execute those resolutions and the means available to commanders in the field."[67]

It may be that the most serious challenge to the viability of a concert-based UN peace operations system resides in the domestic politics of several major powers. In Russia and China domestic instability poses a latent threat to the concert, insofar as a more nationalist Russia and either a disintegrating or a more aggressive China would alter those countries' postures rapidly. In the United States the problem has to do with the fact that no constituency of support for the UN has been rebuilt following the U.S.-UN estrangement of the 1970s and 1980s. Nor have U.S. administrations articulated a compelling vision of the possible benefits of a concert, especially such broad geopolitical objectives as engaging China, facilitating the "normalization" of Germany's and Japan's global security roles, restraining excessive Russian unilateralism, and bringing some of the rapidly developing and militarizing third world countries into a responsible UN role. Nor have they sought to make the UN Security Council a more prominent forum in combating the proliferation of weapons of mass destruction, or in encouraging the creation of regional conflict resolution and peacekeeping mechanisms. Their case for the UN has been made largely on burdensharing grounds, which has simply led Congress to push more of the financial burden onto other UN members, where some of it does rightfully belong, while also pushing the United States further into UN arrearages.

In contrast, domestic opponents of the United Nations have seized on the concert with gusto to make a negative case: that it unduly constrains the United States and requires it to do things it would not otherwise do—that the Clinton administration, in the words of Senate Majority Leader Robert Dole, has "subcontracted" American foreign policy to the United Nations.[68] Actual instances are hard to find, however. One that is often cited, European rejection of the administration's "lift-and-strike" proposal vis-à-vis Bosnia in the spring of 1993—lifting the arms embargo on the Muslims and launching punitive air strikes against Serbian targets—pitted the United States against Britain and France, its closest NATO allies, more than against "the United Nations." And the fatal ambush of U.S. Army Rangers in Mogadishu on October 3, 1993, widely depicted at the time as a tragic instance of the UN entangling the United States in a deplorable situation, resulted from decisions made unilaterally by the U.S. military in an operation that was under its exclusive control from start to finish.[69]

It may be that the United States would not have become involved on the ground in Bosnia without the UN; the desire to salvage the UN's credibility and even more so NATO's helped bring the Clinton administration around. It had been reluctant to act not because it believed that no American interests were affected by the brutal dismemberment of a multiethnic society in early post-cold war Europe, but because it reckoned that the domestic political price of involvement would be too high. Thus, the case inadvertently may illustrate the sort of institutional tripwire function Roosevelt had in mind for the United Nations—albeit in an utterly inept fashion.

At the same time, the means of collective intervention through the UN have not functioned well. Two defects stand out: the lack of an agreed understanding of the nature of nontraditional UN peace operations; and the problem of command and control. Unless they are resolved, the promise of a concert-based UN peace operations system will be short-lived. Below, we take up each in turn.

Operational Doctrine

In several major recent UN peace operations, neither the UN nor its member states strictly speaking have fully known what they have been doing or how to do it. Frustration and failure, therefore, have been inevitable.[70] The UN distinguishes between two purposes for the collective use of military forces: enforcement and peacekeeping. But its role in a rapidly growing number of conflicts has conformed to neither. As a result, these UN operations have floundered in a conceptual void, sometimes with tragic consequences for their participants and for the UN itself. This problem would exist regardless of whether the UN were to have its own rapid deployment force, draws on dedicated stand-by forces, or be obliged to continue with the practice of waiting for countries to volunteer troops. The critical issue is not where forces come from, but the objectives and rules of engagement governing their deployment and employment.

As it was articulated in the UN charter, enforcement is easy to grasp. A specific act of aggression, or a more general set of hostile actions, are collectively identified as a threat to international peace and security and the aggressor state is subjected to an escalating ladder of diplomatic, economic, and military sanctions until its violation is reversed. Ultimately, enforcement involves flat-out war-fighting—for example, the "all necessary means" of Security Council Resolution 678, authorizing what became Operation Desert Storm. The UN does not have an institutionalized military enforcement capability of this sort and is unlikely soon to acquire one. Large-scale UN military enforcement, therefore, will in the future remain episodic and, as in the Korean and Gulf wars, consist of UN authorization and general political oversight together with execution by ad hoc coalitions of the willing.

Peacekeeping is nowhere mentioned in the UN charter, as we noted in chapter 3. It was a practical invention, the doctrinal expression of which was a reflection of the 1956 Suez experience. Above all, peacekeeping is predicated on the consent of the parties, which typically have agreed to cease hostilities before a peacekeeping mission is deployed. Moreover, peacekeepers fight against neither side but play an impartial interpositionary role, monitoring a cease-fire or controlling a buffer zone. Indeed, they do not fight at all. They carry only light arms and are authorized to shoot only in self-defense—and, on occasion, in the defense of their mission if it comes under direct attack. Unlike fighting forces, then, peacekeepers are not intended to create the peace they are asked to safeguard. They accept the balance of forces on the ground and work within it. In short, peacekeeping is a device to guarantee transparency, to reassure each side that the other is carrying out its promises. It is a noncombatant mission carried out by military personnel.

To this classical peacekeeping portfolio the United Nations, starting in the late 1980s, began to add monitoring and sometimes conducting elections, supporting and sometimes performing tasks of civil administration, as well as related services facilitating transitions to elected governments and what the UN calls post-conflict peace building. The most elaborate of these operations were in Namibia, El Salvador, and Cambodia. The future viability of this expanded portfolio depends on governments providing the UN with adequate levels of funding, staffing and materiel. But neither classical UN peacekeeping nor its recent civilian offshoots requires any fundamental doctrinal innovation.

Symbolizing the new post-cold war spirit, in January 1992 the UN Security Council met for the first time ever at the level of heads of state or government. The summit asked Secretary General Boutros Boutros-Ghali to prepare a keynote strategy document for UN peace operations in the new era. Entitled *An Agenda for Peace*, it set out to define more diverse and robust roles for the UN.[71] Two proposed departures from previous practice were critical. First, *An Agenda for Peace* defined peacekeeping as "the deployment of a United Nations presence in the field, *hitherto* with the consent of all the parties concerned. . . . " (par. 20). Here was a clear signal that the UN might, in some instances, seek to deploy peacekeepers without local consent. Second, the document noted that cease-fires had often been agreed to in the past but not always complied with, making it necessary for the UN to try to restore a cease-fire. But because this task on occasion exceeded the capability of peace-keeping forces, Boutros-Ghali continued, "I recommend that the [Security] Council consider the utilization of *peace-enforcement units* in clearly defined circumstances and with their terms of reference specified in advance" (par. 44). Here the Secretary General was calling for a new United Nations military role altogether, beyond peacekeeping, but short of all-out war-fighting.

At the same time, the UN found itself confronting types of conflicts it had not encountered since the Congo operation in the early 1960s, which had nearly destroyed the organization. Of twenty-one peace operations established between 1988 and the end of 1994, thirteen involved what were (or became) primarily intrastate rather than interstate conflicts.[72] Many took place amid the rubble of contested or collapsed domestic authority (Angola, Cambodia, Somalia), and/or they involved large ethnic minorities left exposed when federal political structures disintegrated (former Yugoslavia, Caucasus).

Boutros-Ghali's proposals should have led immediately to joint efforts by the UN and its member states, especially national militaries, to work out their doctrinal implications and practical feasibility. Instead, the traditional peacekeeping modality was simply ratcheted up and projected into uncharted terrain—euphemistically termed "semi-permissive environments." There it was supplemented by ad hoc "peace-enforcement" components, such as the U.S. Quick Reaction Force and Army Rangers in Somalia, or NATO's air-strike capability in Bosnia-Herzegovina. But countries participating in these newer UN peace operations had very different understandings of their nature, sometimes without realizing that this was so.

Doctrinal confusion seriously impeded—and ultimately defeated—the UN's Somalia mission. During its U.S.-led phase, from December 1992 through May 1993, the operation was authorized, under the enforcement provisions of the UN charter, "to use all necessary means to establish as soon as possible a secure environment for humanitarian relief operations."[73] The United States responded by committing up to 28,000 troops. As described by General Colin L. Powell, Chairman of the U.S. Joint Chiefs of Staff, the U.S. forces' mission statement reflected prevailing American military doctrine: an overwhelming force applied decisively over a limited period of time, after which the remaining political and humanitarian tasks would be handed off to the United Nations. Even so, the United States rejected a UN request that it pacify and disarm the warring clans.[74] Paradoxically, after U.S. forces were drawn down and control of the operation was turned over to the UN under a more traditional peacekeeping mandate, the Security Council, urged on by the newly inaugurated Clinton administration, escalated the mission's objectives to include disarming the tribal factions and, in retribution for a deadly attack on Pakistani peacekeepers, implicitly authorized a manhunt for General Mohammed Farah Aidid and an offensive against his clan's leaders.

This escalation dismayed several troop-contributing countries, which had not agreed to a mission that went so far beyond traditional peacekeeping. Italy threatened to withdraw its 2,600-member contingent, Prime Minister Carlo Azeglio Ciampi accusing the UN of pursuing "a military intervention almost as an end in itself, against the wishes of those who are carrying it out."[75] U.S. military leaders were unhappy for a different reason: Secretary of Defense Les Aspin reportedly turned down Gen. Powell's request for tanks and armored vehicles which the military felt the more hostile environment demanded.[76] In the end, three distinct forces with three different missions and three separate command-and-control structures were deployed simultaneously in the streets of Mogadishu: a traditional UN peacekeeping force, supporting the provision of humanitarian assistance; a U.S. Quick Reaction Force, only tenuously connected to UN command, for more muscular action; and to hunt Gen. Aidid, a 400-strong detachment of

U.S. Army Rangers, completely autonomous from the UN, commanded out of Tampa, Florida. "The U.N. will be powerless," a UN official predicted. "They won't know who's fighting who."[77] He was right. An ambiguous and even contradictory set of tasks and means to pursue them forced first the United States and then the United Nations to abandon their military operations in Somalia—and, despite humanitarian successes in the countryside, leaving Mogadishu in much the state they found it.

But it was the Bosnian conflict that became a defining moment for post-cold war cooperative security relations, not solely because of its savagery—Rwanda was a far worse human tragedy—but because the conflict took place in Europe, where expectations were highest, and it humiliated not only the UN but also NATO and the West as a whole. It is well beyond the scope of the present study to analyze the origins and unfolding of this conflict. Once it erupted, the major powers, the UN, and NATO pursued three objectives: to contain it, horizontally and vertically; to relieve civilian suffering; and to help bring about a negotiated settlement—though until about mid-1994 the Clinton administration disagreed with the Europeans on whether that should include partitioning Bosnia-Herzegovina, thus sending mixed signals to the belligerents and diminishing the political effectiveness of UN involvement. In addition, the UN's military involvement in Bosnia was plagued by very different doctrinal understandings held by the main parties.

The United States viewed the issue of possible military intervention in the former Yugoslavia through the lenses of the "all-or-nothing" doctrine that came to dominate its use of force in the wake of Vietnam.[78] As defined by the U.S. Joint Chiefs of Staff, the "all" part of this doctrine stipulates the swift, decisive, comprehensive, and synchronized application of preponderant military force to shock, disrupt, demoralize, and defeat opponents.[79] This doctrine, however, left the United States with the "nothing" option for a growing number of conflict situations that conformed neither to traditional peacekeeping nor all-out war-fighting. In the former Yugoslavia, the U.S. military regarded the Serbian-dominated Yugoslav army (JNA) to be one of the more potent in Europe, barring a swift and decisive victory. Accordingly, even demonstration strikes were ruled out—as when the JNA shelled Dubrovnik and Vukovar in 1991, at which time, according to a subsequent account by Warren Zimmermann, who was U.S. ambassador to Yugoslavia at the time and had advised against U.S. military involvement, they might have deterred Serbian escalation.[80] On the eve of a presidential election year, the Bush administration had little desire to become militarily involved in Bosnia. Once in office, President Clinton decided to limit the U.S. military role to NATO air strikes, except to protect UN troops if they were forced to withdraw, or to implement a peace settlement.[81]

While American and British scholars have speculated in recent years about putative norms of humanitarian intervention in internal conflicts, France has actively sought to shape UN peace operations to give expression to certain of those norms.[82] French strategy has combined pursuit of negotiated settlements at the diplomatic level with the protection of civilian populations, by nonconsensual military means if necessary, from aggression by local warring factions. Thus, France has advocated creating "safe areas" within which civilians can be shielded and humanitarian aid distributed; "humanitarian corridors" through which these areas can be supplied; together with armed protection of humanitarian convoys engaged in "innocent passage" through the corridors. Most notably, the proposal to establish the UN safe areas in Bosnia (Sarajevo, Tuzla, Gorazde, Bihac, and Srebrenica) came from France.

The Bosnian experience taught two lessons about these notions. First, unless "humanitarian intervention" in an internal conflict protects civilians on all sides, it will be regarded as a hostile act by the disadvantaged factions. The Bosnian Serbs frequently harassed and even attacked UN troops in the safe areas for that reason. Second, if the intervening force is regarded as favoring one faction and is also outgunned by others, it merely offers itself up as a target. When the safe areas were created in Bosnia-Herzegovina, the UN Secretary General's military advisers estimated that it would take 34,000 troops to deter Serb attacks; the Security Council could muster only 7,600, and hoped that this symbolic UN presence and Serb fears that an attack on it might trigger NATO airstrikes would suffice.[83] France tried to compensate for the deficiency through heroics—as in Gen. Philippe Morillon's stand to keep Srebrenica from falling—denunciation—exemplified by Gen. Jean Cot's frequent public complaints about the humiliations suffered by UN troops at the hands of the Bosnian Serbs—and threats—that the UN either use greater force or suffer the withdrawal of French forces: "*tirer ou se tirer* (to shoot or to get out)."[84] Until mid-1995, its efforts were in vain.

Britain expended greater effort than any other country to devise a new doctrine for post-cold war peacekeeping, but its attempt to achieve clarity, in the event, merely further muddled the UN's Bosnian operation. Like the United States and France, Britain began with the view that the UN mission there constituted neither traditional peacekeeping nor war-fighting, that it was a "gray area" operation. When Lt. Gen. Sir Michael Rose arrived in Bosnia as UN force commander the press viewed his experience in British Special Forces, together with his own early actions in February 1994 to break the siege of Sarajevo, to signify that the UN was now prepared to use greater force in securing compliance with its mandates.[85] Gradually, however, the new British doctrine took shape, moving sharply away from these expectations. Termed "Wider Peacekeeping," the doctrine categorically rejected the very notion of "gray area" operations as "spurious historically [and] dangerous doctrinally."[86] There are only two types of UN military operations, it asserted, peacekeeping and enforcement, the second of which it deemed a subset of war-fighting. Differentiating the two, the doctrinal statement held, "is not the level of violence," as is typically assumed, "but simply consent."[87] Thus, wider peacekeeping was said to share with traditional peacekeeping the defining feature of being consent-based. By the time he left his command, Gen. Rose had come around to echo this dichotomy: "Patience, persistence and pressure is how you conduct a peacekeeping mission. . . . If someone wants to fight a war here on moral or political grounds, fine, great, but count us out. . . . I'm not going to fight a war in white-painted tanks."[88]

But what, then, was "wider" about "wider peacekeeping?" Apparently, the fact that it did not rule out selective use of force for purposes other than self-defense. As Gen. Rose explained, "Hitting one tank is peacekeeping. Hitting infrastructure, command and control, logistics, that is war."[89] Yet how can hitting even one tank be justified under the requirement of consent, except in self-defense? Here the British doctrine drew a distinction between "operational" and "tactical" levels of consent. Through continual negotiations with the appropriate leadership at the theater level, overall consent for an operation must be sought at all times. Accordingly, "wider peacekeeping" ruled out the *strategic* use of force. At the same time, within a framework of operational consent, the *tactical* use of force is permitted in defense of the mission as well as in self-defense. Moreover, when force is used for these purposes it must be "appropriate, proportionate, demonstrably reasonable and confined in effect to the specific and legitimate target intended."[90]

Insofar as the UN ever conceived of a common doctrine for its Bosnian operation, this was it.[91] The results were not salutary. So-called operational consent carried over poorly to the field level, leaving UN troops deployed in highly vulnerable positions. Their restrictive rules of engagement often made it difficult for these troops to defend themselves, let alone their mission. And when the mission was reinforced by the "peace enforcement" component of NATO airstrikes, as advocated repeatedly by the United States, the troops became, predictably, hostages to retaliation.

In sum, the major powers held very different precepts regarding the appropriate form of UN military intervention in the Bosnian conflict, while the UN's civilian and military command roughly reflected Britain's concept of "wider peacekeeping." If these precepts were not entirely at cross-purposes, they decidedly did not add up to a coherent and sustainable doctrine. In mid-1995, a pervasive sense of failure, coupled with the opportunity created by Croatia's successful sweep through its Serb-inhabited Krajina region, led Britain and France to field a more heavily armed UN Rapid Reaction Force, NATO to launch sustained air attacks, and the United States to take the lead in forging the outlines of a peace agreement.[92]

For the UN to have a viable military role in the domain between traditional peacekeeping and enforcement, it will have to devise a doctrinal basis for these gray area peace operations. The British "wider peacekeeping" team focused on *consent* as the decisive factor, but that seems to settle only the most obvious cases. If a government is in control and consents to a UN peace operation, the traditional peacekeeping modality suffices. But if consent is not granted, breaks down, or is sporadic then *any* UN military intervention must be viewed as a potential act of enforcement, fully capable of achieving compliance with its mission. The truly perplexing cases are those wherein domestic authority is contested and no faction has been collectively branded as the aggressor. Here the UN confronts a critical choice between two principles that it holds equally dear but which are sometimes incompatible: impartial versus minimum use of force.

The *impartial* use of international force in an internal conflict logically implies a "neutralization" strategy.[93] Its political objective would be to prevent local force from becoming the successful arbiter of outcomes on the ground and to persuade local combatants that they have no alternative but to reach a negotiated settlement. In other words, international military force would be employed in support or defense of certain rules of conduct, not the particular parties to a dispute. Ideally, the timely show of sufficient international force would deter the local use of force altogether. If the time for deterrence has passed, or should deterrence fail, international force would be employed in the attempt to deny military success to local combatants. As a last step, the international force would seek to compel offending local combatants to negotiate. To achieve these objectives, the international force must be militarily credible. Neither its size nor technical or operational capabilities can be defined generically, therefore, but will depend on the balance of power on the ground. At the high end of the spectrum, such a force could be virtually indistinguishable from war-fighting units in all respects *except* its political objectives.

UN member states may not be prepared to adopt such a strategy on principle, however, preferring an absolute *minimum use* of force. Or, for a variety of political and financial reasons, they may be willing to provide the UN with only a small and lightly armed force. But if governments ask the UN to intervene in internal conflicts under those constraints, then logically they may have to abandon impartiality in order to achieve success. For, as Richard Betts has argued: "Limited [capability] intervention may end a war if the intervenor takes sides, tilts the local balance of power, and helps one of the rivals to win—that is, if it not impartial. . . . [T]he attempt to have it both ways has brought the United Nations and the United States—and those whom they sought to help—to varying degrees of grief."[94]

Finally, if UN members are unable or unwilling to adopt either of these strategies—or a viable and mutually agreed-upon alternative to them—then they have no business asking the UN to become involved in gray-area operations in the first place. The UN and the world at large would be better off by having the organization lower its military profile and not muddle the strategic calculus of states and substate combatants.

In sum, devising a shared understanding among governments of how to do what they have asked the UN to do is a necessary first step toward greater success. Constructing workable implementation mechanisms is the next.

Command and Control

Perhaps the most hotly contested UN-related issue in American domestic politics today is the command and control of UN forces. Yet in any military operation, personnel, equipment, and procedures somehow must be coordinated in such a way as to achieve unified direction of effort in the field, guided by and in support of overall strategic objectives.

Under traditional peacekeeping, the military role of UN headquarters is limited essentially to management, appropriately vested in the Secretary General. The newer peace operations, however, also require effective performance of critical command functions. The UN charter assigned overall direction of UN military forces to a Military Staff Committee, advising the Security Council, with operational command-and-control issues to be worked out subsequently. Today, the United States is not alone among

Security Council members in believing that the representational character of this Committee—the military chiefs or deputies of the permanent five—renders it inappropriate for command purposes. Be that as it may, command functions in nontraditional UN peace operations are performed poorly.[95]

Problems exist throughout the entire chain of command: the Security Council routinely adopts mandates that do not provide militarily meaningful guidelines to missions; troop-contributing countries have no systematic input into the design of mandates unless they happen to be Security Council members; there is no duly constituted military authority at UN headquarters to command overall operations and serve as the connection between political authorities and force commanders; and the Secretary General acts as both the Council's executive agent in military operations and neutral mediator. In theater, force commanders are required to perform operational tasks without adequate strategic guidance or plans. Their options in employing the troops and equipment governments provide are subject to constraints by national authorities, which they do not always make known in advance. National contingent commanders often seek instructions from their capitals before acting on orders by UN force commanders—a practice that is hardly surprising, but that delays and can jeopardize the success of field actions while further undermining unity-in-command. Linking UN peace operations with non-UN "peace enforcement" components has also proved difficult: attempts to couple UN and NATO commands through a "dual key" arrangement for NATO airstrikes in Bosnia led to confusion and mutual recrimination, degrading the mission of both; decoupling UN and U.S. command structures in Somalia did not produce a model of operational success either. As a result of these difficulties, UN military units have been unable to act strategically, quickly, and on a sustained basis.

Despite national political cross-currents, some improvement should be possible in three areas. First, the UN requires a more effective military staff capacity in New York, responsible to the Security Council and enjoying a sphere of institutional independence from the Secretary General. The current arrangement of military advisers to the Secretary General leaves their functioning entirely at the discretion of the Secretary General, who may or may not ask for or accept their advice, or share it with the Security Council, and which, in any case, is too weak to perform the grand-strategic and operational planning roles that are now lacking. Second, the major troop-contributing countries should be systematically involved in reviewing the operational plans of missions in which they participate, possibly through a subsidiary organ of the Security Council. Greater involvement in the formative stages would reduce the extent that national authorities interject themselves at the field level. Finally, to reduce the incidence of national contingent commanders consulting their capitals before acting on UN force commanders' orders, senior officers of the larger contributing forces should be made part of the field headquarters staff of UN missions, performing liaison and advisory functions outside the operational chain of command. Troop-contributing nations would be asked to deal only through this mechanism on matters affecting their contingents, and if it is warranted by an operation's size they could provide their national representative officers with a staff to support these functions—thus turning what is now a vice undermining missions into a virtue strengthening them.[96]

In conclusion, the end of the cold war *has* created new possibilities for UN peace operations, but they are not nearly as unlimited or unproblematic as the early post-cold war euphoria promised. The concept of a concert can serve as a viable basis for UN peace operations, as we have seen, and it has broader positive effects besides. Significant practical problems afflict these operations, however, which must be attended to if the potential of the concert is to be translated into reality on the ground. For any form of UN military intervention beyond traditional peacekeeping to succeed, a shared doctrinal understanding of the nature of these operations, coupled with improvements in command-and-control arrangements, are absolute requisites.

Cooperative Balances

In Western Europe today, further transformation toward a community of power is a very real possibility, transcending balance-of-power politics as it has been understood historically. Moreover, European Union and trans-Atlantic security ties increasingly may entangle parts of Eastern and Central Europe in a correlative process of creating dependable expectations of peaceful change. Neither outcome is foreordained but remains contingent on several factors, the most critical of which is the future of Russia and of its relationship to the West. At the global level, UN-based concertation of major-power policies with regard to some range of regional conflicts appears feasible, though neither its geopolitical boundaries nor their threshold of intensity has been clearly established. But what of the rest of the spectrum of international security relations—above the reach of the UN yet also well short of possibilities for security-community–building?

What if any means are available for movement toward cooperative security relations there? A brief discussion of some generic mechanisms is followed by illustrative references to East Asia.

In view of our running debate with realism throughout this study, it is perhaps ironic that we find a useful starting point for this discussion in the canonical realist text of Hans Morgenthau, specifically its distinction between associative and adversarial balances of power.[97] The post-World War II U.S.-Soviet balance differed significantly from the historical experience of nearly three centuries, Morgenthau contended, not merely by virtue of being bipolar, but by being framed in two equally expansive yet mutually exclusive sets of values and norms. In contrast, the classical European balance of power, according to Morgenthau, rested in far greater measure on shared beliefs, creating a "common habitat" within which states pursued their rivalries. It was the asocial—or "mechanical"—nature of cold war bipolarity, Morgenthau argued, which imbued it with its particularly adversarial disposition. Losing track of this distinction, subsequent generations of realist scholars slipped into the assumption that the specific character of the U.S.-Soviet balance, rather than being anomalous, was synonymous with the very concept of balance-of-power politics.[98] Hence the bleak prediction in the early 1990s that we would soon miss the cold war.[99] But if Morgenthau was right, then the end of the cold war ought also to provide greater scope for associative or cooperative elements within balance-of-power politics.

What are examples of such cooperative elements, drawn not from a previous century but from recent international experience? At a minimum, cooperative balance-of-power strategies would seek to attenuate security rivalries with measures to increase transparency and build greater confidence, much as the 1986 Stockholm agreement tried to do across the East-West divide in Europe.[100] These measures include regular policy-level security dialogues, the exchange of defense white papers and annual plans of military activities, as well as prior notification of and invitations to observe military exercises, possibly working up to a reciprocal right of direct inspection. Further steps might comprise joint discussions of defense budgets, military-to-military contacts on issues related to doctrines and deployments, and reporting military incidents that could cause misunderstandings. In short, cooperative balances will not emerge spontaneously, but need "to be brought into existence by a self-conscious effort and then carefully nurtured."[101]

Both the need for and receptivity to cooperative measures of this kind will vary by time and place. The East-Asian security context is undergoing fundamental changes today. It is not difficult to conjure up scenarios of serious instability ahead unless practical efforts succeed in building mutual trust and confidence.[102] The region's rate of increase in military expenditures arguably is the highest in the world. Unresolved territorial claims abound. The status of Taiwan and the intensely militarized stand-off in the Korean peninsula remain volatile. Of the major powers, Russia is immobilized by internal turmoil, problems along its Central Asian frontiers, and forging a viable European role. China is widely regarded as a potential regional security threat yet simultaneously views itself as the victim of growing encirclement. Japan continues to be a U.S. military protectorate, which is at once reassuring to Japan's neighbors but also delays the inevitable adjustment within the region and within Japan's domestic polity toward its assuming the role of a normal great power. The United States is generally viewed as a stabilizing influence in the region but doubts do exist about the long-term credibility of its commitments. Strengthening the elements of cooperative security within this fragile balance will not in itself solve outstanding security problems, but it may help shape *how* states decide to solve them.

Multilateral institutions have never been strong in the region and East Asian states consider the intrusive and formal cooperative security mechanisms devised for East-West relations in Europe during the waning years of the cold war inappropriate for their context. Nevertheless, modest regional and subregional building blocks are beginning to take hold.[103] They include the Association of Southeast Asian Nations (ASEAN) and the ASEAN Regional Forum (ARF), a non-threatening confidence- and security-building mechanism to which all the relevant states in the region belong; the Asia-Pacific Economic Cooperation Forum; and the Council for Security Cooperation in Asia-Pacific. The Australian security specialist Paul Dibb points out that solidifying these mechanisms will not be easy, due to the absence of a cooperative tradition in, as well as the sheer strategic complexity of, the region. At the same time, he believes, "there is the sense [in the region] that an opportunity exists that should be exploited before it is too late."[104]

This chapter has not tried to make the case that the world ahead is the best of all possible security worlds. But, while problems do exist today that did not exist during the cold war, so, too, do opportunities for cooperative security relations. Their domain, as we have seen, lies between Wilsonian collective security and classical balance-of-power politics. Hence, that analytical dichotomy, so central to the cold war realist enterprise, is of little practical utility in exploiting the new opportunities. But neither are grand schemes of all-encompassing security orders. Among the practical cooperative security strategies that can help sustain the long peace are consolidating the trans-Atlantic security community and projecting particularly its European institutional web into Eastern and Central Europe; fleshing out a more robust concert-based system of UN peace operations; and incorporating associative mechanisms into potentially adversarial power balances, including, perhaps most critically for the sake of global stability, in East Asia.

5 | Economic Stabilization

E fforts to reconstruct the postwar international economic order began amid raging world war, coupled with painful memories of the Great Depression, beggar-thy-neighbor trade and monetary policies, and outright economic warfare. Understandably, the reconstruction reflected, above all, a quest for normalcy, a search for stability. "Historians often treat stability as a passive coming to rest or a societal inertia that requires no explanation," Charles Maier has written. "In fact, stabilization is as challenging a historical problem as revolution."[1] The challenge was especially acute for the architects of the postwar economic order because they were obliged to reconcile two dimensions of stability that history had shown to stand in contradiction.

The United States sought to create an open and nondiscriminatory international economic order. But a mere return to the gold standard and free trade was rejected on the grounds that they would destabilize the domestic employment and social welfare objectives that had become imperatives of the activist New Deal state and its counterparts abroad. At the same time, the internationally uncoordinated pursuit of domestic objectives was also ruled out because it had triggered the mutually destructive economic spirals of the 1930s, thereby showing itself to be incompatible with international openness and nondiscrimination. This tension between the requirements of international and domestic stability was resolved by the heterodox formula of the "embedded liberalism" compromise. Societies were asked to accept the transitional dislocation attending international liberalization. In turn, liberalization would be constrained by the domestic economic and social policy roles of governments, and its serious adjustment costs socialized. As Karl Polanyi predicted in 1944, anticipating the Bretton Woods monetary agreement: "Out of the ruins of the Old World, the cornerstones of the New can be seen to emerge: economic collaboration of governments *and* the liberty to organize national life at will."[2]

The embedded liberalism compromise was not intended as a one-time fix but as a dynamic equilibrium, a steadily evolving set of practices that would, however, continue to reflect a rough balance of obligations to external and internal stability. Stability in both realms was achieved in due course and a period of unprecedented economic expansion ensued. The cold war, far from being an impediment to instituting this international economic order, facilitated it. The socialist countries dropped out early on, making it easier to devise and implement multilateral monetary and trade regimes in the capitalist world. And bipolarity made it easier for the capitalist West to compromise and make sacrifices for the sake of their common front against the communist East.[3] Even before the collapse of the communist system, several of its constituent states sought entry into the multilateral economic regimes. Since 1989, almost all of the rest have done so, as have most developing countries, making these the first economic regimes in history to achieve virtual universality.

And yet, for nearly a quarter century now serious observers have predicted potentially fatal strains in, if not the imminent collapse of, these economic regimes. On the trade side, the well-known economic policy analyst Fred Bergsten warned as early as 1972 that "the first real international trade war since the 1930s" may be at hand, reminding us that "trade wars could become full economic wars, precisely as they did under similar international conditions in the 1930s."[4] On the monetary side, Robert Triffin, one of the grand academic figures in international monetary relations, dismissed the 1976 Jamaica accords, which codified the move to floating exchange rates, as "slapstick comedy." More recently, he wondered whether the acronym IMS stands for international monetary system—or scandal.[5] An erosion of America's support for economic multilateralism typically is held responsible for these putative threats to the monetary and trade regimes.

By definition, the embedded-liberalism compromise can unravel by one of two routes: if domestic policy measures reverse the commitment to liberalization, producing a move toward protectionism; or if unrestrained liberalization undermines the commitment to domestic economic and social objectives, creating greater societal vulnerability to market forces. Virtually all the policy analysts' attention has focused on the protectionist route, especially on the possibility that shifts in U.S. preferences and policies are generating internationally deleterious consequences. We examine this scenario in the present chapter but find it to be greatly exaggerated. In contrast, relatively little attention has been paid to the "disembeddedness" route toward unraveling the postwar compromise, which we explore in chapter 6. This scenario implicates the United States more fully and potentially poses far greater dangers to the future stability of international economic relations.

Our first task is to sketch out the baseline—the principled and shared understandings on the basis of which the capitalist countries sought to come to grips with the twin desires of international and domestic economic stability in the postwar era. Only then can we discern systematically which practices constitute serious deviations from the embedded-liberalism compromise today, and where fundamental problems reside.

The Bretton Woods Regimes[6]

On the monetary side, by the time of the Anglo-American "Joint Statement of Principles," issued not long before the 1944 Bretton Woods conference, a broad consensus had emerged between these two nations. As summarized in chapter 2, it provided, on the one hand, for free and stable exchanges and, on the other, the erection of a "double screen" to cushion the domestic economy from the strictures of the balance of payments.[7] Indeed, the most intense negotiations were occasioned by the functioning of the cushioning mechanisms, to be instituted in an International Monetary Fund (IMF). With regard to short-term balance of payments financing, the British, in the person of John Maynard Keynes, proposed an international overdraft facility of some $25-to-$30 billion in which one country's credits would have been recorded as another's debits. This arrangement would have been self-clearing unless countries were structurally out of balance, in which case symmetrical corrective measures were called for on the part of surplus countries (stimulate demand) and deficit countries (tighten monetary and fiscal policies). The overall ceiling could be raised by intergovernmental agreement as required to finance the expansion of international trade. The United States, led by Treasury New Dealer Harry Dexter White, originally called for a mere $5 billion Fund though ultimately agreeing to $8.8 billion. However, these funds had to be paid in, as opposed to being created by agreement. Access to the Fund as well as voting rights were limited by quotas, reflecting relative levels of paid-in subscriptions—

the initial U.S. contribution being $3.175 billion. Moreover, a country that sought to draw on the Fund had to make "representations" that it needed assistance to make payments on its current account, and for no other reason. Thus, with the United States, the only major creditor country in sight, seeking to limit its exposure, the first part of the double screen was both more modest and more rigid than Britain and other potential debtor countries would have liked. But there was no question about its being provided.

On the issue of exchange rate changes, Britain was more successful in assuring automaticity and limiting external intrusions into the domestic policy domain. The Fund was required to concur in any change necessary to correct a "fundamental disequilibrium," and if the change was less than 10 percent from initial par values the Fund was given no power even to raise objections. Most importantly, the Fund could not oppose any exchange rate change on the grounds that the domestic social policies of the country requesting it had led to the disequilibrium making the change necessary.

Interestingly, the critical issue of how international liquidity would be provided generated relatively little debate—in all probability for two reasons. First, under the British overdraft scheme liquidity would have become largely a non-issue because accounts automatically balanced out while the ceiling could be raised as needed, and the British were too preoccupied with promoting their scheme to pay close attention to alternative solutions to the liquidity problem. Second, the United States was not keen to have the issue discussed, as it had been counting all along on the U.S. dollar emerging as the chief medium of international currency reserves—which it did. All currencies were valued against the dollar and the dollar against gold; all countries in practice would use dollars to clear their international accounts and the dollar would be convertible into gold on demand. With gold production subsequently being inadequate, and IMF quota increases constrained by U.S. voting power in the Fund, U.S. payments deficits—produced in the first instance by overseas military expenditures, government transfers, and private foreign investments—became the major source of international liquidity.

Lastly, the Bretton Woods monetary regime permitted governments to control capital flows—not merely as a temporary expedient but as a permanent feature. This provision may appear surprising in light of the explosion of international capital markets in recent decades. But it reflected a widespread consensus at the time, outside of banking circles to be sure, which White and Keynes shared. Capital controls were deemed necessary, first and foremost, to safeguard domestic macroeconomic and social policies from the instabilities produced by unrestricted capital flows. Moreover, because of the experience gained in the interwar period, it was believed that the speculative financial movements that restored capital mobility would unleash were detrimental to the maintenance of stable exchange rates. In addition, it was anticipated that the adverse effects of large and volatile capital flows on the external payments positions of countries would increase domestic pressures for protectionism in trade, potentially undermining the trade regime.

Once negotiations on postwar commercial arrangements got under way seriously, nondiscrimination and tariff reduction were affirmed, but so, too, were safeguards, exemptions, and restrictions—all designed to protect the balance of payments and a variety of domestic social policies.[8] The General Agreement on Tariffs and Trade (GATT) made obligatory the most-favored-nation rule, but a blanket exception was allowed for existing preferential arrangements (a U.S. concession to Britain), and countries were permitted to form customs unions and free-trade areas (U.S. encouragement to Western Europe). Moreover, quantitative import restrictions, although prohibited, were deemed suitable measures to safeguard the balance of payments—explicitly including payments difficulties that resulted from domestic full employment policies. They could also be invoked in agricultural trade if they were used in conjunction with a domestic price support program.

The GATT also called for the substantial reduction of tariffs and other barriers to trade, but this was *not* made obligatory, and it was coupled with emergency actions that were allowed if domestic producers were threatened with injury from import competition caused by past tariff concessions. The Agreement also offered a blanket escape from any of its obligations if two-thirds of the contracting parties approved—in 1955 the United States availed itself of this opportunity to exclude its entire agricultural adjustment program from international scrutiny. Lastly, the GATT provided procedures to settle disputes arising under the Agreement, as well as for the multilateral surveillance of the invocation of most (though not all) of its escape clauses. The principle of reciprocity was enshrined as a code of conduct, to guide both tariff reductions and the determination of compensation for injuries suffered.

These efforts to construct multilateral economic regimes did not come to fruition until the late 1950s. Only then had European countries acquired the confidence to undertake the process of liberalization beyond Europe itself. The European Economic Community had been formed, the IMF agreements became fully operational, and GATT rounds of tariff reduction began in earnest. Getting from "here to there" required substantial doses of U.S. financial assistance, security assistance, and deliberate discrimination by Western Europe against the United States in monetary and trade relations so as to promote intra-European liberalization. The United States also intervened more directly in the domestic polities of other countries, through the occupation authorities in Germany and Japan, and through such transnational adjuncts of American civil society as the American Federation of Labor, which was particularly active in France, Italy, and Latin America. The United States sought, thereby, to moderate the structure and ideological direction of political movements, to encourage the exclusion of communist parties from governing coalitions, and generally to keep collectivist impulses within acceptable center-left bounds.[9] Finally, in order to persuade the Europeans to admit Japan into the GATT in the mid-1950s, the United States permitted them to phase in Japan's access to their markets while opening its own market to Japanese goods immediately.

Patterns of Continuity and Change

In a major survey of international monetary reform published in 1985, *The Economist* commented: "How easy to say that, in the early 1970s, the Bretton Woods system 'collapsed' or was 'swept away.' Easy but unfortunate." It went on to explain: "Of course, fixed rates were replaced by floating ones—but was that the change that mattered . . . ? Certainly, governments were freed of the external discipline of maintaining parity; but didn't they still face other disciplines . . . ?"[10] In fact, neither the monetary nor the trade regime ever functioned precisely as designed. Furthermore, countries abandoned specific instruments of the two regimes as time went on; deviations from rules have not been unusual; and even core norms are sometimes disregarded with impunity as governments pursue their policy objectives. All of this is well known and beyond dispute. What remains in contention is what it signifies.

In the sections that follow, I examine several major changes in the monetary and trade regimes that many observers believe constitute serious deviations from the postwar multilateral designs and exhibit a reversion to protectionist tendencies. The purpose of this exercise is not to explain the evolution of the international economy since World War II—a task that is well beyond the scope of this study—but rather to interpret, in the light of the embedded-liberalism compromise, changes in specific practices of governments that were occasioned by that evolution.

The Monetary Regime

When seen against the backdrop of the abusive currency practices of the interwar period, the creation of a nondiscriminatory system of currency exchanges has been a singular achievement of the postwar monetary regime: All major currencies are fully convertible into one another; none is governed by multiple exchange rates or other rationing schemes; the former socialist economies are undergoing the wrenching process toward full convertibility; and the remaining deviations consist mainly of third world currencies that do not affect the overall functioning of international monetary relations. This core attribute of monetary multilateralism, the desire for which so animated the Bretton Woods negotiators, is so deeply instituted and taken for granted today that it is rarely even mentioned in assessments of the monetary regime.

When analysts today speak of the collapse of the Bretton Woods monetary regime they typically have in mind these factors: ending fixed rates of exchange; closing the gold window; exchange rate volatility; and the erosion of external discipline more generally. Their combination suggests to many analysts that the monetary regime has been replaced by, in Susan Strange's term, "casino capitalism"—largely pushed by the United States, according to Strange, because it has had most to gain from this new game.[11]

Floating Exchange Rates

We would do well to remind ourselves that under a system of truly fixed exchange rates governments are expected to subordinate their domestic policies to the maintenance of external parity: "monetary policy, as usually conceived, ceases to be a discretionary instrument of policy. The money supply on any meaningful definition must be altered if necessary to preserve the exchange rate."[12] It is safe to say that no government at Bretton Woods would have accepted this stricture had it been proposed—which, of course, it was not. Under the Bretton Woods regime, exchange rates were *expected* to change if necessary to correct fundamental disequilibria.

Thus, exchange rates were on an "adjustable peg," an arrangement that proved flawed for several well-known reasons. Surplus countries, particularly Germany and Japan, enjoying the competitive advantage of undervalued currencies and basking in the presumed virtue of positive payments balances, refused to revalue upward as much or as frequently as required. Deficit countries, such as Britain, were afraid of losing face and waited until the last minute to devalue. And the United States was prevented from changing the value of the dollar because its price was fixed in terms of gold.

For all practical purposes, then, there never was any effective means of routinely realigning currency values in response to fundamental disequilibria. The adjustable peg system, therefore, was inherently unsustainable once economic recovery in Europe and Japan took off; only the timing of its demise was in doubt.

What is more, although controls on capital flows were not formally mandated by Bretton Woods, the internal logic of the regime required them and they were expected to remain in place.[13] This arrangement, too, was unsustainable in the long run, Cooper suggests, insofar as it presupposed the ability to differentiate sharply between current and capital account transactions, a distinction that, if nothing else, the growing volume of direct foreign investment would have eroded.[14] More important, governments chose to liberalize capital flows as a matter of policy preference—in the first instance largely because capital controls were becoming ineffective due to the emergence of international capital markets, beginning with the London-based "offshore" Eurodollar market in the 1960s, as well as the expansion of multinational enterprises.[15] The combination of capital mobility and discrete exchange rate changes, in turn, produced the celebrated one-way option for currency speculation that was responsible for the recurrent exchange rate crises of the 1960s—when decisions to change rates were delayed so long that their inevitability provided a sure bet to speculators.[16] Sooner or later either capital mobility or pegged exchange rates had to be abandoned.

Governments abandoned the adjustable peg. But by the time they moved to floating exchange rates in 1973, their choice as they understood it was, according to Rachel McCulloch, "not between floating and fixed rates, but between rates changing by small amounts on a day-to-day basis and those changing at longer intervals by substantial percentages and usually only after macroeconomic policy debacles, welfare-reducing direct controls, and repeated foreign exchange crises."[17] Moreover, having come to prize financial liberalization as a policy goal, governments now looked to floating rates as the means to restore greater domestic policy autonomy while also preserving the relatively open trading order. These aims surely were in keeping with the underlying objectives of Bretton Woods.

The Dollar Standard

We saw above that the liquidity provisions of Bretton Woods were ambiguous from the start and inadequate in the event. As a result, the dollar exchange standard was already in trouble when the monetary regime first began to function without restraints. In 1958, just as the Europeans resumed full convertibility of their currencies, U.S. gold reserves fell permanently below U.S. overseas liabilities.[18] Throughout the 1960s, a seemingly endless series of stop-gap measures was devised to defend the gold-convertibility of the dollar. Roughly speaking, these measures were intended to make conversion financially unattractive, to increase the capacity of the IMF to supply liquidity, and to increase the capacity of central banks to neutralize the flow of speculative capital. The United States also "taxed" its allies for military services provided by obtaining offset payments from them as well as through the exercise of seigniorage. In addition, the United States undertook limited domestic measures to reduce its payments deficits while pressuring surplus countries to revalue their currencies. By 1968, however, the dollar had become in effect inconvertible into gold; it was declared formally so in 1971.

It is critical to note, however, that while the link of the dollar to gold may have been "psychologically important," it was also, Cooper contends, "technically tenuous."[19] This was so because it had not provided a principled basis for determining the overall world monetary condition in the first place. As Cooper explains, pegging the value of currencies in the manner of Bretton Woods "determines the price level of each country in relation to the others, but it does not determine the world price level."[20] So long as the United States pursued domestic economic policies that were conducive to international monetary stability the problem remained masked. Once it became unable or unwilling to perform that international public service the problem became unmasked. Surging inflation in the Johnson era, created by outlays for Vietnam and Great Society programs that were funded by monetary expansion rather than taxes, forced the issue. But it had been no more resolved before; it had existed throughout the life of the Bretton Woods regime. Today, the world is, in effect, on a dollar standard—or a "Greenspan" standard, Thomas Friedman has quipped, referring to the Chairman of the U.S. Federal Reserve Board.[21]

Nevertheless, none of the major monetary powers has rushed forward with solutions to this congenital defect of the Bretton Woods regime. Like the United States, they have been content to patch things up around the edges. When the dollar has gone on one of its periodic wild gyrations—the sharp depreciation of 1978 and the staggering appreciation of 1981–85 being prime instances—they have shown irritation; they have jawboned the United States; and the West Europeans have sought to limit the dislocating effects among themselves by striving, haltingly, for a European Monetary Union. From time to time, governments have also coordinated extensive exchange market interventions in support of the dollar. But no other government has been prepared to have its own currency play a significant international reserve currency role—at the height of Japan's financial bubble in the late 1980s the yen played, in the words of an American banker in Tokyo, "only a laughably small role as a settlement or reserve currency."[22] Nor is there any desire among the leading economic powers to return to a fully fledged gold standard. Nor is there any consensus among them to construct a different commodity-based reserve asset, or to expand significantly the use of the IMF collectively created Special Drawing Rights. Even so modest a proposal as the 1979 IMF Substitution Account, whereby some portion of "unwanted" dollars could have been traded in for an IMF asset, was rejected by governments in part over squabbles about the allocation of exchange rate risks and interest payments—just before the dollar glut was overtaken by a renewed scramble for dollars as a result of the second oil shock. The scramble continues today, boosted this time by the dollar's use in the economies-in-transition: as of mid-1994, sixty percent of all U.S. currency bills printed was destined for circulation abroad, a twenty percent increase from the 1970s.[23]

Volatility

Even most critics of the current international monetary arrangements concede that they helped absorb the extreme duress of the 1970s: the two oil shocks, double-digit inflation in the industrialized world, and a sudden reversal in prevailing current account balances that was unprecedented in peacetime. Floating exchange rates and liberalized capital markets were the major mechanisms of adjustment; the formal apparatus of the IMF played a relatively minor role. At the same time, there exists a growing unease that these mechanisms have increased the volatility of exchange rates which, it is felt, undermines the efficiency, stability, and domestic monetary autonomy their advocates promised. Once again, the facts are relatively clear but the implications for the monetary and trade regimes are ambiguous.

For better and for worse, international capital flows have been cut loose from their role as servants to international trade. The relative magnitude of international capital market transactions, according to a recent estimate by *The Economist*, now dwarfs world trade flows by a ratio of 60:1.[24] Moreover, whereas capital movements historically reflected business decisions to finance trade or establish production facilities abroad, from the mid-1970s on it became increasingly apparent, as Robert Roosa, former U.S. Treasury Under Secretary, put it a decade ago, "that the dominant proportion of the investment funds actually in movement internationally today reflects instead decisions concerning portfolio holdings . . . , shifts among holdings of various kinds of intangible assets."[25] In other words, the world's major currencies have become one among many tradable intangible assets.

It is intrinsically troublesome for some observers that national curren-cies are treated in this manner, though others applaud the development. McCulloch's conclusion may not mollify the former: "while exchange rates have indeed been volatile, their volatility has been less than that of stock prices."[26] But it does raise the issues of relative volatility, and how it is man-aged. Directly comparing different monetary regimes over time, Allan Meltzer finds that on some measures of stability the period since floating exchange rates actually compares favorably with the pre-World War I gold standard. In addition, though some measures of volatility may be higher today, Meltzer contends that because of better risk management strategies and instruments, risk and uncertainty are uniformly lower.[27]

Meltzer's findings go some way toward explaining why the volatility of exchange rates in recent years has had relatively limited effects on trade and investment flows as well as on the attitudes of governments.[28] A senior executive of Gillette, the multinational consumer products firm, puts it this way: "In the long run, these currency fluctuations, up and down, don't mean a whit in the decision where to manufacture."[29] For now, at the global level governments in the leading currency countries apparently prefer liv-ing with prevailing levels of volatility to the cost of trying to fix it. Fixing it would require new capital controls, without guarantees that they would work, and/or unacceptably intrusive levels of domestic policy coordination. Even in the European Union, movement toward monetary integration is driven as much by political considerations as economic conviction.

Policy Coordination

The reluctance of governments to move toward closer policy coordination is often taken as an indication that such coordination has declined over time. Here, too, the evidence is ambiguous. Indeed, it suggests two distinct developments, in two different directions. First, under the old rules, the IMF was involved in policy coordination when it concerned balance-of-payments financing and exchange-rate changes. The Fund retains a powerful role vis-à-vis developing countries and the former socialist economies-in-transition that continue to borrow from the Fund. But since the 1970s, it has lacked this formal leverage over the industrialized coun-tries because they get whatever financing they need from the markets. There is also a second development, however: the *objects* of policy coordi-nation among countries have changed, from "external" to "internal"

adjustment mechanisms.[30] In the 1960s, macroeconomic policy coordination largely concerned the balance-of-payments and exchange rates—
which are external mechanisms. By the 1980s, the focus of collective concern came to include monetary and fiscal policies—very much internal
matters. This type of policy coordination is, of course, far more difficult to
achieve: under Bretton Woods, monetary and fiscal policies were solely
domestic concerns; they have widespread domestic ramifications and so
face greater domestic political constraints; and policymaking is shared
among several domestic institutions including central banks, which typically enjoy substantial statutory independence.

The significance of this second shift, it is true, may be partially offset by
the first. But even in the past the IMF's regulative role operated only on
industrialized countries requiring its assistance, with Britain and Italy
being the most frequent customers. And the Fund's current normative role
in relation to the industrialized countries should not be entirely discounted. It consists of policy surveillance, revived and adapted after the
monetary upheavals of the early 1970s largely at the initiative of the
United States and France.[31] Governments reaffirmed, as a binding principle, the commitment to avoid manipulating exchange rates in the attempt
to evade adjustment or gain competitive advantage. In addition, they
endorsed coordinated exchange market intervention to counter disorderly
conditions. Extensive albeit soft IMF oversight of these provisions was provided for, and is complemented by consultations within the Organization
for Economic Cooperation and Development (OECD), among central
banks, and at the annual economic summits of the seven major capitalist
countries.[32] Quite apart from these official deliberations, foreign-exchange
markets impose a degree of external discipline on domestic policies, especially if those policies depart too radically from the norm. As a French commentator said of France's attempt in the 1980s to rouse its economy by fiscal stimulus: "The message came through loud and clear that go-it-alone
Keynesianism was no longer possible."[33] Lastly, when the monetary system
as a whole is threatened, as it was in 1982 by the prospect of first Mexico
and then other countries defaulting on their external debts, and again by
political and financial instability in Mexico in 1994, the IMF's coordination role quickly assumes a more active form.[34]

What all is said and done, what can we conclude about the evolution of
the Bretton Woods monetary regime? The question needs to be answered
at three levels of analysis. In one sense the regime clearly has "collapsed":
none of its core instruments is in place any longer, a state of affairs that has
persisted for more than twenty years, nor have these instruments been

replaced by ones that closely resemble the originals. This answer is consistent with the assessment by observers who view the post-1973 reforms as slapstick comedy and even scandal—with the proviso, however, that governments in the leading currency countries seem to take these efforts seriously enough but, thus far, have concluded that the available remedies are more costly than living with the afflictions. At a deeper level, it may be said that the regime has changed—not collapsed—from being rule-based to being discretion-based. That is, many of the core norms embodied in the regime are no longer expressed in explicit rules—specifying, for example, how the possibility of manipulating exchange rates for competitive advantage should be limited—but are now subject to greater discretion by national authorities. That makes it more difficult to judge, objectively, when norms are being violated. But the focus of collective scrutiny has also shifted, as we noted, from external to internal adjustment mechanisms. Consequently, domestic policies that drive external imbalances are now more likely to become transparent than before. The regime appears to exhibit greatest continuity at its deepest level of the underlying commitments to monetary multilateralism and domestic stability. Indeed, if there is a tendency to deviate from this principled basis today it is not toward beggar-thy-neighbor policies, pursued for neoprotectionist purposes, but in the direction of neoliberalism. It is undoubtedly the case that governments enjoy less domestic policy autonomy today than the architects of the regime intended and expected—though they probably also enjoy higher levels of economic welfare.

Finally, what can we conclude about the role of the United States in the evolution of the monetary regime? For starters, it is hard to disentangle the two. The United States was critical in getting the regime functioning. And the recovery of Europe and Japan made the earlier American policy posture unsustainable, thereby forcing the changes of the early 1970s. In the 1980s, the United States, followed by Britain, became the driving force for neoliberalism, but international capital markets had emerged earlier—initially triggered, ironically, by governments, including the Kennedy and Johnson administrations, attempting to maintain domestic capital controls. The United States paid little regard to the international monetary regime in the first half of the 1980s, as both its budget deficits and trade deficits soared while the exchange rate of the dollar *appreciated* by over fifty percent in real terms. But the charge that the United States behaved in a predatory manner thereby, becoming the world's largest debtor country, is as simplistic as the counter claim that it merely served as an attractive investment haven. Currency manipulations for competitive advantage have been rare all around. The major instances in which the United States can be implicated concern Japan's immovable trade surplus, which is addressed below. As for America's economic power—the relative decline of which is stressed by liberal and realist political economists alike to explain monetary disorder—it has shown little variation of late: the U.S. share of world product has held relatively steady since the 1970s.[35]

The Trade Regime

Thanks to successive rounds of GATT reductions, tariff levels have been lowered to the point where they no longer constitute a significant barrier to international trade: some 5 percent on industrial products, down from an average of more than 40 percent in the immediate postwar years. As a result, exclusive preferences have also become irrelevant, though generalized preferences for developing countries are in place by international agreement.[36] Growth in world trade has averaged over 5 percent per annum throughout the postwar era and continues to outpace growth in world output. Moreover, many developing countries that had stayed out of GATT, preferring the more statist orientation of the UN Conference on Trade and Development, have now joined. The former socialist countries uniformly have turned their backs on more than forty years of central planning and now strive to integrate into the world economy. Lastly, GATT's Uruguay Round, its first to venture systematically into the uncharted terrain of services, intellectual property rights, and agriculture, produced an overall agreement and recommended the creation of a World Trade Organization (WTO), which has since come into being, and which has a greater capacity than GATT for dealing with trade policy disputes.[37]

The concerns observers express about the world trade order taking a protectionist turn focus on a different side of recent trade policy history: the imposition of various forms of nontariff barriers by the leading industrialized countries on imports from one another and from the newly industrializing countries, as well as "results-oriented" market access initiatives, on behalf of domestic producers. The United States is usually cited as a chief culprit, undermining the multilateral trade regime it helped to create.[38] And while the WTO may restrain some of these practices, it is not likely to be able to do away with them altogether. As in the case of the monetary regime, there is little disagreement about the particulars in question. Here, too, however, what the particulars signify lends itself to very different interpretations depending upon the base-line from which one starts. Below, we survey four alleged patterns of neoprotectionist deviation from

the vantage point, not of the textbook model of free trade, but the embedded-liberalism compromise: process protectionism; managed trade; aggressive unilateralism; and regionalism. Though grounds exist for concern and
vigilance, we find that scenarios depicting a decisive shift away from multilateralism and liberalization are greatly exaggerated.

Process Protectionism

Serious tariff reductions began with the GATT's Kennedy Round in the
1960s. Studies suggest that, right from the start, movement toward greater
economic openness in the OECD countries has been closely associated
with governments expanding their domestic role to manage the adjustment costs. What is more, openness overrides virtually all other economic
and political factors in explaining governments' active policy roles—
including economic size, level of affluence, rate of unemployment, and the
presence of left-wing parties in the electoral system.[39] Lastly, in the words
of one such study, governments on the whole "merely attempt to mitigate
the negative effects of trade liberalization on specific industries and not to
offset them entirely."[40] Though governments have never defined a precise
metric, in terms of the overall balance of international and domestic objectives this is, as we have seen, more or less how the trade regime was
expected to function.

The United States differs from other industrialized countries in its size,
the still relatively modest share of trade in its national product, and the
more liberal character of its state. Accordingly, it has relied more heavily
on means of externalizing the burden of adjustment.[41] But the pattern is
similar, and its markets are among the world's most open. In a comprehensive survey, Judith Goldstein has shown that "[a]s tariffs decreased and
imports increased their market share in the 1960s and 1970s, American
producers did react by petitioning the bureaucracy for protection"[42]—that
is, by seeking protection through administrative processes. Nevertheless,
the government's response did *not* simply mirror the increased petition
activity:

> When confronted by a choice between giving aid or not, the
> executive gave no aid. When protectionism was mandated by
> the bureaucracy, the president often chose to give a transfer
> payment, to give less than recommended or, in the case of
> countervailing duties, to sanction a tariff waiver. In dumping
> findings, legislation leaves no recourse but to assess a duty.

However, every effort was made to convince the exporter to
halt the practice.[43]

Voluntary export restraints, negotiated directly with the exporting country,
became the instrument of choice for the executive branch to avoid mandated actions. But while the U.S. government may have provided adversely
affected domestic industries with many things thereby, Goldstein concludes that effective protection was not one of them.

From the 1970s on, Congress, as a condition for approving further liberalization, began to change the domestic rules so as to make it easier for
import-affected industries to obtain trade relief: in 1974, as part of legislation authorizing U.S. participation in the GATT's Tokyo Round, and in
1979, as the price for implementing its results; and similarly in connection
with the more recent Uruguay Round. Many more petitions have been
filed as a result. But into the 1980s, according to I. M. Destler, "in terms of
actual relief granted, industry petitioners were again to be disappointed."[44]
So the rough balance continued to hold. The stagflation of the Carter years
put enormous pressure on the trade relief system in the United States. During the first Reagan administration, process protectionism exploded.
William Niskanen, a member of President Reagan's Council of Economic
Advisers and a strong defender of the administration's overall economic
program, summarizes the episode in these terms:

> Trade policy in the Reagan administration is best described
> as a strategic retreat. The consistent goal of the president was
> free trade, both in the United States and abroad. In response
> to domestic political pressure, however, the administration
> imposed more new restraints on trade than any administration
> since Hoover.[45]

The domestic political pressure had two main sources. The first was the
consequences of the administration's own macroeconomic policies. As
noted previously, the value of the dollar appreciated by over 50 percent in
real terms from 1981 to 1985. Not surprisingly, imports surged during the
same period, from 18.9 percent to 25.8 percent of total U.S. goods production, and exports plummeted by "a drop nearly as great as that precipitated
fifty years earlier by the Great Depression and the Smoot-Hawley Act."[46]
The resulting trade deficit dwarfed all previous peaks. "Not only was this
imbalance unprecedented for modern America; it was the worst imbalance
experienced by any advanced industrial nation since the 1940s."[47] It is vir-

tually axiomatic that recourse to domestic trade relief measures should have soared to equally unprecedented levels. For a brief time new trade impediments actually may have outweighed market opening trends.

The second source was electoral. The Reagan imbalances created irresistible opportunities for entrepreneurial politicians in both parties to seek support on platforms of "level playing fields," protecting American industries and jobs from "unfair" foreign competition. When the Democrats regained control of the Senate in 1986, this general political mode took on a directly partisan cast. A president from the other party who seemed invincible in so many other respects was exceedingly vulnerable on the trade issue. The trade bills that emerged in both the House and Senate, in Niskanen's words, "threatened the most substantial reversal of U.S. trade law since the United States took the lead in rebuilding the world trading system in 1934."[48]

And yet, in the end, the Omnibus Trade and Competitiveness Act of 1988 that was finally passed into law veered off that dangerous course—perhaps aided by Wall Street's "Black Monday," when the Dow Jones average went into a 500 point free-fall. Contrary to predictions, that Act "did not impose statutory protectionism, and it did not [re]impose direct congressional control over trade."[49] Indeed, a reversal had already begun to set in, first in monetary policy, as we saw above, then in the trade imbalance and requests for relief.[50] Destler draws up a judicious assessment for the decade as a whole: "the most reasonable conclusion is that American trade protection increased sharply in the early 1980s but receded somewhat thereafter. The net increase over the decade was less than one might have expected given the pressures at play."[51] The cost of legal and lobbying services generated by the trade relief system continues to grow, however, and to distort economic incentives while also serving as an outright impediment to smaller or weaker importers into the American market.[52]

Finally, and with the aim of overcoming this lingering problem, the Uruguay Round produced new provisions to discipline the invocation of the most frequently employed process protectionist measures, including countervailing duties, antidumping, and safeguards, and it created new dispute-settlement procedures within the WTO.[53] It remains to be seen how effective they will be in practice.

Managed Trade

Another criticism of certain trade policy practices is that they represent "managed trade," potentially undermining both the open character and nondiscriminatory principles of the international trade regime. Examples

cited include voluntary export restraints (VERs), frequently resorted to by
the United States in recent years; the multilaterally organized Multifibre
Arrangement; and results-oriented market-access initiatives, which have
become pronounced in U.S.-Japan trade relations. We look at each briefly.

The Uruguay Round accord prohibits future use of VERs—agreements
between importing and exporting countries setting quantitative limits on
the import of products such as autos, consumer electronics, footwear, and
steel—as a result of which this practice will be phased out. A loophole does
exist permitting VER-like actions in circumscribed instances, but they
must be consistent with the WTO's new safeguard provisions and are subject to sunset clauses. In essence, the Uruguay Round kept some positive
features of VERs while limiting their costly and disruptive ones. Voluntary
export restraints, it should be noted, never sought to fix bilateral or overall market shares, but to limit the rate of increase in imports in the attempt
to give domestic industry time to adjust to new competitive environments.[54] Moreover, in many cases VERs did less collateral damage to the
multilateral trade regime than their multilaterally sanctioned alternative,
Article XIX of the GATT, would have done, because they were targeted at
the actual sources of surging imports while the officially prescribed remedy
must be applied in a nondiscriminatory manner to all imports of the product concerned.[55] At the same time, importing countries, led by the United
States, came to use VERs too freely and without adequate multilateral surveillance. In addition, by setting quantitative limits VERs raised import
prices, imposing the cost of the restrictions on consumers in the importing
countries. And because exporters remained free to shift into higher priced
versions of the numerically restricted products—Japanese automobile
manufacturers, for example, moved from exporting relatively inexpensive
models to capturing a large share of the American luxury market—some
VERs also raised the exporters' profit margins.[56]

In contrast to voluntary export restraints—which are temporary limits
on increases in imports—the Multifibre Arrangement (MFA) is a clear
case of managed trade. The difference is this: under managed trade schemes
governments go well beyond merely cushioning the burden of domestic
adjustment; they negotiate or otherwise fix market shares. The MFA, for
instance, is a vast web of multilaterally coordinated bilateral quotas, stipu-
lating who can sell how much of which textiles and apparel to whom. But
the Uruguay Round resolved that the MFA will be phased out over a ten
year period. As a result, the single most significant instance of managed
trade will be eliminated.

A relatively novel form of managed trade, however, has been on the rise:

bilaterally targeted market-access initiatives. One type of market-access policy is relatively benign: it seeks a generalized opening of impediments on the part of a country suspected of rigging access to its markets, and typically enjoys legitimacy among most everyone else. Another is not benign: it seeks specific market shares or specific progress in market penetration for a particular trading partner, and it is nearly universally condemned. In recent years, the United States on occasion has slipped from the first into the second in its approach to trade relations with Japan. The costs have been high and successes low. The controversial side-letter to a 1986 U.S.-Japan semiconductor agreement, which the United States believed promised its exporters a 20 percent share in Japan's domestic market within a five-year period, triggered a series of trade disputes with Japan and is no longer in force. The 1995 U.S.-Japan "agreements" governing American access to Japan's market for autos, auto parts, and dealerships, reached under the threat of 100 percent tariffs on Japanese luxury-car imports into the U.S. market, similarly was no stirring victory for the United States. None of its trading partners supported the U.S. position; and knowing that it could not win, the United States did not take its case to the WTO.[57] Furthermore, the final texts may be unique in commercial diplomacy: for each issue, they consist of a statement by the United States summarizing what it understood had been agreed to, followed by a statement on the part of Japan indicating that it did not see things the same way.[58] In light of this record, one would assume that the United States will reassess this strategic posture in its Japan trade policy.

Thus, all along managed trade has been, by many orders of magnitude, an exception to the rule. The Uruguay Round accord as well as recent bilateral experience suggest that this pattern is unlikely to change fundamentally in the immediate future.

Aggressive Unilateralism

We come, next, to a tendency in recent American trade policy that critics have labeled "aggressive unilateralism."[59] At issue here are unilateral means the United States has adopted to achieve objectives which themselves may be perfectly valid. The chief culprit is Section 301 of the U.S. trade code, especially the so-called Super 301 variant. From its original version on down, Section 301 has been intended by Congress to circumscribe executive branch discretion. In the past, as we noted above, the executive branch typically avoided imposing the full array of actions permitted under domestic law. Initially enacted with Europe in mind, for the past two decades East Asia has been a more prominent target of Section 301 cases.

Regular 301 identifies "unfair" trade practices abroad that adversely affect U.S. producers; it requires the United States to go to GATT when GATT rights are affected; but it retains the option to impose unilateral remedies if the results of GATT's deliberations are not satisfactory. One justification for regular 301 action that even its critics have trouble refuting is that GATT processes for dealing with unfair trade claims have been exceedingly clumsy and slow, cases are difficult to prove and harder to settle, while prospects for reforming the procedures in the absence of external pressures, such as 301, have been modest.[60] In any event, detailed studies of the history of 301 cases document that they exhibit patterns which are broadly consistent with the core objectives of the multilateral trade regime. The United States has typically deployed 301 in support of American industries that are globally competitive, and that should not, therefore, experience commercial impediments to market access abroad; and it has tended to do so if it determined foreign practices to be in noncompliance with GATT rules, or where GATT rules are weak or nonexistent.[61] Moreover, third parties have tolerated 301 actions despite their unilateralism because these actions have had a net liberalizing effect on world trade, and they have prodded GATT besides—the creation of the WTO's new "Dispute Settlement Understanding" being but the latest instance.[62]

Super 301 began on a different note. Legislated for a two-year period in 1988 and then reinstated by executive order in 1994, Super 301 bypasses GATT altogether. It not only unilaterally identifies unfair trade practices, but also lists target countries and requires the executive branch to take timely action against them. Under Super 301, the United States completely arrogates to itself the right to act as accuser, judge, and jury in assessing which trading practices by others are unfair and imposing punishment on those it deems guilty. Abroad, the introduction of Super 301 had the effect of shifting concern from unfair trade practices that affected all, to U.S. trade relief procedures that potentially threatened all.

Thus far, however, the actual use of Super 301 has aroused less controversy. The reason can be simply put: Japan. Even though Super 301 is written in universalistic language and three "unfair" traders were identified in its first year of operation, it would not have been adopted were it not for Japan.[63] Specifically, it was animated by a growing consensus in U.S. political circles that Japan's domestic structures, policies, and practices keep Japan's market relatively sheltered against foreign competition and boost Japan's exports, thereby contributing to the high and seemingly permanent trade imbalance by Japan vis-à-vis the United States and Europe. Europe could hardly disagree.

Discussions of U.S.-Japan trade relations are often politically and even emotionally charged. On one extreme are Japan-bashers, on the other the so-called Chrysanthemum club. Periodic outbursts of racist commentary occur in both countries. Yet when all else is stripped away, one dimension of Japan's trade flows stands apart from the other major industrialized economies: its relatively low levels of intra-industry trade. Yet intra-industry trade has been a privileged area for trade liberalization by the industrialized countries. Therefore, Japan's difference produces serious political friction, no matter what its causes may be. This subject requires a closer look.

Governments in successive GATT rounds have actively promoted the liberalization of intra-industry, in contrast to inter-industry, trade. As a result, international specialization in the industrialized world has been achieved not by countries abandoning entire industrial sectors, but "mainly by individual firms narrowing their product lines."[64] There are, of course, straightforward economic reasons why intra-industry trade among industrialized countries should have expanded throughout the postwar era, having to do with similarities of production structures and the existence of scale economies. But there are also strong political reasons for governments in those countries to encourage such trade: the domestic social and political adjustment costs of intra-industry trade are lower because entire sectors of producers and the work force are not threatened with displacement by it, and yet all the while it offers gains from trade. In a word, the liberalization of intra-industry trade is more compatible with the political economy of embedded liberalism.

This puts the "Japan problem" in a somewhat clearer light. As Edward Lincoln shows, Japan tends to import least precisely in those areas in which it exports most, so that its level of intra-industry trade is at or near the bottom in virtually every industrial sector.[65] Granted, Japan is resource-poor and needs, therefore, to import raw materials as well as export manufactured products to pay for those imports. Even here, though, Japan exhibits a much stronger preference than other resource-poor industrialized countries for entirely unprocessed or the simplest refined forms of raw-materials imports. On the manufactured-exports side, Japan exhibits a far higher level of export concentration in selected high value-added products than its competitors. In addition, as Louis Pauly and Simon Reich have shown, Japan's already low level of intra-industry trade is conducted overwhelmingly within Japanese firms and among affiliates, further limiting opportunities for other producers of intermediate products.[66] Lastly, while the lowering of formal trade barriers and the maturing of Japan's multinational firms, according to both economic theory and the historical experiences of the other industrialized countries, should have led to the erosion of these patterns, they have not.[67] It is these differences that have led even non-Japan-bashers to single out Japan's trading pattern as "adversarial"[68]—a charge that is not without irony because Japan, in a certain sense, is merely "follow[ing] the principle of comparative advantage," as *The Economist* notes plaintively.[69]

The "Japan problem," then, is not a matter of Japan cheating on the formal trade rules. Japan's tariffs are low, its quotas are few, and its outright violations are less frequent than in many other industrialized countries. Nor is Japan primarily responsible for America's trade deficit; a far larger share is accounted for by macroeconomic factors in the United States itself. But the structure of Japan's trade deviates significantly from the behavioral norm around which the trade regime revolves and from which Japan derives great benefits. Leave aside for now the thorny questions of why Japan exhibits this structure of trade and how it is sustained. Whatever its causes, the result is that Japan poses serious problems for its trading partners. As Lincoln puts it: "The fact that intra-industry trade has become a normative pattern of behavior for other countries means that Japan's failure to conform imposes adjustment costs on the industries of other countries that they do not expect to bear."[70] It also imposes political costs on governments as they struggle to cope with pressure from the affected domestic industries.[71] Finally, other countries have found it hard to compensate for restricted trade access to Japan by means of direct foreign investment access.[72] With both routes into Japan's market constrained, the U.S. Congress felt it had little choice but to act.

Super 301, then, may be seen as an attempt by the United States to devise a tit-for-tat strategy vis-à-vis Japan intended to induce Japan to change its trade and investment patterns.[73] Moreover, the measure can be plausibly justified as substituting for gaps in the available multilateral mechanisms that prevent them from handling fairness claims arising out of structural asymmetries of the kind posed by Japan. As Robert Hudec points out, "there are relatively few international agreements regulating the substance of such claims, and there is no recognized tribunal to adjudicate them in common law fashion."[74] GATT is silent on the subject, and progress within the WTO is likely to remain modest.

When targeted by Super 301, Japan made no move to retaliate against the United States or even to bring the case to GATT. While refusing to negotiate formally under Super 301, Japan reached several accords with the United States under a parallel Structural Impediments Initiative—one of the more successful in the long series of U.S.-Japan trade negotiations because it examined practices on both sides, and also because it drew in the Japanese consumer.[75] Hudec has proposed that America's trading partners should hold the United States accountable to its own 301 standards, in the attempt to increase demand all around for more collectively legitimated fair trade mechanisms.[76] Indeed, a 1992 report of an industry advisory council to Japan's Ministry of International Trade and Industry (MITI) accused the United States of engaging in no fewer than nine unfair trade practices. Being new to the game, the Japanese group outdid even the U.S. Congress in hyperbole, accusing the United States of being "the most unfair" trading nation of them all. But the real intention, a MITI official added quickly, "is to use GATT more frequently" in the hope of devising a common definition of fairness.[77] That in itself constituted a concession by Japan, which had never before acknowledged fairness to be an issue.

In sum, the "aggressive unilateralism" of regular 301 has been neither as unilateral nor as aggressive as critics claim. Super 301 does pose a greater risk to the multilateral trade regime, but its one serious deployment has been against Japan, which constitutes a very special problem. However, if the United States abandons the objective of nondiscriminatory market access abroad and couples its unilateral measures with demands for specific U.S. market shares it loses all international support, and permits the target country to frame its defense in the rhetoric of free trade—as Japan did successfully in 1995 when it brushed aside the Clinton administration's quest to achieve numerical targets in Japan's automotive sector for the American industry.

Regionalism

From 1948, the first full year of GATT's operation, to the end of 1994, its members reported signing 109 regional free-trade agreements—nearly one-third of which were reached in the last four years.[78] In January 1995, with the accession of Austria, Finland, and Sweden membership in the European Union (EU), the world's biggest and most deeply integrated trading bloc, grew to fifteen. The United States became an active initiator of free-trade areas in the 1980s, negotiating such an accord with Canada, which was later expanded to include Mexico in the North American Free Trade Area. NAFTA, in turn, has begun membership discussions with Chile. In 1991, Brazil, Paraguay, Uruguay, and Argentina formed Mercosur, a regional customs union. And at the 1994 Miami summit of the Americas, the 34 leaders agreed to establish a hemispheric free-trade zone by 2005— stretching from Alaska to Tierra del Fuego, as President George Bush enthused when he first proposed the idea. Across the Pacific, the United States has been a major force behind pledges by the Asia-Pacific Economic Cooperation (APEC) forum to establish free trade among all eighteen participating countries by 2020, with the richer countries reaching that goal by 2010. And the seven-member Association of South East Asian Nations (ASEAN) has agreed to set up a free-trade area by 2003. Many other agreements are on the way. The most ambitious idea to date is for a free-trade accord between North America and the EU.

Clearly, regionalism is proliferating. This fact has led some observers to raise concerns about its impact on the global trading order.[79] The press has spun vivid tales of "fortress Europe," a "moat" around North America or the Western hemisphere, and in the case of East Asia, "flying geese" in formation with Japan in the lead. At issue is whether regionalism is a "stumbling block" or a "building block" on the road toward a more integrated global economy—at the extreme, whether regionalism casts the shadow of the 1930s over the future of multilateralism in trade. Free-trade liberals fear this scenario; many realist analysts have long predicted it.[80]

The founders of GATT actually spent a good deal of time and energy worrying about this issue. The GATT's constitutive principle is nondiscrimination; yet customs unions, free-trade areas, and other forms of preferences inherently discriminate against outsiders. The potential incompatibility was resolved in 1947 by drawing a distinction between an arrangement which, in the words of Clair Wilcox, a principal U.S. negotiator of the GATT, "removes obstacles to competition [and] makes possible a more economic allocation of resources," and one that "is set up for the purpose of conferring a privilege on producers within the system and imposing a handicap on external competitors."[81] GATT placed customs unions and free-trade areas into the first category, preferential arrangements into the second. And to qualify as a customs union or free-trade area an arrangement had to be designed to facilitate trade, not to raise barriers; it had to cover substantially all trade among the parties; and whatever barriers were imposed on outsiders could not, on the whole, be higher or more restrictive than those that were in place before the arrangement was created.

Economists came to express this distinction operationally as the trade-creating vs. trade-diverting effects of regional arrangements—that is, where lower barriers encourage members, on the one hand, to buy goods from each other that they previously produced at home, or, on the other hand, to switch imports from outside suppliers to members. The empirical evidence does not strongly favor the trade-diversion scenario. Intraregional trade is up, but in most instances not decisively.[82] In addition, trade among near-neighbors naturally grows more rapidly, especially after trade barriers and in some cases political walls have come down. And intra-regional trade has increased even in such areas as East Asia, where no formal agreements are yet in place.[83]

More importantly, the very concept of regional trading *bloc* conjures up atavistic objectives which are not widely warranted today. As Stephen Kobrin notes, "the primary motivations for [regional] integration are efficiency and scale rather than containment" or exclusion—which did prevail in the 1930s.[84] Particularly for strategic industries with escalating research and development costs, Kobrin contends, there is no reason to assume that this process will stop at the regional level and not embrace even more inclusive economic units in the future. Beyond that, countries have constructed free-trade areas for a variety of complementary reasons: to push GATT into speedier progress; to liberalize domains not yet well covered globally, such as investment and intellectual property; and as insurance should global multilateralism unravel.

Finally, both the growing volume and mobility of capital flows among the major regions—North America, Europe, and East Asia—make it difficult to imagine that exclusive trading blocs could emerge within them. The United States, EU, and Japan now account for some eighty percent of the world's total outward stocks and flows of direct foreign investment. During the 1980s, this triad also increased its share as host to such investments to well over one-half of the world's total—and nearly two-thirds if intra-EU figures are included—so that investment interactions among the triad "have outpaced both interactions in the rest of the world, and interactions between the triad and the rest of the world."[85] A major unraveling would have to occur in the structure of global capital flows, then, for either natural or negotiated regional trading clusters to shift toward becoming exclusionary blocs.

A question mark does hang over Japan. That nation hosts a relatively low level of direct foreign investment, is the source of high levels of investments in the East Asian region, while Japanese multinationals tend to purchase inputs disproportionately from related-party suppliers and distributors. A system of tightly coupled East Asian production structures has resulted, facilitated and reinforced by Japan's policy of closely tying its foreign aid to opportunities for its firms.[86] These characteristics limit the ability of investment flows to outweigh inward-looking trade arrangements focused on Japan, though the Asia-Pacific region as a whole is far more open to extra-regional investment.

In short, the issue of whether regional trade arrangements may become inward-looking trading blocs depends on the future dynamics of production structures, flows of direct foreign investment, and the intentions of countries. The current geographical clustering of international trade may not be optimal if viewed through Ricardian lenses, but any resurgence of centrifugal forces comparable to the 1930s seems far fetched. Nor does regional free trade appear to impede global multilateralism in any other fashion.

Let us step back now and assess the overall evolution of the postwar trade regime. To begin with, despite proliferating instruments of the so-called new protectionism, the markets of the industrialized countries are more open than ever before. This poses a puzzle. As Bhagwati has put it: "the growth of protectionism appears significant but its consequences do not."[87] Within the embedded-liberalism framework, however, the puzzle is easily resolved: many instances of the "new protectionism" are seen as predictable adaptations to further international liberalization in very different competitive contexts.

Nevertheless, some of the regulatory mechanisms of the trade regime, never strong, became weaker in the face of increased national trade relief actions. For example, in its entire history GATT took up barely 200 cases under its dispute settlement procedures. That number was matched by U.S. unilateral antidumping and countervailing duty cases in their peak year of 1982 alone.[88] Moreover, Congress has gradually restricted, but not eliminated, the range of executive-branch discretion. Delicate maneuvering between the two branches of government turned into an avalanche of trade protection in the early Reagan years. But by the late 1980s, the situation had begun to return to a more stable equilibrium. And innovations in the WTO's dispute settlement procedures should enhance its efficacy in the future.

The Uruguay Round provisions for nontariff barriers should also help reduce some of the longer-term erosion in the rules of the trading game. Its provisions for agriculture and investment, though modest, mark first steps in extending multilateral rules to these domains.[89] And this Round's results are uniformly applicable to all GATT members, which differs from the earlier Tokyo Round, whose plurilateral codes for nontariff barriers held only for those countries that specifically agreed to sign them, thus producing a more fragmented trade regime—an outcome that realist political economists at the time attributed to declining American hegemony.[90]

Changing industry preferences reinforce these equilibrating tendencies. All economies, including the American, have become more internationalized. For obvious reasons, export-dependent industries and multinational firms in general are less likely to demand protection even if they are under pressure from import competition in a specific sector. To the extent that they seek help from their governments, it is more likely to be for access to markets abroad. Some of the most advanced industrial sectors, including semiconductors, commercial aircraft, and telecommunications, exhibit this pattern.[91] The net effect of such pressure should be liberalizing. However, if it were to result in negotiated market shares, as in the U.S.-Japan semiconductor and automotive negotiations, it would increase the incidence of managed trade, violating both the spirit and letter of postwar norms.

Finally, these changed industry preferences are also reflected in recent Congressional alignments. The One Hundredth Congress (1987–88) voted on more trade legislation than any other in the postwar era. An analysis of those votes reveals several instructive patterns.[92] The partisan effects of divided government were evident; a traditional protectionist coalition retained some influence in the House; and conventional free trade had little support outside the Republican party. The balance of power, however, was held by "fair traders" in both parties who "are not simply protectionis[ts] in disguise."[93] Indeed, they opposed protectionism and were more likely to receive campaign contributions from internationally oriented businesses.

The major permanent shift in the posture of the United States is its adopting a more strategic orientation to trade policy, as a result of which America has become less likely than in the past to "lock its doors open" irrespective of what others do.[94] This shift was an inevitable consequence of the economic resurgence of Europe and Japan, the emergence of entirely new entrants in the tournament of major economic countries, as well as the end of the cold war, which reduced the security rationale for tolerating significant deviations from postwar behavioral norms by America's allies.

To bring this chapter to a close, recall that for the capitalist countries the primary job of the postwar monetary and trade regimes was to achieve the twin goals of international and domestic stability through a form of liberalization that was consistent with and constrained by domestic intervention. The two regimes have managed their liberalization task about as well as can be expected in a world of sovereign states, and in a period of serious economic dislocations and major shifts in the international division of labor. Scenarios depicting the contrary are greatly exaggerated and are compelling only from the cosmopolitan vantage of a centralized world monetary system and the textbook model of free trade—worlds that no government has agreed to inhabit. Nor have governments been inclined, in Robert Aliber words, to "risk sacrificing the state to save the constitution"—that is, to adhere rigidly to rules, no matter what the conditions or the consequences, merely because they were written down, and even when viable and apparently acceptable alternatives exist.[95]

Largely due to the success of these regimes, point-of-entry barriers to international economic transactions have been virtually eliminated, financial markets are globally integrated, and entire sectors of production have become transnationalized. This very success of international liberalization, however, poses potential threats to its embeddedness twin in the postwar compromise: the policy frameworks, institutional structures, and domestic social compact on which the commitment to liberalization was conditioned. While many observers stand on guard to warn of protectionism's dangers, relatively little attention has been paid in think tanks, the academy, or in political circles to the potential danger for international and domestic stability alike of society's vulnerability to increasingly disembedded market forces. We examine those critical issues in the following chapter.

6 | Economic Transformation

On December 24, 1993, London's *Financial Times* published an unusual editorial.[1] While rejoicing in "the most capitalist Christmas in history," the *FT* nevertheless urged governments to devise "new structures" and find "new methods" to sustain what it termed welfare capitalism. "The world is changing rapidly," the editorial noted; "the Atlantic nations in general and Europe in particular face competition from the younger, harsher, more robust capitalism of south Asia." And the domestic consequences in the mature capitalist countries, it conceded, are not uniformly good: "Even the middle classes, who have benefited most from economic growth, fear that they may lose what they have, while those outside note that however rich the super-rich may get, large-scale unemployment persists. Lower down the income scale the picture is far worse." Reversing these trends, the editorial concluded, will require "radical policies" by governments, including new ways to ensure that "the fruits of capitalism" reach all segments of society. Similar sentiments had already been expressed by *The Economist*, applauding what it detected as the new Clinton administration's grand economic proposal to the American people. "Its outlines are simple: you accept change (such as the North American Free Trade Agreement) and we'll help to give you security"—occupational, health care, and personal security.[2]

These two British publications are among the most irrepressible and articulate advocates anywhere of free markets and free trade. What, then, moved them to worry about the economic security of the middle classes and the poor—and, even more curiously, to suggest that governments have an active role to play in achieving it? The answer is surprisingly simple. Both realize that the extraordinary success of postwar international liberalization has hinged on a compact between the state and society to mediate its domestic effects. Both sense that this compact is fraying throughout the western world. And both fear that if it unravels altogether, so too may domestic public support for sustaining the international economic order. In short, out of a firm commitment to economic multilateralism these stalwarts of laissez-faire have developed grave concerns about the growing inability or unwillingness of governments to perform the domestic policy roles they were assigned under the postwar compromise.

This shift in governments' policy postures runs deeper than swings in ideological moods and preferences, though such a swing is underway. It is also structural in character and, ironically, at least in part reflects the very success of the postwar trade and monetary regimes whose sustainability may hang in the balance. Point-of-entry barriers to international economic transactions have been virtually eliminated, financial markets are globally integrated, and entire sectors of production have become transnationalized. This transformation in the world economy has generated positive welfare effects for countries. But it has also undermined key conceptual and institutional premises of the postwar economic regimes as well as related aspects of national economic policymaking on the basis of which governments mediated the relationship between international and domestic stability: that the international economy consists of territorially distinct and disjoint national economies linked by "external" transactions; that these transactions are carried on at arms-length; that border measures are effective policy tools; that governments enjoy considerable policy autonomy within their domestic sphere; and that a relatively coherent and consensual policy framework exists for domestic governmental intervention.

Each of these premises has been rendered problematical and several irrelevant, even in an economy as large as the American. In this chapter, we explore how, why, and with what consequences. The first section examines the collapsing boundaries between domestic and international economic policy domains, and predicts a period of "economic border conflicts" in the years ahead. The second section provides a schematic sketch of economic globalization, and relates globalization to the pervasive sense of insecurity in domestic economic life. And the third section addresses the end of the New Deal state, the domestic foundation of the postwar regimes for money and trade, and flags the dangers for the government's capacity to mediate between the newly unleashed transnational economic forces and domestic welfare.

To anticipate: the *nation-based* world economy was effectively stabilized; but realignments in the *global* world economy are only just beginning.

Disputed Boundaries

It was no secret to economists in the 1930s that imperfect competition, and patterns of domestic industrial organization more generally, produced significant effects on international trade.[3] Articles 46–54 of the Charter of the International Trade Organization (ITO) reflected these concerns, curtailing a variety of restrictive business practices that might shape trade flows. By virtue of Article 46, for instance, ITO members pledged to prevent "business practices affecting international trade which restrain competition, limit access to markets, or foster monopolistic control, whenever such practices have harmful effects on the expansion of production or trade."[4] In the immediate postwar years, however, these concerns were removed from the international trade agenda by a two-step process. The first was the defeat of the ITO in the U.S. Senate, which left conventional point-of-entry barriers as the portfolio of the quickly assembled General Agreement on Tariffs and Trade (GATT). Second, GATT then avoided the related conceptual problems posed by state-trading nations, such as the Soviet Union, by calling for state-trading enterprises in their external purchases and sales simply to behave like private economic units: "solely in accordance with commercial considerations," in the words of Article XVII of the GATT, that is, in response to factors such as price, quality, transportation costs and similar terms of purchase or sale.[5] Thus, the external significance of domestic economies' divergent institutional features was assumed away. And the postwar economic regimes were given the tasks of removing or lowering point-of-entry barriers such as quotas, tariffs, and currency-exchange restrictions, as well as banishing deliberate acts of cheating such as export subsidies, dumping or currency manipulation.

Now that point-of-entry barriers have become progressively lowered or eliminated, the impact of domestic economic arrangements and policies on international economic transactions has soared in salience. Over a decade ago, Richard Blackhurst, a well-known GATT staff economist, already detected "the twilight of domestic economic policies."[6] A shift was taking place, Blackhurst noted, in distinguishing between "international" and "domestic" economic policy: from a definition of international as border measures, to *any* policy, no matter what the instrument or where it was applied, which had an "important" impact on international transaction flows. Blackhurst ventured the prediction that, "barring either a major retreat into protectionism such as occurred in the 1930s or a massive reduction in the level of government intervention in the economy, the reclassification will continue into the foreseeable future, aiming towards an end point where few economic policies of any consequence will be considered primarily domestic."[7]

This trend affects monetary relations as well as trade. But it impinges more directly in trade and also is more intense, because domestic trade relief measures make compensatory and retaliatory moves more readily accessible. That, in turn, poses serious problems for the conduct of trade relations. GATT was designed, in the words of one legal scholar, "to maintain a balance of [external] concessions and obligations, not to restructure nations."[8] Yet "restructuring nations"—at least, aspects of nations—is what commercial policy increasingly has become about. Below, we describe briefly some of the main issues at stake.

Domestic Structures

One contested issue is domestic economic structures—defined broadly to include both patterns of government policies and policy networks, as well as private-sector industrial organization. Sylvia Ostry, a former Organization for Economic Cooperation and Development (OECD) official, differentiates three stylized forms among the leading capitalist countries: the pluralist market economy of the United States, the social market economy of continental Europe, and Japan's corporatist market economy.[9] For the purposes of regulating their trade effects, Ostry would take as "given" the behavior, tastes, and institutions in each that have "cultural and historical roots," because the "appropriate domain for international policy co-operation is government policy."[10] But even if one accepts Ostry's concession to culture and history, achieving policy convergence in the remaining areas on her list is a daunting task. For reconciling the most serious trade effects arising from them, Ostry indicates, requires convergence in competition policy, including merger law; research and development policies, especially state subsidies; asymmetries in access of direct foreign investment; and financial regulation as it relates to corporate governance, such as bank ownership of firms.

Moreover, no agreed framework of principles, norms, and rules exists to guide the proposed convergence, posing additional problems. First, governments, with equal legitimacy, may seek to advance or protect domestic objectives that are inherently difficult to reconcile internationally. "Some countries stress consumer welfare and efficiency as the highest priorities while others include social goals such as protection of small and medium size industries."[11] Who, or what, is right?[12] Second, few algorithms and metrics exist on the basis of which to harmonize such domestic differences. When cases emerge under the "fairness" rubric, for example, virtually by definition they are expected to yield unilateral concessions on the part of the accused party: "To say that certain conduct is unfair is to say that the guilty party must correct it for that reason alone."[13] But the "guilty" party typically has its own views of fairness and its own targets for fairness claims.

Even apart from the fairness issue, the central conceptual pillars of the postwar trading order offer relatively little guidance for the more elusive and often very micro-level issues that make up the new commercial policy agenda—for example, whether government policies or, more difficult still, industry practices favoring neighborhood shops or long-standing affiliated party transactions should be viewed as trade restraints. Finally, as the Japan debate makes abundantly clear, it is hard to know where to stop in the quest for convergence. At issue in that debate are the organization of Japan's labor market, capital markets, as well as ownership, production, and distribution systems; the economic roles of the state; and, indeed, Japan's multimember-district electoral system. All of these have been adduced as affecting Japan's trade and investment posture—and not only by "Japan-bashers" but also by dispassionate analysts.[14] Even the more narrow U.S.-Japan Structural Impediments Initiative comprised no fewer than 240 items.

A decade ago, Blackhurst recommended that governments adopt new multilateral rules to defend themselves from pressures originating at home no less than abroad: "[G]eneral international rules are at least as useful in protecting a government from domestic interest groups as they are in protecting it from abuses by other governments. It is no paradox that the observance of general rules *increases* a government's freedom and ability to pursue genuine national interests."[15] But the process is more difficult than he thought. The very definition of this emerging policy domain remains subject to strategic manipulation by firms and governments, capture by protectionist forces, and competition among domestic as well as international agencies over which of them will play lead roles in devising new rules. No comprehensive agreement on meaningful multilateral frameworks is imminent.[16]

Intangibles Transactions

The erosion of boundaries between domestic and international policy domains is hastened and deepened by the growing significance of services in international trade. Services used to be the "invisibles" appendage to goods trade: shipping, insurance and the like, as well as tourism. Today the list is longer and the magnitude higher. It includes information services, various financial, professional, and business-related services, construction, cultural services, and many more. Their volume has reached somewhere between one fifth and one quarter of total world trade, though because of accounting anomalies the balance of world services imports and exports routinely is off by $100 billion or so per annum—and that still understates hard-to-measure services that are embodied in traded goods, such as design, engineering, and data processing. This expansion of traded services is due to the transnationalization of goods production; technological developments, especially the informatics revolution; as well as domestic deregulation, particularly of capital markets and the telecommunications sector.

The institutional challenge posed by traded services is, however, not quantitative but qualitative. The GATT was designed for merchandise trade: ball bearings and bananas cross frontiers, passing through customs houses on the way. Invisibles were left uncovered by GATT. Indeed, according to an etymological survey by Drake and Nicolaidis, services were not generally regarded as being "traded" prior to 1972, when they were first so construed in an OECD experts' report: "the group took a huge leap by suggesting tentatively that the transactions in services could be considered trade, that the principles and norms for trade in goods might apply, and that the challenge in the emerging transition was to avoid 'protectionism.'"[17] As the world's largest producer and "exporter" of services, the United States quickly embraced these notions. It pushed for GATT rules to govern traded services as early as the Tokyo Round of the 1970s, but with little success. The United States also had difficulty getting services onto the agenda of the Uruguay Round, and when it did the victory initially seemed to be largely symbolic.[18] In the end the Round succeeded in producing a General Agreement on Trade in Services (GATS).[19]

Essentially, the GATS consists of a set of broad principles, a number of special conditions or exceptions, and initial liberalization commitments. Traded services generally are to be governed by the classical GATT principles of nondiscrimination and transparency of domestic rules and regulations, but countries may exclude specific services from national treatment and the right of market access. Safeguards provisions are included and mechanisms for dispute settlement provided for. In short, trade in services will be brought under the GATT/WTO umbrella with an ultimate balance of obligations between domestic and international objectives that is more qualified than for merchandise trade, and also more individualized.

The GATS, however, merely marks the conclusion of a chapter in a continuing story of economic realignment. It brings within the conventional trade framework that portion of traded services which countries are willing to include. A number of highly contentious issues remain beyond the reach of this framework. Intrinsically, this fact has little to do with what are normally regarded as trade barriers, protectionism, or cheating—though services readily lend themselves to each—but stems from the unique attributes differentiating services from goods.

First, because the concept of services has no well-established place in economic theory, its definition tends to be ad hoc and arbitrary: the residual activity not included in agriculture, mining, and manufacturing. With tongue only half in cheek, *The Economist* once proposed defining services as "[t]hings which can be bought and sold but which you cannot drop on your foot."[20] Attempts to define services theoretically have focused on the attribute of their being nonstorable, therefore requiring simultaneity in provision and use.[21] But in practice even this definition has done little more than generate variable and ultimately contested lists. In short, unlike the case of goods trade, in traded services the phenomenon itself is open to deliberate manipulation by, as well as genuine disagreements among, governments. There is no reason to expect that contested definitions will yield to consensus because a GATS has been signed.

Second, governments typically regulate domestic service industries more rigorously than other economic activities. Entry into many services, such as medicine, law, and accounting is strictly licensed; governments often reserve the right to approve utilities prices, which in many places include transportation and telecommunications; financial institutions, such as banks, insurance firms, and securities traders are subject to prudential supervision; and in some countries the state still owns outright certain service industries. Most of these regulatory objectives and instruments were not instituted with trade in mind, though they affect transactions that are now construed as trade. The principles of nondiscrimination, transparency, and national treatment, where they apply, should moderate somewhat the impact of differences in national regulatory environments, but they will not eliminate the problem.

Finally, despite what Drake and Nicolaidis characterize as the "revolution in social ontology" that reconceived services as trade, the fact remains that relatively few services are "traded" in the conventional sense of that term. In merchandise trade, the factors of production and the consumers stand still while the finished product moves. In traded services, the factors of production or the consumer do the moving while the product is fixed in location. But no economic theory justifies, however, why provider mobility should encompass U.S. banks and insurance firms offering financial services in Seoul, for example, but not South Korean construction workers providing their services in Seattle—an issue that exercised developing countries during the GATS negotiations, and which will remain contentious in the future.

Thus, the expansion of traded services reinforces the growing trend in international commercial policymaking whereby, not "external" transactions, but the boundaries between domestic and international issues and processes are becoming a central concern. The GATS represents a first step, but little more, in instituting some degree of order.

Environmental and Labor Standards

When trade ministers and other high-level officials from 109 countries assembled to sign GATT's Uruguay Round accord in Marrakech, Morocco, in April 1994, Vice President Al Gore announced that Washington would seek to address the relationships between trade and the environment as well as trade and labor standards in future WTO negotiations—neither had gone far in the round itself.[22] A smaller-scale preview of such negotiations took place when Congressional pressure forced the Clinton administration to conclude supplemental environmental and labor accords with Mexico as the price of securing adoption of the North American Free Trade Agreement (NAFTA). Here, too, difficulties lie ahead.

The trade-environment nexus is conceptually ill-defined, substantively complex, and highly subjective.[23] Furthermore, it pushes the transgression of domestic policy domains well beyond institutional features which may or may not affect trade, to include what economists like to call "tastes," or economically and culturally conditioned preferences and values, but which environmentalists view as overriding concerns of universal validity. For present purposes, it is useful to distinguish three classes of cases.

One concerns the trade effects of differing domestic environmental standards.[24] This issue has generated the most political heat. Representative Richard Gephardt has promised to push for a "Green 301" provision, which would permit the imposition of "ecoduties" on imports produced under conditions that are inferior to U.S. environmental standards. The European Union has indicated that it will not negotiate rules on eco-dumping—and it is powerful enough to retaliate, possibly targeting low U.S. energy costs as an actionable subsidy. International trade economists and officials predict that the already fragile trade regime could well unravel under the strains of such ecocountervailing wars. And policymakers in developing countries fear that the additional costs of higher environmental standards will impede their development prospects.

A second class of cases concerns, not the environmental context within which goods are produced, but goods' environmental "content." That content can be defined as a product standard or a process standard. Product standards are hardly new, and exploiting their environmental variants for competitive advantage, while troublesome, poses no fundamental conceptual challenge to international commercial policymaking.[25] What is new and difficult to accommodate is the notion that goods must be produced in accordance with certain *processes* that are deemed environmentally sound. At the very core of nondiscrimination in international trade is the most-favored-nation norm, requiring that like imports are treated alike, together with national treatment, requiring the no-less-favorable treatment of imports than of like domestic products. "A car, for GATT, is a car. No, say the greens, it is also an assembly of metals and chemicals produced in certain ways"—and they would treat cars and other imports differentially depending on the environmental attributes of their production.[26]

Yet a third class of cases involves the use of unilateral trade sanctions against countries in support of environmental objectives. If those objectives are internationally set, trade sanctions are likely to be tolerated even though they may be on soft legal grounds. For example, few other countries objected when the United States imposed such sanctions on Norway for flouting the international whaling moratorium. Punitive trade measures for environmental goals are an open invitation to retaliation, however, when both the ends and means are unilaterally determined, and when they simply seek to impose the domestic preferences of one country on others.

In coping with trade-related environmental concerns the WTO will have to become environmentally more literate and better staffed than GATT has been. It was GATT's orthodoxy in the Mexican tuna-dolphin case that first fully mobilized the environmental movement against the trade regime.[27] In addition, the WTO needs to reform its adjudicative processes (as distinct from substantive rules) to permit interested parties to submit amicus briefs, for example, and to provide greater transparency of its deliberations. Beyond that, only stronger environmental agreements can reduce the heavy environmental burden the trade regime bears—though some environmental groups will continue to oppose trade liberalization on principle because they regard it as intrinsically inimical to environmental quality.

The other new trade-related issue that Vice President Gore sought at Marrakech to place on the WTO's future agenda was labor standards. In doing so, the *Washington Post* editorialized, "the Clinton administration is blowing a kiss to unions that are still sore about the free trade agreement with Mexico"[28]—a gesture undoubtedly also aimed at the broader electoral base of Ross Perot, still agitated about the predicted "giant sucking sound" of jobs moving south. The United States is unlikely to demand convergence with Europe in this area of policy, however: workplace conditions do not diverge significantly, and worker amenities often favor the Europeans.[29] Hence this will become almost entirely a north-south affair.

Once again, linking trade privileges to established international norms —banning slave labor, child labor, prison labor, and the like—is not at issue. Nor are accords such as the Generalized System of Preferences Act (GSP), whereby developing countries are granted duty-free access to the U.S. market for many products provided they meet certain labor standards: freedom to associate; freedom to bargain collectively; the prohibition of forced or compulsory labor; the prohibition of child labor; and a process for establishing a minimum wage, taking into account prevailing levels of economic development.[30] But domestic political pressure from American labor—which, as we discuss below, bears a heavy burden under the industrial restructuring of the U.S. economy—in effect seeks to offset the "natural" comparative advantage of developing countries in relatively inexpensive labor, on the basis of which their prospects for future higher living standards rest. And that violates the most elemental principle of all international trade.

What conclusions can we draw from this discussion of the contested boundaries between domestic and international economic policy domains? To begin, it is important to recall that the postwar economic regimes were intended to balance external obligations and concessions among nations, not to restructure their domestic economies. Indeed, both the trade and monetary regimes promised a substantial degree of domestic policy autonomy as long as certain rules concerning adverse international effects were observed. That premise has eroded. In the area of monetary relations, the capitalist countries are experiencing the erosion indirectly, largely through constraints imposed by financial markets. In trade, restructuring aspects of domestic economies is what international policymaking increasingly has come to be about.

To the public at large, the first-order effects of the virtual elimination of point-of-entry barriers to trade appear in the form of what we might call "economic border conflicts," with countries reaching deep into one another's domestic policy domains in the quest to neutralize perceived advantages. Disputes typically feature charges of unfairness, cheating, and environmental as well as social dumping. At the institutional level, the growing salience of domestic structures and practices has yielded arrangements which are, at best, partial extensions of prevailing multilateral frameworks. Many foundational concepts of the trade regime—including most-favored-nation treatment and nondiscrimination—are ambiguous guides in this contested terrain, and it is uncertain what if any substantive principles of multilateralism will take their place.

The process of international commercial policymaking similarly is moving away from single focal points, such as GATT/WTO, toward shifting policy networks simultaneously involving multiple forums and covering several areas of policy—for example, the nexus among trade, environment, and competition policy. Direct lobbying at the national level is a central instrument of collective policymaking, with Washington serving as the major world node and Brussels playing an analogous role for the European Union. Lastly, transnational private actors—be they environmental groups, industry associations, bond-rating agencies, or Anglo-American law firms—play a growing role in filling multilateral policy voids. The long-term pattern of conflict and cooperation these developments may generate is not yet clear. As a British scholar observes: "We are only now in the first stages of a complex worldwide evolutionary process."[31]

The removal of border barriers to trade and capital mobility has had an even more profound second-order consequence: to facilitate the processes and structures of economic globalization.

Globalization

Much has been written about the internationalization of economies and nearly as much has been dismissed as "globaloney." Milton Friedman, as is his custom, has put the negative case most categorically: "The world is less internationalized in any immediate, relevant, pertinent sense today than it was in 1913 or in 1929."[32] Friedman contends that the divergence between the price of the same good in different countries, which became pronounced after the Great Depression, has remained in place despite steadily decreasing transportation costs, thus "demonstrating vividly how powerful and effective government intervention has been in rendering the law of one price far less applicable after 1931 than it was before."[33] The "myth" of internationalization has long been a staple of realist analysis as well.[34]

Friedman's observation that the world economy today is less of a single economy, governed by the law of one price, than it was earlier in this century may be largely correct. But it hardly disposes of the issues at hand. Economic internationalization in recent decades has taken the form of increasingly extensive, diverse, and integrated institutional links forged between markets and within firms across the globe. Illustrating the poverty of conventional concepts, the result is typically described as the emergence of "off-shore" markets and "off-shore" production, as if they existed in some ethereal space waiting to be reconceived by the economic equivalent of relativity theory. Moreover, the American and other publics in the capitalist world widely hold these institutional changes responsible for heightened economic uncertainty, vulnerability, and loss of policy control, fears that are unlikely to be alleviated by the observation that the world economy is merely turning "back to the future."[35] What, specifically, are these institutional changes, and what are their consequences?

The simple typology of markets, hierarchies, and networks will help us grasp intuitively the changes underway.[36] Begin with markets, and take first the financial sector. The popular image of globally integrated markets—functioning "as if they were all in the same place," in real time and around the clock[37]—is most closely approximated by foreign-exchange transactions. At $1.3 trillion in daily volume, this is also the biggest global market, towering over world trade, as noted in the previous chapter, by a ratio of more than 60:1.[38] International bank lending began to take off in the 1960s; its net stock grew from $265 billion a decade later to $4.2 trillion by 1994. Bond markets became globally integrated in the 1980s, and international transactions in U.S. Treasury bonds increased from $30 billion to $500 billion over the course of the decade. Equity markets are integrating more slowly and cross-national equity holdings remain relatively modest.[39] As for the integration of markets in goods and services, the best available indicator, in addition to the reduction of border barriers itself, is average annual trade as a proportion of gross domestic product; for a group of 15 OECD countries, the ratio increased from roughly 45 percent in the 1960s to 65 percent twenty years later.[40]

Thus, not only are economic boundaries more open than ever before in the postwar era. Markets have also become more directly linked with one another, from goods and services on up to the most liquid—and globally most integrated—foreign-exchange markets, in which "rates are set by armies of bellowing 22-year old traders, amid flailing arms, blinking screens and flashing telephones."[41] But in some ways an even more pivotal shift has occurred in the global organization of production and exchange of goods and services: increasingly, it takes the form of "administrative hierarchies rather than external markets."[42]

This shift began simply enough. For a variety of reasons, starting in the 1960s more and more firms began to set up subsidiaries abroad to serve local markets. Since then, this outward movement progressively trans-

formed into a process of constructing "the global factory."[43] Led initially by
the automobile and consumer electronics industries, components production, input sourcing, assembly, and marketing by multinationals spread
across an ever broader array of countries, exploiting shifting advantages of
different locales. The pattern came to include even advanced technological sectors. For example, the once-popular IBM PS2 Model 30–286 contained: "a microprocessor from Malaysia; oscillators from either France or
Singapore; disk controller logic array, diskette controller, ROM and videos
graphics from Japan; VLSI circuits and video digital-to-analog converter
from Korea—and it [was] all put together in Florida."[44] Consequently, by
the 1980s international production—that is, production by multinational
enterprises outside their home countries—began to exceed world trade. By
the early 1990s, worldwide annual sales of multinational firms reached \$5.5
trillion, only slightly less than the entire U.S. gross domestic product. U.S.-
based multinationals play the leading role in global production, and their
revenues from manufacturing abroad are now twice their export earnings.[45]
It follows that intrafirm trade—trade among subsidiaries or otherwise
related parties—is growing more rapidly than arms-length trade. It now
accounts for about one third of all world trade, and a far higher share of
U.S. trade.[46]

Consequently, even as country borders have become more open to the
flow of economic transactions, in an institutional sense the international
division of labor is becoming increasingly *internalized* at the level of firms.[47]
Administrative hierarchies that span the globe manage the design, production, and exchange of component parts and finished products; the syn-
optic plans that orchestrate these processes, including their location; the
allocation of strategic resources, such as capital and skills; and the information as well as telecommunications systems that make it possible to
manage globally in real time.

Analysts and policymakers are still struggling to understand these globally integrated structures of production and exchange, but the corporate
world has already generated the next wave of institutional innovation. It
has been described as network forms of organization, more commonly
known as strategic alliances. This organizational form is regarded to be
"especially useful for the exchange of commodities whose value is not easily measured," including "know-how, technological capability, a particular
approach or style of production, a spirit of innovation or experimentation,
or a philosophy of zero defects." Such qualitative matters "are very hard to
place a price tag on. They are not easily traded in markets nor communi-
cated through a corporate hierarchy."[48] In addition, the sheer size of invest-

ments and magnitudes of risks in many rapidly changing areas of high technology increasingly are beyond the capacity of even the largest firms, driving them to establish strategic alliances—as in, for example, the automobile, commercial aircraft, semiconductors, and telecommunications industries.[49] Numerous questions attend the future of strategic alliances, not the least being their long-term viability: "Managing such vaguely defined relationships is difficult enough at the best of times; distance, language and culture bring added complications. Add to this the fact that many networks are in the business of closing plants and refashioning markets, and you have a recipe for trouble."[50]

Contrary to the nostrums of orthodox economists and realist political scientists, then, there *is* something new under the world economic sun: a profound institutional transformation in the global organization of markets as well as structures of production and exchange. But how justified are fears that these changes adversely affect the working public and the processes of economic policymaking? Because the state of the art on this subject is still in infancy, our answer is necessarily stylized and contingent.

Writing in the *Wall Street Journal*, Paul McCracken, who chaired President Richard Nixon's Council of Economic Advisers, has struck a somber note about the current labor market situation: "Those entering the work forces in Western Europe and even in the U.S. confront labor market conditions more nearly resembling those of the late 1930s than those prevailing during the four decades or so following World War II."[51] Indeed, average real wages for most categories of workers in the United States have been stagnant since the mid-1970s; during the twelve-month period ending in September 1995, they rose at the lowest annual rate ever since the U.S. Department of Labor began to collect these statistics.[52] Official studies also indicate that income disparities have grown significantly in the United States over the past two decades, and are now the widest of any industrialized country.[53] Both wage levels and income distribution have held up better in Western Europe, but unemployment has been greater there—indeed, at ten-percent-plus, it has reached postwar highs.[54] In light of such conditions, the following finding by the University of Michigan's Consumer Surveys is not surprising: "For the first time in 50 years, we are recording a decline in [Americans'] expectations. And their uncertainty and anxiety grow the farther you ask them to look into the future."[55]

The heated NAFTA debate in the United States indicated that the public as well as many politicians blame globalization for this state of affairs, attributing job losses and stagnant wages to competitive pressures unleashed by the institutional transformation in the world economy that we have been describing. Their belief is only partially borne out by the evidence. But it contains enough truth to sustain uncertainty and anxiety, and also to provide an inviting issue for entrepreneurial politicians to exploit.

We should note to begin with that the American economy has suffered from low rates of economic growth since the 1970s, while the labor force has expanded rapidly. That alone would put downward pressure on wages. The most direct cause of slow economic growth has been anemic productivity increases.[56] Foreign competition is only one contributing factor, however; domestic economic practices and policies together with demographic changes are more significant.[57] At the same time, it is true that recent productivity improvements have come "largely from record layoffs"—from fewer workers doing more work and jobs migrating overseas.[58] The outward migration affects not only semiskilled and skilled labor, but also growing numbers of white-collar positions.[59]

Evidence directly linking low rates of wage increases and greater income disparities in the United States to outsourcing production to lower-wage countries remains elusive for a number of technical reasons.[60] Moreover, fundamental skills-biased technological changes in the economy—what some commentators are calling the third industrial revolution—are bound to exert a more decisive effect. Nevertheless, globalization is implicated. Jagdish Bhagwati has proposed a highly suggestive formulation. Globalization has narrowed, or made more thin, he observes, the margins of comparative advantage many industries in the OECD countries enjoy. Those industries, therefore, are becoming "more footloose than ever," redeploying production as marginal advantages shift. That, in turn, results in higher labor turnover and frictional unemployment, which logically implies flatter earnings for labor.[61] More generally, the capitalist economies may be experiencing a trend toward "kaleidoscopic" (Bhagwati's term) labor markets, as opposed to continuous and cumulative employment patterns, a trend that further diminishes the already-weakened structural bargaining power of labor. The proliferation of strategic alliances, which are intended from the start to be project-based, reinforces this kaleidoscopic pattern.

A vivid—albeit inadvertent—illustration of the growing disjuncture between global production relations and the American work force appears in a recent U.S. Department of Commerce study. It sought to gauge what the American position in the overall world market for goods and services would be if the standard balance-of-trade measure were combined with net sales by U.S.-owned companies abroad less sales by foreign-owned companies in the United States. The study found that on this more inclusive indicator of global sales "the United States" consistently has been earning a surplus, rising from $8 billion in 1981 to $24 billion in 1991, even as its trade deficit deteriorated during the same period from $16 billion to $28 billion.[62] This was reported as up-beat news about the competitive performance of American industry, an antidote to gloomier balance-of-trade figures, which in some sense it is. Indeed, the valuation of U.S.-owned multinationals by the stock markets reflects their broader—the "American"—position in the world market. The problem is, however, that the surplus so generated does not accrue to "the United States" as such, especially not to immobile factors of production like labor, which remain fixed in the conventional world measured by standard balance-of-trade figures.

In sum, globalization is not, in itself or even primarily, responsible for the "funk de siècle," to borrow Ikenberry's clever phrase, that afflicts the working public in the capitalist countries.[63] But it is a contributing factor.

Studies also show, however, that policy demonstrably affects outcomes. In his presidential address to the Canadian Economics Association, Richard Harris compared globalization and wage trends in Canada and the United States. Even though Canadian industry is relatively more internationalized, wage growth has slowed less and income distribution is more equal. "Public policy," Harris concluded, "accounts for a large part of this difference."[64] Similarly, Geoffrey Garrett, in a statistical analysis of 15 OECD countries, finds that the political strength of social democratic parties as well as organized labor results in policies that compensate for potentially deleterious effects of globalization.[65]

But, is not the efficacy of key public-policy instruments itself undermined by the forces of globalization, reducing their compensatory capacity? "When markets evolve to the point of becoming international in scope," Richard Cooper, the distinguished Harvard economist, has written, "the effectiveness of traditional instruments of economic policy is often greatly reduced or even nullified."[66] Cooper's claim has not gone unchallenged, but it seems to be supported by the best available evidence. We take up first some key policy effects of capital mobility, and then of globalization in production and exchange.

Financial integration has several significant policy effects. First of all, governments enjoy greater access to capital and can borrow more cheaply than earlier in the postwar era, as reflected by growing public-sector debt in the OECD countries for the past twenty years.[67] There is, of course, a point at which markets decide, often quite suddenly, that debt is too high. Concurrently, however, governments are less free to deploy monetary policy in the pursuit of desired domestic outcomes "independent of external constraints."[68] This is so because the markets will demand higher bond yields from governments of whose policies they disapprove, or drive down their currency exchange rates. In the long run, then, capital mobility increases market-based pressure for policy convergence within a range of acceptability that the markets determine. Moreover, globalization restricts governments' ability to increase taxes, especially on business. As a result, *The Economist* concedes, "if governments need to cut budget deficits, they have to look mainly to public spending."[69]

Advocates of these changes feel that little is lost because the markets take away from governments the power only to do "wrong" things.[70] But the markets have not demonstrated that they are sufficiently sophisticated and function sufficiently smoothly to discriminate among policy objectives at the margin any better than governments in the past were able to fine-tune the economic cycle. In any event, whether they like it or not, governments seem stuck with their lot: "the costs of resisting capital mobility either in isolation or in combination have dramatically escalated, with the results that states have by and large chosen to accommodate the phenomenon."[71]

Global capital markets also pose entirely new policy problems. Existing systems of supervision and regulation as well as tax and accounting policies were created for a nation-based world economic landscape.[72] Steps have been taken to coordinate the supervision of international banking by establishing capital adequacy standards and a lender-of-last resort understanding through the Bank for International Settlements. But international securities trading, as well as the international banking and securities clearance and settlements systems, remain weak and vulnerable. Moreover, although markets in exotic financial derivative instruments help manage risks for individual firms and investors, they may make the system as a whole more vulnerable. George Soros, a leading global financier, testified to this effect at Congressional hearings on hedge funds, which he has helped to promote: "The instrument of hedging transfers the risk from the individual to the system. . . . So there is a danger that at certain points you may have a discontinuous move"[73]—which, when it occurs in stock markets, is called a crash. But to date only some derivatives markets have the margin requirements or "circuit-breakers" that have long existed in stock markets.

By liberalizing regulations governments facilitated the emergence of global capital markets. Private and public economic actors derive benefits from these markets. But their expansion and integration have also eroded traditional instruments of economic policy while creating wholly new policy challenges that neither governments nor market players yet fully understand let alone can fully manage.

Globalization in production relations also has had significant effects on traditional policy instruments. One of its byproducts, as noted above, is the growth of intrafirm trade. Studies indicate that this form of trade is far less sensitive than conventional trade to such policy instruments as exchange rates.[74] It also lends itself more readily to transfer pricing for the purposes of cross-subsidization and minimizing tax obligations[75]—indeed, within global firms these become core objectives of strategic management. Intrafirm trade also reduces the effectiveness of "process protectionism" which, as described in the previous chapter, has allowed governments to maintain public support for trade liberalization by cushioning surges in imports.

Furthermore, globalization has turned some aspects of American trade policy into virtually metaphysical exercises—poignantly captured by Robert Reich's question: *Who* is Us?[76] Symbolizing this existential state, the U.S. International Trade Commission not long ago found itself confronted with antidumping charges brought by a Japanese firm producing typewriters in Bartlett, Tennessee, against an American company importing typewriters into the United States from its off-shore facilities in Singapore and Indonesia.[77] But the "who is us" issue is not limited to minor irritants like portable typewriters. The tendency by American firms to forge strategic alliances for costly high-technology projects has raised serious—and as of yet unresolved—concerns in the defense community.[78]

Finally, globalization of production challenges what was perhaps the central policy premise guiding the postwar domestic American political economy. As Cowhey and Aronson depict it, the federal government assumed that its primary role was to manage levels of consumer spending, support research and development, and otherwise help socialize the costs of technological innovation by means of military procurement and civilian science programs. America's corporations would take it from there.[79] Today, it is getting harder not only to determine whether something is an American product, but more critically whether the legal designation, "an American corporation," describes the same economic entity, with the same positive consequences for domestic employment and economic growth, that it did in the 1950s and 1960s. In the absence of viable alternative policy frameworks, the major default option for governments is to adopt the "denationalized" posture of competing with other, similarly situated, capitalist countries in providing a friendly policy environment for transnational capital irrespective of ownership or origins. A British scholar calls this model "the residual state."[80]

Thus globalization is real; it contributes to, though it does not decisively cause, the sources of economic uncertainly and anxiety experienced by the American public; and in some measure it does diminish the efficacy of certain traditional policy instruments by means of which the U.S. and other governments have mediated between international economic forces and domestic policy objectives.

Retrenchment

A residual state in economic life is, of course, the political objective of conservatives in the United States and abroad—the present-day descendants of nineteenth-century laissez-faire liberals. Quite apart from the diminished capacity of governments to employ traditional policy instruments due to the effects of globalization, a pendulum-like swing in political preferences and mood has been gaining momentum back in a neo-laissez-faire direction. This ideological thrust is still too fluid for us to explore it fully here. But we do need to take up those aspects of it that relate to the subject at hand.

The New Deal state was America's version of the universal reaction against the collapse of laissez-faire capitalism in the Great Depression and the international economic warfare that preceded the outbreak of military hostilities in World War II. It was also the platform from which the United States sought to reconstruct the postwar international economic order. The current domestic political struggle over what kind of American state should replace the remnants of the New Deal state, therefore, has profound implications not only domestically but internationally as well. It is exceedingly doubtful whether the residual state model would suffice to sustain domestic political support for the liberal international economic order. Let us see why.

The New Deal state was considerably more modest in aims and less intrusive in means than European-style social democracy and corporatism, let alone socialism.[81] Its objective was to stabilize the capitalist order, not transform it, and its means were largely limited to Keynesian-type monetary and fiscal policies, employed in pursuit of the principle of full employment, together with a safety net of social services for those in need. The Great Society initiatives of the 1960s added several layers of social welfare programs onto this base. They were rendered politically acceptable, however, only by strict and extensive specification of the boundaries delimiting state intervention, eligibility requirements, and the modalities of provision. Over time, this conditionality produced "the paradox of liberal intervention," in Mary Ruggie's felicitous phrase, whereby the state was drawn into ever-deeper and clumsier intervention, spawned a sizable bureaucracy, fought legal battles with advocacy groups, and incurred escalating costs— all initially necessitated by its desire for the scope of intervention to be as contingent and circumscribed as possible.[82] Today, anti-government senti- ment in the United States is driven, at least in part, by this paradoxical experience. The West European states, in contrast, avoided this problem by making many of the same programs universally available, though increased costs have now forced stricter limits there as well.

Several routes link the future domestic policy role of the American state, not simply to social and economic welfare at home, but to stability in the world economy at large. One involves the virtual abandonment of labor market policies. In keeping with its underlying commitment to pri- vate sector institutions, the New Deal state remained relatively unintru- sive on this front.[83] In the 1950s, then-Senator John F. Kennedy took up the cause of trade adjustment assistance for labor, and gained its enactment when he became President. This provided workers hurt by imports with federal financial and technical assistance for job retraining and relocation, thereby securing labor support for the trade liberalization that was about to unfold.[84] Trade adjustment assistance was enhanced in the 1970s with the same objective in mind. However, the policy had done progressively less and less to promote actual "adjustment"—by the 1970s it amounted to lit- tle more than extending the duration of unemployment benefits.[85] The Reagan administration sharply reduced it. The Clinton administration has proposed eliminating it altogether, and using the savings for more produc- tive worker retraining efforts.[86] But for now, virtually nothing is in place.

Compared to its OECD trading partners, the U.S. government does a poor job in helping the American workforce prepare for the new global economy.[87] Indeed, the United States ranks dead last among them in pub- lic spending for job training and placement, as a percent of GDP[88]—lower even than Japan, which, until recently, has required no such policy thanks to lifetime employment practices by firms. Moreover, U.S. health-care ben- efits for workers are more precarious, less generalized, and less portable, while pension benefits are less secure. Outside the military, vocational training programs are episodic and typically of low quality; Germany, with less than one-third the U.S. population, has nearly six times the number of industrial apprenticeships.[89] At the same time, the competitiveness of the American economy is threatened by a dearth of skilled workers. Finally, corporate downsizing and off-shore outsourcing, as we have noted, have begun to displace white-collar clerical and managerial positions as well as manufacturing jobs. It is hardly surprising, then, that American labor for some time now has been an implacable foe of trade liberalization, and that the economic nationalist appeals of Ross Perot in 1992 and Pat Buchanan in 1996 resonated with growing numbers of middle-class voters as well.

A second and related link between the domestic role of the state and international economic stability is via the social safety net more generally. It was a cardinal belief of New Dealers that society seeks protection from the disruptive and destructive effects of unmediated market forces, and that it will hold government responsible for providing that social protection. There were, and remain, sound historical grounds for that view.[90] But budget deficits and tax-averse publics make it impossible for governments to expand or even to maintain the web of social policies that have characterized welfare capitalism since World War II. Even for the most social-democratic and neocorporatist welfare states, the costs have become too high.[91] Moreover, there is a growing belief that some of these policies have become part of the problem, not a solution, not only because of their financial burden but also because many are perceived not to work well any longer or to create perverse disincentives. U.S. Labor Secretary Robert Reich reflects a growing sentiment in proposing that several job-related social programs be terminated: "Investing scarce resources in programs that don't deliver cheats workers who require results and taxpayers who finance failure."[92]

And yet, simply to "slash and trash" the social safety net, rather than "review and redesign" it, as Lloyd Axworthy, Canada's Minister of Human Resources, posed the options in a House of Commons debate on Canadian welfare reforms,[93] is to invite a populist upsurge that would shock proponents of neo-laissez-faire. Publics in kaleidoscopic labor markets, slipping through a tattered social safety net, and witnessing income disparities that are unprecendented in their lifetimes at some point inevitably will turn against the most visible manifestation of unmediated market forces today: those emanating from the global economy. Should the slash-and-trash option prevail, a siren song of protectionism awaits the mainstream political singer.

A third and potentially promising link between the post-New Deal state and the international economic order may be found, perhaps ironically, in the work of some of the same economists who did so much to demonstrate the inability of Keynesianism to deliver on its macroeconomic promises. Robert Lucas, the 1995 economics Nobel prize winner, showed in the 1970s that economic actors—business owners, investors, and consumers—learn to anticipate governments' actions and to incorporate those "rational expectations" into their own behavior, thus confounding the policies' efficacy. Lucas subsequently turned his attention to the determinants of economic growth. Here, he and fellow "new growth" theorists have found that an active role of the state can be critical in providing the collective goods that the market undersupplies, such as education, infrastructure, and research and development.[94] The policy recommendations that follow from this work are not to return to unfettered laissez-faire but to rethink and reconfigure the political economy of the advanced capitalist state.

In a word, the gravest danger for the international economic order lies in its growing "disembeddedness" from the domestic social compact that sustained it throughout the postwar period.

And so we come back, in the end, to the embedded-liberalism compromise, the ingenious heterodox creation of Franklin Delano Roosevelt's New Dealers. Its accomplishment within the *nation-based* world economy is historic. Stabilization was achieved and has withstood intense international strains that would have destroyed previous international economic orders. Within the *global* world economy, however, its borders are shredded: it is surpassed and enveloped by forces it cannot easily grasp, and it finds itself being hollowed out from the inside by a political philosophy it was intended to replace. What Charles Kindleberger, in his classic study of the Great Depression, called a "transition trap," a moment of discontinuity when things could go terribly wrong, lurks ahead.[95]

7 Polarity, Plurality, and the Future

"**N**ow is the unipolar moment," a triumphalist commentator crowed after the collapse of the Soviet empire and the defeat of Iraq in Desert Storm. "There is but one first-rate power and no prospect in the immediate future of any power to rival it."[1] Looking at the growing array of international trouble spots, however, including Bosnia, a senior Clinton administration official soon demurred: "We simply don't have the leverage, we don't have the influence, we don't have the inclination to use military force," Under Secretary of State Peter Tarnoff said in what were intended as off-the-record remarks to a group of journalists. "And we certainly don't have the money to bring to bear the kind of pressure that will produce positive results any time soon."[2] Post-cold war U.S. foreign policy, in short, got off to a confused start—so much so that the Congressionally funded United States Institute of Peace drew an overflow crowd for a 1995 conference on the subject of "managing chaos" in international affairs.[3]

If anticommunist ideological fervor provided the attitudinal adhesive linking together otherwise disparate political orientations in support of an active U.S. world role during the cold war, the condition of bipolarity was the analytical anchor for its geopolitical strategies. Deprived of both when the Soviets conceded the superpower contest, U.S. foreign-policymakers in the 1990s found themselves confronting the same challenge their predecessors had struggled with in 1919 and 1945: securing sustained engagement by the United States to help achieve a stable international order, one that is conducive to the continuation of the long peace and the further realization of such quintessential American objectives as economic liberalization, democratization, and the vindication of human rights.

America's leaders in 1919 and 1945, as we saw in chapter 1, understood that as a result of the country's geopolitical constitution, variants of isolationism remained an ever-present possibility, and that the core mission of foreign-policy strategy, therefore, was to frame America's international role in a manner that promised to avoid sliding down isolationist paths. In this final chapter, I contend that the widespread realist-inspired practice of deriving the contours of post-cold war U.S. foreign policy from the emerging global power balance offers a relatively poor safeguard against any possible resurgence of that danger. Instead, I conclude that the pre- and early-cold war articulation of America's role in the world by FDR, Truman, and to some extent Eisenhower—linking America's international project with its sense of self as a nation—serves as a surer source of insight. In short, this chapter affirms the hunch of Terry Deibel, professor of strategy at the U.S. National War College, that "strategies designed to serve U.S. interests *before* the Soviet threat dominated American statecraft may well prove suggestive for strategists attempting to further those interests *after* the Soviet threat has disappeared."[4]

The discussion is organized as follows. First, I recapitulate briefly the two main roads to possible neo-isolationism that our study has uncovered, one via the field of security relations, the other through the terrain of political economy. Next, I summarize the academic and policy discussions concerning shifting alignments of international power—whether the world now is, or is becoming, unipolar, bipolar, or multipolar—and show why this factor serves as a poor guide for future U.S. foreign policy. The third section identifies several major patterns of domestic political realignment in America from the vantage point of what kind of foreign-policy orientation they may or may not support. Lastly, in the fourth section I suggest that, under the prevailing conjunction of international and domestic circumstances, an appropriately modified multilateral world order program may resonate among the American public today, and also indicate its limits.

Two Roads to Neo-isolationism

For a generation that was reared on running debates about the possible overextension of American commitments abroad, witnessed the growing international interdependence of economic activities, and experienced the early phases of the global information revolution, even to raise the issue of neo-isolationism may seem oddly anachronistic. In political circles, more-over, it is a loaded term, prone to trigger sharp rejoinders from those so accused. Yet our look at American isolationism during the interwar period taught us to be leery of the common view that isolationism requires, liter-ally, seeking to insulate oneself from the world, or that it is necessary to harbor isolationist intentions to produce the result. Both sentiments existed in the 1930s, but neither was dominant. "In matters of trade and commerce we have never been isolationist and never will be," said Senator William Borah, a leading isolationist, in a 1934 speech. "In matters of finance . . . we have never been isolationist and never will be. When earth-quake and famine, or whatever brings human suffering, visit any part of the human race, we have not been isolationists, and never will be."[5] What, then, can neo-isolationism possibly mean today?

That earlier experience suggests at least two plausible future neo-isolationist scenarios, though others exist as well.[6] One is in the field of security relations. It would begin, as it did in the 1930s, with strictly con-strued unilateralism—"in all matters political," as Borah put it, "in all com-mitments of any nature or kind, which encroach in the slightest upon the free and unembarrassed action of our people, or which circumscribe their discretion and judgment."[7] A current expression of such a unilateralist dis-position, described briefly in chapter 1, is legislation introduced to enact part of the Republican Party's 1994 "Contract With America" that would severely restrict timely and effective U.S. participation in UN peace oper-ations even as it would free the president from the Vietnam-inspired War Powers Act's constraints on the unilateral use of American force abroad. Indeed, generalized anti-cooperative security sentiments are quite strong in the legislative branch of government, particularly on the Republican side of the House.[8]

The next step in this a neo-isolationist security scenario, again as in the interwar years, would be to set such a high threshold for what constitutes a vital or important American interest that few threats to peace and security would trigger an American response—short of a direct challenge to Amer-ican territory or assets. The excruciating controversy in the United States regarding the forcible dismemberment of Bosnia illustrates the problem only too well. It stands to reason that American lives and treasure must not be lightly risked. But several consequences of the high-threshold require-ment should be factored into the decisionmaking process. First, when it is coupled with an insistence on strictly unilateralist means, the vital-interest test axiomatically will be still more demanding and less frequently met, while the possibility of sharing the burdens of acting and diversifying its risks will be diminished. Second, it is often the case that the United States, by virtue of its size, importance, and multiple commitments either influences or is otherwise drawn into conflicts it has sought to avoid, but by the time it does the "easy" options may long since have passed, leaving only the tougher and costlier ones. And third, a threshold of interests that is set too high—especially when coupled with unilateralism—permits the international milieu to deteriorate incrementally, local conflict by local conflict, "no one of which," as Deibel notes, "is sufficient to engage American interests in a major way, but which together have the potential to endanger Americans' physical security around the world and to disrupt the trade and manufacturing links so vital to economic prosperity."[9]

The final step would consist of unqualified future adherence to the Powell doctrine—the all-or-nothing position—governing the use of American force. If U.S. troops are never to be deployed in ongoing conflicts unless they can be brought to bear swiftly, decisively, and in overwhelming numbers to defeat an adversary then they simply will not be a significant factor in the most frequent threats to international peace and security in the years ahead. For virtually all strategic analysts predict that what I called "gray area conflicts" in chapter 4—beyond the capacity of traditional peacekeeping, short of all-out warfighting, and involving elements of collapsed states—will continue to proliferate.

Thus, in the security field it is not necessary for America overtly to turn its back on the world, or for policymakers explicitly to pursue isolationist objectives, for that result to come about: strict unilateralism, an unrealistically high vital interest threshold, and an all-or-nothing military doctrine can yield the same outcome.

A second possible neo-isolationist scenario suggested by our study concerns the evolving American political economy. But for a quarter century, I argued in chapter 5, economic policy analysts have been looking for it in the wrong place: trade wars triggered by U.S. neoprotectionist policies, in turn animated by the desire to satisfy import-competing producers or those aiming for greater market access abroad. Market-access issues are the more serious of the two, I noted, because it is tempting to resolve them through bilateral managed trade deals, thereby undermining the multilateral trade regime. Yet, by and large, those neoprotectionist fears, for reasons I enumerated, are greatly exaggerated. And presidential campaigns built on that platform, such as Richard Gephardt's in 1988, have not done well.

The more dangerous route, I warned in chapter 6, is through the combined effects of continued wage stagnation, widening income gaps, increasingly kaleidoscopic labor markets, and the growing inability or unwillingness by the government to moderate the deleterious consequences of unfettered global market forces and corporate deployments—or to prepare, or at least compensate, the working and middle classes for these economic forces. If left unattended, this set of developments may give rise to, not producer-initiated "fair trade" demands—which are, in any case, declining because importers increasingly are also exporters, and cross-investments result in further cross-pressures—but a potentially significant, populist rather than partisan, and highly volatile pool of disaffected voters clamoring for "social protection" against globalization.

Elements of such a potential coalition exist in the American electorate. What is left of organized labor is responsive to virtually any form of protectionism. The appeal of Ross Perot's 1992 campaign was based largely on "social protectionist" grounds: declining economic opportunities and grave social uncertainties produced by the "giant sucking sound" of high-wage jobs moving out. In a similar vein, Pat Buchanan, in a 1995 Labor Day speech, lashed out against "stagnant wages of an alienated working class," promised to "insulate" those wages from externally induced downward pressure, and proposed a "social tariff" to accomplish that end.[10] The successful resurgence of neo-laissez-faire attitudes regarding the role of government in the United States, which Buchanan embraces, would make it all the more likely that the sole vent for the "alienation" of which he speaks would be economic neo-isolationism—or what he, proudly, calls economic nationalism. The combination of an abiding bias against government yet a declared desire to enhance economic stability and opportunities for working America, leaves Buchanan with no alternative but a 1990s version of the 1930 Smoot-Hawley tariff, which caused the entire system to unravel. To reach its full potential, this latent electoral coalition awaits only a more mainstream political figure to lead it.

In short, many people believe that globalization has rendered economic neo-isolationism an oxymoron. That may be so for the producer-induced variety. It is not for social protectionism, the populist kind.

Polarity

It is a canonical realist principle that states balance power—or threats posed by power. The configuration of power and attendant threats among states are, accordingly, deemed the decisive determinants of international outcomes, and hence the most useful frame of reference for grand strategy—as U.S.–Soviet bipolarity was after about 1947. Geopolitical strategizing of this sort, as we have seen on several occasions in this study, has never had much appeal to the American public, and there is no reason to assume that it holds greater sway today. But even putting that fact aside, trying to deduce an overall foreign-policy strategy from the current global balance runs into two further impediments.

To begin with, for the foreseeable future no military threat similar to that posed by the Soviet Union during the cold war is likely to confront the United States. Indeed, according to the War College's Terry Deibel, over the course of the next decade or two any "catastrophic military dangers to American physical security seem hard to imagine."[11] Shifting global, and some regional, power balances will be of concern to the United States, but their perceived stakes will be lower than they were under bipolarity. Proliferation of nuclear and other weapons of mass destruction—and nonproliferation failures—will pose specific flashpoints of danger, in some instances requiring direct American responses. But this is not the stuff of threat-induced grand strategy.

In addition, realists do not, alas, fully agree among themselves what the emerging global power balance is, what it is likely to become—or what it should become, insofar as it is subject to policy volition. And even when they do agree, their policy prescriptions are frequently contradictory, or otherwise problematic.

In the early 1990s, the condition of unipolarity was celebrated by Charles Krauthammer, as quoted above.[12] The objective of maintaining unipolarity was stipulated by a Bush administration Pentagon team under the leadership of Paul Wolfowitz, Under Secretary of Defense for Policy.[13] In what may have been its most controversial passage, the team's draft report called for the United States "to establish and protect a new order" that accounts "sufficiently for the interests of the advanced industrial nations to discourage them from challenging our leadership," while also maintaining a military dominance capable of "deterring potential competitors *from even aspiring to* a larger regional or global role."[14]

The draft policy guide, on the whole, was not well received at home or abroad. Bush administration officials themselves felt obliged to describe it as "dumb," and the final report dropped all references to the objective of seeking to perpetuate a world with only one superpower.[15] Interestingly, among the harshest critics were fellow realists, for whom the "unipolar moment," in the words of Christopher Layne, "is just that," certain to be progressively replaced, in the normal course of power balancing, by a multipolar structure.[16] The idea of deterring even others' *aspirations* for larger international roles correctly was singled out as a particular folly, a recipe for American bankruptcy, not primacy.

Though strategic bipolarity went out with the Soviet collapse, the possibility of a new and different strain of it has been raised from time to time since. John Le Carré expresses it crisply in his novel of post-cold war Transcaucasian covert intrigue, *Our Game:* "the demonization of Islam as a substitute for the anti-Communist crusade."[17] Harvard's Samuel Huntington formulates it more broadly as a "clash of civilizations," the most serious of which, nevertheless, he believes will be between Islam and the West[18]— and so, bipolarity redux. Because intercivilizational wars deal mainly in such nonnegotiables as identities, Huntington contends, they will be "more frequent, more sustained and more violent than conflicts between groups in the same civilization."[19]

It is hard to tell from Huntington's description what defines civilizations and determines their interrelationships; how certain civilizations differ from a state (he calls Japan a civilization) or region (ditto for Latin America); under what circumstances culture and religion are linked to become paramount drivers of states' policies; and how all of these relate to the desire and ability to project organized force.[20] It is easier to see that his analysis holds considerable potential for generating self-fulfilling prophecies: treating all of Islam, for example, from Indonesia to Morocco, from Hamas to the House of al-Sabah, as a coherent and hostile force, determined to oppose and degrade Western interests and values, might go some way toward making it so.

By far the most common expectation of realists is that the international political order inevitably will become multipolar. Christopher Layne and Kenneth Waltz both predict the recurrence of multipolarity sometime during the first decade of the next century.[21] By then Japan and Germany will have reached great-power status, they foresee, acquiring "the full spectrum of great power capabilities, including nuclear weapons."[22] Russia will likely remain among the great powers, while China will enter their ranks if it manages to sustain an effective central government. "Germany, Japan, and Russia will have to relearn their old great-power roles," Waltz concludes, "and the United States will have to learn a role it has never played before: namely, to coexist and interact with other great powers."[23]

As plausible as the multipolarity scenario may appear, it has not gone unchallenged. Much of the controversy has focused on Japan and Germany, neither of which to date has shown any inclination to embrace the new roles that balance-of-power theory has in store for them, particularly renouncing their non-nuclear status and preferences.[24] But other factors give pause as well. For one, the multipolarity scenario equates, as being equally "polar," an integrated Europe, and an ascendant Germany without

European Union (EU) and NATO ties. For practical purposes, however, the two are worlds apart. And though it is possible to conjure up an EU that is a reflection of German dominance, the same cannot be imagined of NATO, the military forums of which France rejoined in 1995 after a thirty-year absence. For another, Richard Betts observes that a U.S. defense budget growing at a post-cold war rate of "only" 3 percent "is still larger than those of the other great powers in the world *combined*; it is far higher than those of all states in the world combined that are unfriendly to the United States; and it is astronomically higher than it ever was in peacetime before the Cold War."[25] If this trajectory suggests multipolarity, it is unlike any the world has seen.[26]

Analysts, of course, prescribe diverse and often incompatible foreign-policy strategies depending on which form of polarity they believe is most likely to emerge. What is worse, however, is that even those realists who agree on multipolarity invoke it to justify very different policy directions—ranging all the way from U.S. strategic independence, to active global power balancing, to the "carefully managed" proliferation of nuclear weapons to certain countries that may, according to the academic theorist, at some point develop a sense of insecurity without them.[27] Even on so concrete—and critical—an issue as the future of NATO no consensus exists among realists: Kissinger holds it to be as indispensable in the future as in the past; according to Mearsheimer it should already be fading into oblivion; and Waltz predicts its gradual marginalization as multipolarity sets in.[28]

Lastly, the multipolarity scenario provides little practical guidance in matters of economic relations. Waltz offers up a disquisition on the current relevance of Friedrich List, the mid-nineteenth-century German writer on the subject of mercantilist economic practices, while Huntington predicts, at best, an economic cold war between the United States and Japan: "In the 1930s Chamberlain and Daladier did not take seriously what Hitler said in *Mein Kampf*," he reminds his readers sternly, even histrionically. "Americans would do well to take . . . seriously both Japanese declarations of their goal of achieving economic dominance and the strategy they are pursuing to achieve that goal."[29] More generally, realists tend to assume that the recurrence of multipolarity will go hand in hand with a resurgence of economic blocs. But none of these postulates, predictions, and predilections are linked in any way to a serious analysis of economic globalization—the significance of which, as noted in chapter 6, realists discount if not reject.

When all is said and done, it seems prudent to assume that the future international distribution of power will lie somewhere between unipolarity and multipolarity, as the latter has been understood historically. More than this we cannot squeeze out of the concept of polarity. It does not, therefore, comprise a compelling frame of reference for U.S. foreign policy in the new era. Indeed, little has changed in this regard since the mid-1970s, when U.S.-Soviet détente, U.S.-Soviet-China triangular balancing, and the termination of the Vietnam war and with it the domino theory first raised questions in some scholars' minds about the utility of the concept of bipolarity—and polarity itself. Political scientist Joseph Nogee, for example, found polarity to be "ambiguous" and models utilizing it "imprecise and vague." Already then, he concluded that polarity could not "predict the characteristic or modal behavior of the system—much less predict the behavior of individual nations or be a guide to policymaking in the real world."[30]

Coming belatedly to this recognition, Henry Kissinger, the master realist practitioner, now concedes that the United States "cannot base its policy on the balance of power as the sole criterion for a new world order."[31] Sustained American involvement, he acknowledges, also requires a dose of what he calls "American idealism"—which, as pointed out in chapter 1, has less to do with mushy moralizing than with certain ideas about how the international order should be organized, ideas which have meaning not only in terms of the interests but also the identity of America.

Plurality

Franklin Roosevelt had already reached much the same conclusion in the early 1940s, when he first began to imagine the postwar organization of international security and economic relations. Harry Truman took the interest-plus-identity premise to heart in designing the Marshall Plan and constructing NATO. And Dwight Eisenhower acted on it in his commitment to transform permanently the European security order via a European Defense Community and EURATOM.

We would expect the identity dimension of foreign policy to become particularly salient in the absence of a compelling external security threat, as is the case for the United States before the cold war and again today. But America is a very different place than it was a half century ago. Has not its fundamental sense of self fragmented significantly over that period, thereby providing weak if not contradictory attitudinal signals for the nation's post-cold war foreign policy orientation? Indeed, at least three partially related sources of unresolved tension may be identified in the American polity today that are likely to affect the domestic climate of opinion concerning future U.S. foreign policy.

First, wars in American history have tended to produce both expansion and centralization of the federal government.[32] Far from being the exception, the cold war generated the most active and comprehensive American state form yet, raising fears, in its early days, that the United States might turn into a "garrison state."[33] Now that the cold war is over, it is quite natural, therefore, for America's "national security state" to be scaled back, for its dominance over the individual states to diminish, for its relationship to the private sector to be reconfigured, and for some of the rationales that justified its prior scope and structure to be successfully challenged. However, no natural equilibrium point exists on which new sets of relationships will settle; this is a matter of political contestation, in which foreign-policy needs are unlikely to be the central considerations.

A second as-of-yet unresolved source of tension is the electoral realignment that began in 1968, when George Wallace split the white Southern vote and catalyzed, thereby, its gradual conversion by and to the Republican party.[34] This realignment affects foreign policy directly. Ever since FDR, the South had been solidly Democratic and its Congressional representatives a mainstay of support for the party's internationalist agenda. Neither is the case any longer. In addition, the Wall Street wing of the Republican party, equally outward looking, withered long ago. In its place is a Main Street contingent, coming mostly out of small, entrepreneurial businesses, and holding the view that past "business-government partnerships," including trade policy, have excluded their interests while government regulations impeded their efforts.[35] These changes are accompanied by the steady decline of "wise men" in the foreign-policy process, and the greater involvement of innumerable grassroots organizations.[36] It does not follow that an isolationist mindset has seized the electorate and its representatives. However, fewer predictable bases now exist among them for a consistent and sustained internationalist foreign policy.

This electoral realignment also affects foreign policy indirectly. At its core is a deep skepticism of the efficacy of government, a greater skepticism of the federal government than of state and local levels, and a new receptivity to more nongovernmental answers.[37] And yet, these views remain coupled with, according to Everett Ladd, "high expectations that large national problems be vigorously addressed," including health care, education, crime, and national defense. "In these and other areas, they [the public] see large governmental responsibility. . . . The public will continue to be cross-pulled, even while the underlying balance of sentiment has shifted."[38] Again, this ambivalence in attitudes toward government does not necessarily imply an isolationist turn. But it is bound to pose uncertainty in matters of foreign policy, which is, after all, conducted by the federal government, and which inevitably reflects its domestic role and legitimacy.

Yet a third source of tension concerns the so-called cultural wars that have riven American public discourse and political life since the late-1960s, splintering the ideational project of American community into multiple, competing, and often-presumed mutually hostile identities.[39] In the academy, this movement took aim at the "canon," the established curricula in the humanities and some social sciences. Its advocates have sought to decenter, detotalize, and deconstruct that canon, so as to lay bare underlying hierarchies based on race, gender, sexuality, as well as other forms of real and imagined domination. In its place, under the rubric of multiculturalism, they have affirmed and prized the particularisms of the exploited, disadvantaged, or merely ignored. At the extreme, the history of America was reduced, thereby, to a history of diasporas. In the political realm, a parallel movement, which began with the objective of extending the rights of individuals that inhere in the constitution, ended with institutionalized entitlements in behalf of categorical victims.[40]

The inevitable backlash was led initially by neoconservatives, many of whom had started their adult lives on the political left, many from second or even first generation immigrant families, many Jewish. They had gained their upward mobility through the educational system and believed deeply in civil rights, equal opportunity, and American exceptionalism—and they took grave exception to assaults on these very features of American life. The neoconservatives were followed before long by what is now known as the "social" or "Christian" right, comprising largely evangelical Protestants, typically white, typically from Southern or border states, fundamentally conservative in outlook, and aiming to establish an America that fits within their parameters—that is to say, one considerably more sectarian than the objects of multiculturalists' ire had been in the first place.

It is difficult to decipher what affirmative foreign-policy missions would self-evidently command support within a nation defined by such competing identity preferences. It is somewhat reassuring, then, to recall that these cultural conflicts are not nearly as severe as earlier ones in this century have been.[41] In addition, there are also theoretical reasons and survey data to suggest that considerably more common ground exists than has been supposed in these debates.

In the realm of theory, the Berkeley intellectual historian David

Hollinger, a participant observer of multiculturalist movements, sees hope that their drive toward "promiscuous pluralism" is nearing a halt, and that the debate is circling back in search of new means for a "stretching of the we."[42] What might those means be? The United States does not have an ethnos of its own, Hollinger observes, but it is more than a mere container for ethno-racial and other cultural communities. Pluralism does not suffice as a common ground, he holds, because "it endows with privilege particular groups, especially the communities that are well established at whatever time the ideal of pluralism is invoked."[43] A "cosmopolitan" basis for American we-feeling is necessary, Hollinger contends, one that shares with all varieties of universalism "a profound suspicion of enclosures," but which also embraces a "recognition, acceptance, and eager exploration of diversity."[44] And where does Hollinger propose to locate such a construct? In "the civic character of the American nation-state," he insists, in a "nationality [that is] based on the principle of consent and is ostensibly open to persons of a variety of ethno-racial affiliations," a "civic nation . . . built and sustained by people who honor a common future more than a common past."[45] Multiculturalists, it would appear, are (re)discovering the idea of America and, to paraphrase T. S. Eliot, getting to know the place for the first time.

If the academy is rediscovering America, the American people, a Berkeley social science team documents, never lost its sense of core identity.[46] No state in the Union is more ethnically diverse than California. Asked whether there are unique American qualities, and what they were, 80 percent in a statewide poll responded in the affirmative, and 85 percent of those mentioned specific civic traits "familiar to the readers of de Tocqueville."[47] In a national poll, respondents divided between "assimilationist" and "distinct cultures" views as the preferred model for America by roughly 5:3, and "[s]trikingly, whites, blacks, and Hispanics did not differ in their responses to this question." Nor were blacks or Hispanics any more likely to reject the idea that "speaking English is a defining element of being American."[48] Nativist impulses, not surprisingly, were most pronounced on the issue of immigration, though the perceived threat is far more likely to be defined in economic (loss of jobs, higher taxes to pay for welfare and social services) than cultural terms. The research team also constructed "nativist" and "multicultural" indices, composites of responses to questions on immigration, language, and maintaining distinct cultures. "Clearly, both outlooks are minority viewpoints."[49] Blacks and Hispanics scored higher on multiculturalism, but it was decisively a minority viewpoint within those groups as well. Finally, with regard to the issue of foreign policy the researchers conclude, on the basis of the available survey data, that the core—what they call "cosmopolitan liberal"—American sense of national identity "remains a relative bedrock that could provide support for diverse foreign policy positions, especially "instrumental" though not "ideological" support for multilateralism.[50]

These sources of domestic tension are among the major factors that constitute the overall attitudinal context within which America's leaders must maneuver as they define the future of U.S. foreign policy—and in the process advance their own electoral chances, the prospects of their political parties, and the interests of the nation as they see them. Overt isolationism does not appear to be a major problem. And the American sense of self as a nation, while under some duress, remains relatively intact. But uncertainties for foreign policy attend the inevitable devolution of the cold war national security state. And fluidity in patterns of party alignment and ambiguity in the preferences of the electorate have reduced the predictable bases of support for an internationalist agenda.

Foreign Policy in the Era of Realignment

On Sunday morning TV talk shows Beltway pundits repeat, as if chanting a mantra, that it is necessary for this country to articulate a new set of interests that are deemed vital and sufficiently compelling to mobilize the country behind sustained foreign-policy efforts. But the aims, objectives, aspirations, and truisms these entreaties generate clearly have not proved persuasive, because the chants continue unabated. The reason for the failure should not be hard to grasp, however: interests have meaning, and can be ranked, only within an overall frame of reference, but the end of the cold war evaporated the overall frame of reference for U.S. foreign policy along with the Soviet Union and the threats and challenges it posed. Not since the immediate post-World War II period have American foreign-policy-makers had to address the far more basic, underlying issue confronting them today: borrowing David Fromkin's words, "what the United States ought to be and ought to do" in the world.[51]

Answering that question requires not simply making *à la carte* calculations, as is too often assumed, but fashioning a deeper understanding of guiding principles and values which, at one and the same time, make sense externally and can command domestic support. Broadly defined interests will flow from such an understanding, though their realization in any particular instance inevitably will be subject to political toing-and-froing concerning perceived costs and benefits.

I have argued that in the current conjunction of international and domestic circumstances, the world order agenda of that earlier generation of American leaders offers a better source of inspiration for the overall direction of U.S. foreign policy than the available alternatives, and their unfinished institutional program, appropriately adapted to the unique features of the new era, provides a viable focal point for more concrete foreign-policy initiatives. A brief recapitulation of the main implications of this proposition concludes this study.

The relatively benign global security environment implies two major consequences for American foreign-policy strategy. First, the "pull" factor eliciting U.S. political and military engagement will be diminished. The danger of American overcommitment is reduced, thereby, but the danger of undercommitment increases. Second, the scope for what classical realists used to call "milieu goals"—longer-term interests and values, as opposed to direct and immediate threats—in U.S. foreign policy will be enhanced. At the same time, no state willingly pays high costs for milieu goals unilaterally unless it so towers over others in the system that its own interests, and those of the system, become very nearly synonymous—which is not the case for the United States today. This combination of factors suggests an overall foreign-policy posture that puts the United States in a position to defend and vindicate, on its own if need be, both its immediate interests and core values, while working actively with coalitions of the willing to pursue broader and longer-term milieu goals.

The domestic attitudinal context is compatible with such a prudential yet progressive foreign-policy orientation. The public continues to support a relatively strong national defense, so that maintaining the military capacity to meet the nation's needs should not prove inordinately difficult. But the public is also reluctant to use those capabilities unilaterally in the pursuit of milieu goals, insisting on burden-sharing and risk-diversification with allies and friends. Finally, in framing milieu goals the evocative significance of multilateral world order principles—a bias against exclusive bilateralist alliances, the rejection of discriminatory economic blocs, and facilitating means to bridge the gaps of ethnos, race, and religion—should resonate still for the American public, insofar as they continue to reflect its own sense of national identity.

Concretely, what types of policies are implied by these predispositions? The United States currently is prepared to fight two major regional conflicts at the same time, and on its own. Whether the formula remains "win-win" or becomes "win-hold-win," that is, whether they must be fought truly simultaneously in all respects or can be sequenced, ultimately will be as much a political as a military matter, but the general objective seems firmly in place. Beyond this core defense of direct interests lie the cooperative security strategies sketched out in chapter 4.

A core element is continued U.S. involvement in and support for NATO. But this should aim at strengthening NATO's European pillar so that Europe can provide for a greater share of its own defense, and also come to act more coherently and effectively in future crises than it did, for instance, during the early stages of the Bosnian conflict. As of now, the European Union (EU) remains too fragmented in political and military terms to do so—in contrast to the area of international trade. While the EU is slowly moving toward greater integration in security matters through the West European Union, its defense arm, and WEU's relationship to NATO, this objective requires active U.S. support.

As for Eastern and Central Europe, unless strategic exigencies take a sudden turn for the worse, there is no compelling logic to extend NATO's indivisible security commitments before greater consolidation of NATO's European pillar has taken place. Indeed, as suggested in chapter 4, consolidation may be undermined by precipitous expansion. Joint participation in peace operations, joint training through the Partnership for Peace, association agreements with the WEU, and building up the conflict resolution potential of the Organization for Security and Cooperation in Europe provide a full portfolio of security cooperation for the region. When individual East Central European states begin the accession process to EU membership—and thereby to the WEU—it will be appropriate to deal with NATO membership as well.

Active American involvement in East Asia is every bit as necessary from a strategic vantage. But it will be more difficult to sustain on domestic political grounds. Unlike in Europe, there is no common entity that the American public can be told will assume greater indigenous responsibility down the road, and which will, as NATO and the EU have done in Europe, help transform the regional security arena in a more cooperative direction. There being no other grounds, the case for continued U.S. engagement in East Asia has to be made almost entirely in balance-of-power terms, rarely a persuasive discourse for the American public outside the cold war context. What is more, in East Asia the United States is assigned the critical role of balancer in a region that includes its toughest economic competitors, several of which are perceived not to play by fair trade rules, and many of which are hostile to, while none is strongly supportive of, such American milieu goals as human rights. Here, the politically most viable U.S. options, as discussed in chapter 4, are supporting cooperative balancing mechanisms, encouraging regional security organizations, and ending U.S. treatment of Japan as though it were an American military protectorate.

The United States will frequently find itself wishing to help contain or settle regional disputes beyond Europe and East Asia, but without wanting to undertake the job on its own. Here the United Nations must enter the picture. American critics of the UN express a recurring preference for regional organizations "like NATO" to do the job. But there are none. There is only NATO. And NATO is no more likely to become the world's police force than the United States is. Hence, few if any alternatives exist for strengthening the ability of the UN to play a larger role. Several Nordic countries, Holland, and Canada, for example, are exploring designating national battalions for UN peace operations. Indeed, the U.S. military quietly but effectively has been working with the UN to upgrade its operational military capacity—which, during the cold war, there was no reason for it to have had. And, the UN Security Council offers considerable opportunities to engage major developing countries in assuming greater responsibility for regional conflict management, opportunities which the United States has done little to exploit.

The problem largely is a political time warp in the U.S. Congress. The UN occupies an anomalous place in American domestic politics. Its support in public opinion polls is consistently high, and in recent years has reached all-time highs.[52] Yet Congress routinely engages in UN-bashing and withholds U.S. financial obligations—now in excess of $1 billion. It may be that public opinion on this subject is not very intense to begin with. But it is also the case that, whereas anti-UN efforts are effectively organized inside the Beltway, no pro-UN lobby is in place to balance them— the UN's third world majority back in the 1970s undermined what there was of it. In time, the organization's diplomatic and conflict resolution potential, combined with the example of U.S. allies and friends as well as the continued support of the U.S. military, may lead Congress to restore a measure of rationality to U.S.-UN policy.

We explored the multilateral dimensions of future international economic policy in chapter 6. The agenda for the United States seems relatively clear, though parts of it will be exceedingly difficult to achieve. One direction consists of strengthening or extending the rules of the World Trade Organization in services, intellectual property, agriculture, and competition policy—all in a context where point-of-entry measures have lost their effectiveness and competition is fierce. The other concerns the even more problematic issue of coming to grips with the forces of globalization. Here, large segments of the American public and its leaders alike are trapped by their own ideological predispositions, which make it difficult for them to see the contradiction between espousing an increasingly neo-laissez-faire-attitude toward government and the desire to safeguard the nation from the adverse effects of increasingly denationalized economic forces. What is needed is a new "embedded liberalism" compromise, a radically new formula for combining the twin desires of international and domestic stability, one that is appropriate for an international context in which the organization of production and exchange has become globally integrated, and a domestic context in which past modalities of state intervention lack efficacy and often legitimacy.

Finally, a foreign-policy agenda premised on multilateral world order principles is inherently better equipped to deal with certain milieu goals that are assuming a central place in the hierarchy of human concerns, but which we have been unable to take up in the present study. Global environmental change is the most pressing of these in the decades ahead.

Considering the complex of conceptual, ideological, political, and practical challenges in constructing the overall contours of U.S. foreign policy without a Soviet threat, it is small wonder that FDR, in his last State of the Union message, warned against perfectionism above all else. Insisting on perfect solutions after the previous war, he reminded Congress, America gave up on the good and the possible, and in the end got none. In words that Congress would do well to heed again today, Roosevelt urged: "We must not let that happen again."

Notes

Introduction

1. Quoted in Robert A. Divine, *Second Chance: The Triumph of Inter-nationalism in America During World War II* (New York: Atheneum, 1967), p. 47.

2. Quoted in David McCullough, *Truman* (New York: Simon and Schuster, 1992), p. 920.

3. For a discussion of "resurgent Wilsonianism" at cold war's end, see Tony Smith, *America's Mission: The United States and the Worldwide Struggle for Democracy in the Twentieth Century* (Princeton: Princeton University Press, 1994), chap. 11; also see Robert W. Tucker, "The Triumph of Wilsonianism?" *World Policy Journal*, 10 (Winter 1993/94).

4. "'A New Security—Built on Integration,' Excerpts from President Clinton's public address in Brussels at the time of the NATO summit," as reprinted in the *Washington Post*, January 10, 1994, p. A11.

5. See, for example, Anthony Lake, Assistant to the President for National Security Affairs, "The Price of Leadership," Address to the National Press Club, Washington, D.C., April 27, 1995; and Arthur Schlesinger, Jr., "Back to the Womb? Isolationism's Renewed Threat," *Foreign Affairs*, 74 (July/August 1995).

6. See Mark Z. Barabak, "GOP capitalizes on fear of U.S. troops under U.N. command," *San Diego Union-Tribune*, April 1, 1995, p. A23. According to Barbara Crossette, *New York Times*, July 9, 1995, p. D1, "not a single elected Republican, including Gov. Pete Wilson of California," attended the fiftieth anniversary celebration of the signing of the UN charter held in San Francisco.

7. The bills in question are H.R. 7 in the House and S. 5 in the Senate, setting stringent requirements for prior Congressional approval of U.S. participation in UN missions, limiting the discretion of the president to place U.S. troops under multinational control, and reducing U.S. financial contributions to peacekeeping. (See United Nations Association of the United States of America [UNA-USA], *Washington Weekly Report*, February 3, 1995, and February 24, 1995). President Clinton vowed to veto the legislation on the grounds that it contravenes the constitutional prerogatives of the president as commander-in-chief of the armed forces. As of the time of writing, the issue remains unresolved.

8. In Senate debates of the State Department's authorization bill during the summer of 1995, Senator John Kerry (D-MA) noted: "We are going from $36.8 billion in 1985 to $14.6 billion in the year 2002, and we are somehow going to pretend that we are going to represent the domestic interests of the United States abroad with that budget while simultaneously . . . being the leader of the free world. I do not think it makes sense." Quoted in UNA-USA, *Washington Weekly Report*, August 7, 1995, p. 3.

9. See, for example, "Pat Buchanan's happy days," *The Economist*, September 9, 1995, p. 37; and Robert Kuttner, "Look Who Wants to Tinker with Market Forces," *Business Week*, October 2, 1995, p. 26.

10. Henry A. Kissinger, *Diplomacy* (New York: Simon and Schuster, 1994).

11. A recent example is Ronald Steel, *Temptations of a Superpower* (Cambridge: Harvard University Press, 1995).

12. Quoted in John Milton Cooper, *The Warrior and the Priest: Woodrow Wilson and Theodore Roosevelt* (Cambridge: Harvard University Press, 1983), p. 286.

13. Kissinger, *Diplomacy*, pp. 833–835; citation on p. 835.

14. David Fromkin, *In the Time of the Americans: The Generation That Changed America's Role in the World* (New York: Knopf, 1995), p. 7.

15. Steel, *Temptations of a Superpower*, p. 120.

16. Fromkin, *In the Time of the Americans*, quoting the subtitle.

1. An American Dilemma

1. Ed Gillespie and Bob Schellhas, eds., *Contract with America* (New York: Times Books), p. 109.

2. Mark Z. Barabak, "GOP capitalizes on fear of U.S. troops under U.N. command," *San Diego Union-Tribune*, April 1, 1995, p. A23.

3. Quoted in United Nations Association of the United States of America, *Washington Weekly Report*, May 15, 1995, p. 3.

4. "Current United Nations Peace Operations & U.S. Troop Levels," Project on Peacekeeping and the United Nations, Council for a Livable World Education Fund (Washington, D.C., May 31, 1995), with data compiled from U.S. Department of Defense, Department of State, and United Nations.

5. Barabak, "GOP capitalizes," p. A23, quoting pollster Glen Bolger. The public may have recalled televised images of an American soldier's dead body being dragged through the streets of Mogadishu on October 3, 1993, after his contingent of Army Rangers was ambushed while hunting for clan leader Mohamed Farah Aidid. But the Rangers in Somalia were under the direct command and control of U.S. Special Operations Command in Tampa, Florida, entirely bypassing and not even coordinated with the UN's Somalia command structure—which was the main reason it took so long for Pakistani and Malaysian troops to come to their assistance. Washington insiders knew that, yet President Clinton blamed the operation's failure on the UN; already anti-UN Republicans can hardly have been expected to do otherwise.

6. As, for example, in the address by Anthony Lake, Assistant to the President for National Security Affairs, "The Price of Leadership," National Press Club, Washington, D.C., April 27, 1995, which was particularly harsh on what it called back-door isolationists: "Under the cover of budget-cutting, they threaten to cut the legs out from under America's leadership."

7. The major protagonists are fully aware of this fact but choose to vie for the more emotive "internationalist" label. See Lake, "The Price of Leadership," and Bob Dole, "Who's an Isolationist?" *New York Times*, June 6, 1995, p. A25.

8. Robert O. Keohane, "Associative American Development, 1776–1860," in John Gerard Ruggie, ed., *The Antinomies of Interdependence: National Welfare and the International Division of Labor* (New York: Columbia University Press, 1983), p. 90.

9. Quoted in Walter LaFeber, *The American Age: United States Foreign Policy at Home and Abroad Since 1750* (New York: Norton, 1989), p. 80.

10. Felix Gilbert, *To the Farewell Address: Ideas of Early American Foreign Policy* (Princeton: Princeton University Press, 1961).

11. Quoted in David Fromkin, *In the Time of the Americans: The Generation That Changed America's Role in the World* (New York: Knopf, 1995), p. 23.

12. Quoted in Robert Dallek, *The American Style of Foreign Policy* (New York: Oxford University Press, 1983), pp. 34–35.

13. Fromkin, *In the Time of the Americans*, p. 12.

14. Dallek, *The American Style of Foreign Policy*, p. 35.

15. John M. Cooper, Jr., *The Warrior and the Priest: Woodrow Wilson and Theodore Roosevelt* (Cambridge: Harvard University Press, 1983).

16. Ibid., especially chaps. 17 and 18; also see Tony Smith, *America's Mission: The United States and the Worldwide Struggle for Democracy* (Princeton: Princeton University Press, 1994), chap. 4.

17. Quoted in Dallek, *The American Style of Foreign Policy*, p. 56.

18. Cooper, *The Warrior and the Priest*, p. 281.

19. Quoted in Thomas J. Knock, *To End All Wars: Woodrow Wilson and the Quest for a New World Order* (New York: Oxford University Press, 1992), p. 97.

20. Ibid. p. 112.

21. Ibid., pp. 121–122.

22. Ibid., p. 149, emphases in original.

23. Ibid., p. 207.

24. "Peace without Victory" address, as quoted in Lloyd E. Ambrosius, *Wilsonian Statecraft: Theory and Practice of Liberal Internationalism during World War I* (Wilmington, Del.: Scholarly Resources, 1991), p. 80.

25. Knock points out that conservative internationalists "made up the largest and, generally speaking, the most influential segment of the broad American league movement." *To End All Wars*, p. 55. They felt that unconditional German surrender was essential to postwar peace, whereas Wilson wished to avoid humiliating Germany; they saw no wrong in empires, which Wilson sought to dismantle; and they rejected any diminution in American military might that might be entailed in Wilson's arms reduction plans.

26. Lawrence E. Gelfand, "The Mystique of Wilsonian Statecraft," *Diplomatic History*, 7 (Spring 1983), p. 89.

27. Quoted in Knock, *To End All Wars*, p. 254.

28. Ibid., p. 229.

29. Fromkin, *In the Time of the Americans*, p. 17.

30. *Report on Reciprocity and Commercial Treaties*, as quoted by William Diebold, Jr., "The History and the Issues," in Diebold, ed., *Bilateralism, Multilateralism and Canada in U.S. Trade Policy* (Cambridge: Ballinger, for the Council on Foreign Relations, 1988), pp. 3–4.

31. Henry Kissinger, in *Diplomacy* (New York: Simon and Schuster, 1994), chap. 2, describes Roosevelt and Wilson in these terms, and calls them the "hinges" of American foreign policy in the twentieth century.

32. Cooper, *The Warrior and the Priest*, p. xiv.

33. Knock, *To End All Wars*, pp. 258–267.

34. Lloyd E. Ambrosius, *Woodrow Wilson and the American Diplomatic Tradition* (New York: Cambridge University Press, 1987), p. 208. Ambrosius offers the only rational explanation for Wilson's uncompromising stance by speculating that Democratic Senators would have wanted to introduce reservations of their own had he not insisted on trying to defeat all reservations. Most accounts also refer to Wilson's deteriorated state of physical and possibly mental health—he suffered a debilitating stroke just as the treaty fight was getting underway—coupled with the fact that, other than Colonel House, with whom he had since had a falling out, Wilson never delegated responsibility for foreign policy to any person or team.

35. Indeed, Knock believes that the primary reason for Lodge's actions is to be found in domestic politics. Seen from a Republican vantage, control of the Senate "was as slim as could be, perhaps ephemeral. What would become of the party—indeed, of the country—if Wilson got his League, if the Democrats could boast of 'the greatest constructive world reform in history'?" *To End All Wars*, p. 240, quoting from a letter by former Republican Senator Albert J. Beveridge to Lodge.

36. Dallek, *The American Style of Foreign Policy*, p. 91.

37. Manfred Jonas, *Isolationism in America* (Ithaca, N.Y.: Cornell University Press, 1966).

38. Quoted in ibid., p. 7.

39. Ibid., p. 5.

40. Quoted in Dallek, *The American Style of Foreign Policy*, p. 117.

41. Jonas, *Isolationism in America*, p. 27.

42. Dallek, *The American Style of Foreign Policy*, p. 122.

43. Ibid., p. 113.

44. Charles P. Kindleberger, *The World in Depression, 1929–1939* (Berkeley: University of California Press, 1973).

45. Jonas, *Isolationism in America*, chap. 6.

46. Ibid., p. 49. Ever since the publication of E. H. Carr's classic critique of liberal internationalism during the interwar period, realists have attributed such acts of idealist foolishness to the Wilsonian legacy. The irony is striking, for Borah had been a leading "irreconcilable" in 1919, forming what he called a "Battalion of Death" to prevent ratification of the League's covenant. See Edward Hallett Carr, *The Twenty Years' Crisis, 1919–1939* (New York: Harper [1939] 1964).

47. This discussion draws heavily on Jonas's excellent analysis in *Isolationism in America*.

48. Ibid., p. 259.

49. See Fromkin, *In the Time of the Americans*, for a lively anecdotal discussion of their respective relationships.

50. Quoted in Warren F. Kimball, *The Juggler: Franklin Roosevelt as Wartime Statman* (Princeton: Princeton University Press, 1991), p. 96.

51. For a more technical treatment of the issues covered in this section, see John Gerard Ruggie, "Multilateralism: The Anatomy of an Institution," in Ruggie, ed., *Multilateralism Matters: The Theory and Praxis of an Institutional Form* (New York: Columbia University Press, 1993).

52. On Hull, see Diebold, "The History of the Issues," pp. 7–11; and on Schacht, Albert O. Hirschman, *National Power and the Structure of Foreign Trade* (Berkeley: University of California Press, 1945).

53. Kimball, *The Juggler*, p. 104.

54. Arthur Salter, *Security* (London: Macmillan, 1939), p. 155; emphasis in original.

55. The institutional difference between bilateral alliances and collective security schemes can be put schematically: in both instances, state A is pledged to come to the aid of state B if B is attacked by C. In a collective security scheme, however, A is also pledged to come to the aid of C if C is attacked by B. Consequently, as Hudson points out, "A cannot regard itself as the ally of B more than of C because theoretically it is an open question whether, if an act of war should occur, B or C would be the aggressor. In the same way B has indeterminate obligations toward A and C, and C towards A and B, and so on with

a vast number of variants as the system is extended to more and more states."
G. F. Hudson, "Collective Security and Military Alliances," in Herbert But-
terfield and Martin Wight, eds., *Diplomatic Investigations* (Cambridge: Harvard University Press, 1968), pp. 176–177.

56. Quoted in Knock, *To End All Wars*, p. 149

57. Madeleine K. Albright, on the MacNeil-Lehrer Newshour, August 30, 1993.

58. See Kissinger, *Diplomacy*, especially chaps. 1, 2, and 3.

59. George F. Kennan, *American Diplomacy, 1900–1950* (Chicago: University of
Chicago Press, 1951), especially p. 95ff.

60. Quoted in Hans Gerth and C. Wright Mills, eds., *From Max Weber* (New
York: Oxford University Press, 1946), p. 280.

61. Kenneth N. Waltz, *Theory of International Politics* (Reading, Mass.: Addison-
Wesley, 1979), p. 200.

62. See, for example, Ambrosius, *Woodrow Wilson and the American Diplomatic
Tradition*, and *Wilsonian Statecraft*.

63. For example, Knock, *To End All Wars*.

64. On the economic side, see Michael J. Hogan, "Revival and Reform: America's
Twentieth-Century Search for a New Economic Order Abroad," *Diplomatic
History*, 8 (Fall 1984); and on the administrative/legal dimension, Anne-
Marie Burley, "Regulating the World: Multilateralism, International Law, and
the Projection of the New Deal Regulatory State," in Ruggie, ed., *Multilater-
alism Matters*.

65. See Jeff Frieden, "Sectoral Conflicts and U.S. Foreign Economic Policy,
1914–1940," *International Organization*, 42 (Winter 1988).

66. Tracy B. Strong, "Taking the Rank with What Is Ours: American Political
Thought, Foreign Policy, and Questions of Rights," in Paula R. Newberg, ed.,
The Politics of Human Rights (New York: New York University Press, 1980), p.
34. Also see the classic study by Louis Hartz, *The Liberal Tradition in America*
(New York: Harcourt, Brace, 1955).

67. David Rieff, "A Global Culture?" *World Policy Journal*, 10 (Winter 1993/94),
p. 78.

68. Quoted by Strong, "Taking the Rank with What Is Ours," p. 50.

69. Ibid., p. 50. Animated by antipathy to similar notions held by leaders of the
French Revolution, the conservative philosopher Joseph de Maistre wrote:
"No assembly of men can constitute a nation. An attempt of this kind ought
even to be ranked among the most memorable acts of folly." Quoted in Alain
Finkielkraut, *The Defeat of the Mind*, trans. Judith Friedlander (New York:
Columbia University Press, 1995), p. 13. Yet that is precisely how America
constituted itself as a nation.

70. Peter F. Cowhey, "Elect Locally—Order Globally: Domestic Politics and Multilateral Cooperation," in Ruggie, ed., *Multilateralism Matters*, p. 169.

71. Reported by Fromkin, *In the Time of the Americans*, p. 118.

72. See Dallek, *The American Style of Foreign Policy*, chap. 4.

73. Edward Hallett Carr, *The Bolshevik Revolution*, vol. 3 (New York: Macmillan, 1953), pp. 123–125. Arno J. Mayer goes too far, however, in reading 1919 through the lenses of post-1945 cold war politics when he claims that "the allies drafted the charters of the International Labor Organization and the League of Nations with a view to immunizing the non-Bolshevik Left against the bacillus of the Bolshevik Revolution." See his *Politics and Diplomacy of Peacemaking: Containment and Counterrevolution at Versailles, 1918–1919* (New York: Knopf, 1967), p. 9. Knock, *To End All Wars*, notes that "the Bolsheviks played a primary role only insofar as the timing of the Fourteen Points was concerned" (p. 145), not in regard to their substance.

74. The new standard work on the Soviet threat in the early postwar years, and U.S. perceptions of it, is Melvyn P. Leffler, *A Preponderance of Power: National Security, the Truman Administration, and the Cold War* (Stanford: Stanford University Press, 1992).

75. Quoted in David McCullough, *Truman* (New York: Simon and Schuster, 1992), p. 549.

76. "Gorbachev at Stanford: Excerpts from Address," *New York Times*, June 5, 1990, p. A6. The related passages in Wilson's 1917 speech read: "I am proposing . . . that all nations henceforth avoid entangling alliances which would draw them into competitions of power, catch them in a net of intrigue and selfish rivalry, and disturb their own affairs with influences intruded from without. . . . When all unite to act in the same sense and with the same purpose all act in the common interest and are free to live their own lives under a common protection." Quoted in Ambrosius, *Wilsonian Statecraft*, p. 80.

2. The Postwar Compromises

1. Robert A. Divine, *Second Chance: The Triumph of Internationalism in America During World War II* (New York: Atheneum, 1967), chap. 5.

2. Quoted in David McCullough, *Truman* (New York: Simon and Schuster, 1992), p. 316.

3. Ibid., p. 402.

4. See Warren F. Kimball, *The Juggler: Franklin Roosevelt as Wartime Statesman* (Princeton: Princeton University Press, 1991).

5. Robert C. Hilderbrand, *Dumbarton Oaks: The Origins of the United Nations and the Search for Postwar Security* (Chapel Hill: University of North Carolina Press, 1990), p. 1.

6. Robert Dallek, *The American Style of Foreign Policy* (New York: Oxford University Press, 1983), p. 124.

7. William T. R. Fox, *The Super-Powers: The United States, Britain, and The Soviet Union* (New York: Harcourt, 1944).

8. William C. Widenor, "American Planning for the United Nations: Have We Been Asking the Right Questions?" *Diplomatic History*, 6 (Spring 1982).

9. Hilderbrand, *Dumbarton Oaks*, p. 7.

10. Quoted in Divine, *Second Chance*, p. 61.

11. Kimball, *The Juggler*, p. 96; also see Robert Dallek, *Franklin D. Roosevelt and American Foreign Policy, 1932–1945* (New York: Oxford University Press, 1979), pp. 434–435; 439; 508.

12. For a time, Roosevelt entertained the notion of a three-tiered UN: an executive committee of the four; an advisory council of an additional six or eight representatives; and an assembly. From British Foreign Secretary Anthony Eden's report to Churchill on a conversation with Roosevelt in March 1943, as cited in Kimball, *The Juggler*, p. 86.

13. John Lewis Gaddis, *Strategies of Containment* (New York: Oxford University Press, 1982, p. 9.

14. Widenor, "American Planning for the United Nations," p. 251.

15. Quoted in Hilderbrand, *Dumbarton Oaks*, p. 65.

16. Hans Kelsen, *The Law of the United Nations* (New York: Praeger, 1951), pp. 756–761. Technically, Article 106 is still in force.

17. Quoted in Hilderbrand, *Dumbarton Oaks*, p. 122.

18. Kimball, *The Juggler*, p. 127. According to Tony Smith, "the best the Americans were willing to allow the Europeans was an orderly retreat from empire." Smith, *America's Mission: The United States and the Worldwide Struggle for Democracy in the Twentieth Century* (Princeton: Princeton University Press, 1994), p. 126. Also see Hilderbrand, *Dumbarton Oaks*, pp. 170–181.

19. Dallek, *FDR and American Foreign Policy*, p. 513, emphasis added.

20. *Complete Presidential Press Conferences of Franklin D. Roosevelt*, vol. 24, (New York: De Capo Press, 1972), p. 183.

21. A concert of power, such as prevailed in Europe following the Napoleonic wars, has been defined as "a scheme for the continuous management of the international system by the great powers." Richard Langhorne, "Reflections on the Significance of the Congress of Vienna," *Review of International Studies*, 12 (October 1986), p. 317. It differs from conventional balance-of-power politics by virtue of the fact that the great powers act in concert rather than rivalry. Kimball discusses the connections between Roosevelt's thinking and the post-1815 concert: *The Juggler*, p. 103.

22. As a sign suggesting that this may well have been a conscious effort on Roosevelt's part, consider the foreign policy team he put in place after the 1940 election. At the State Department, both Secretary Hull and Under Secretary Sumner Welles were Wilsonian Democrats. At the War Department, "[t]he secretaries of the armed forces were TR Republicans; indeed, the new navy secretary . . . had been one of TR's Rough Riders . . . The new Vice President was from TR's faction of the Republican party, the Progressives, as was William Donovan, who was about to head the forerunner of the CIA." David Fromkin, *In the Time of the Americans: The Generation that Changed America's Role in the World* (New York: Knopf, 1995), pp. 410, 420, 428.

23. Freshman Senator J. William Fulbright took to the Senate floor only days after charter ratification to lament this flaw in Roosevelt's design. Randall Bennett Woods, "Internationalism Stillborn," *Diplomatic History*, 16 (Fall 1992), p. 611, notes the episode and agrees with Fulbright's assessment.

24. Divine, *Second Chance*, p. 251.

25. In 1942, the Republicans had their best showing since the 1920s, coming very close to taking control of the House, and all but 5 of 115 members with isolationist voting records were reelected. Ibid, p. 73. Roosevelt also faced a challenge from a small but highly vocal constituency of liberal internationalists who, he felt, might constitute the swing voting bloc in 1944.

26. See Divine, *Second Chance, passim*; and Philip A. Grant, Jr., "Roosevelt, the Congress, and the United Nations," *Presidential Studies Quarterly*, 13 (Spring 1983).

27. Divine, *Second Chance*, p. 208.

28. Ibid, p. 251.

29. *The State of the Union Messages of the Presidents*, vol. 3 (New York: Chelsea House-Hector, 1966), pp. 2891–92.

30. Kelsen, *The Law of the United Nations*, p. 755. This provision was part of the U.S.-UN participation act and remained unchallenged until 1994, when the Republicans' "Contract With America" vowed to repeal it.

31. Smith, *America's Mission*, p. 103.

32. Quoted in Hilderbrand, *Dumbarton Oaks*, p. 250.

33. For a sampling, see Smith, *America's Mission*, pp. 103–105. This avalanche of criticism was started by the British scholar E. H. Carr, in his influential work, *The Twenty Years' Crisis, 1919–1939* (New York: Harper [1939] 1964). American realists, like Carr, failed to differentiate the internationalist and isolationist strands of idealism, and they pinned both on an ideological construct they termed Wilsonianism.

34. Quoted in Robert A. Pollard, *Economic Security and the Origins of the Cold War* (New York: Columbia University Press, 1985), p. 2.

35. Quoted in Thomas G. Paterson, *Meeting the Communist Threat: Truman to Reagan* (New York: Oxford University Press, 1988), p. 21.

36. The classic, and appropriately titled, study of the Nazi trade regime is Albert O. Hirschman, *National Power and the Structure of Foreign Trade* (Berkeley: University of California Press, 1945). Several major states, including Great Britain and the United States, had limited *Sondermark* agreements with Germany—marks that foreigners could earn through the sale of prescribed products to Germany but which Germany in turn restricted to prescribed purchases from Germany. See Leland B. Yeager, *International Monetary Relations: Theory, History, and Policy* (New York: Harper & Row, 1976), chap. 18.

37. Pollard, *Economic Security*, p. 168.

38. They are discussed in Herbert Feis, "The Conflict Over Trade Ideologies," *Foreign Affairs*, 25 (July 1947), and Raymond Mikesell, "The Role of the

International Monetary Agreements in a World of Planned Economies," *Journal of Political Economy*, 55 (December 1947).

39. See Harold James and Marzenna James, "The Origins of the Cold War: Some New Documents," *The Historical Journal*, 37 (September 1994), pp. 615–622. Based on recently opened Soviet archival material, the Jameses suggest that Soviet bureaucrats were ready to sign on to Bretton Woods until the issue was taken to Stalin for approval.

40. See Richard N. Gardner, *Sterling-Dollar Diplomacy in Current Perspective* (New York: Columbia University Press, 1980). chap. 1.

41. In that classical system, balance-of-payments deficits were supposed to result in domestic monetary contraction, and thus in a slowdown of domestic economic activity, and surpluses in a corresponding expansion. In that sense, the domestic economy was subordinated to the desire to maintain external balance.

42. In the 1942 draft of the plan, as quoted by G. John Ikenberry, "A World Economy Restored: Expert Consensus and the Anglo-American Settlement," *International Organization*, 46 (Winter 1992), p. 298.

43. Jacob Viner, "Conflicts of Principle in Drafting a Trade Charter," *Foreign Affairs*, 25, No. 2 (January 1947), p. 613. Hull, the administration's most ardent free trader, was an exception to this heterodoxy. However, by the time the trade negotiations got seriously under way, Hull had already retired.

44. Stephan Haggard, "The Institutional Foundations of Hegemony: Explaining the Reciprocal Trade Agreements Act of 1934," in G. John Ikenberry, David A. Lake, and Michael Mastanduno, eds., *The State and American Foreign Economic Policy* (Ithaca: Cornell University Press, 1988), p. 102.

45. John Gerard Ruggie, "International Regimes, Transactions, and Change: Embedded Liberalism in the Postwar Economic Order," *International Organization*, 36 (Spring 1982). The historian of the Marshall Plan, Michael J. Hogan, has argued similarly that U.S. postwar planners "married Hull's free-trade dictums to the new theories of economic regulation and countercyclical stabilization." Hogan, "One World Into Two: American Economic Diplomacy from Bretton Woods to the Marshall Plan," Ohio State University, unpublished paper, n.d., p. 7.

46. Richard N. Cooper, "Prolegomena to the Choice of an International Monetary System," *International Organization*, 29 (Winter 1975), p. 85.

47. The classic account remains William Diebold, Jr., "The End of the ITO," *Princeton Essays in International Finance*, 16 (October 1952). Among the most important issues excluded, thereby, were the regulation of commodity markets, restrictive business practices, and international investments.

48. Exceptions were allowed for existing preferential agreements (a U.S. concession to Britain), and countries were permitted to form customs unions and free trade areas (U.S. encouragement to Western Europe). The relevance of both exceptions was expected to decrease as overall tariffs declined.

49. Dallek, *The American Style of Foreign Policy*, p. 157.

50. Quoted in John Lewis Gaddis, *The Long Peace* (New York: Oxford University Press, 1987), p. 58; the quotation marks are Kennan's.

51. All quotations are from Dean Acheson, *Present at the Creation* (New York: Norton, 1969), p. 219.

52. Emily R. Rosenberg, "The Cold War and the Discourse of National Security," *Diplomatic History*, 17 (Spring 1993).

53. See, among many other sources, John Gimbel, *The Origins of the Marshall Plan* (Stanford: Stanford University Press, 1976), and Michael J. Hogan, *The Marshall Plan* (New York: Cambridge University Press, 1987). For an account that is critical of U.S. motives and which discounts the effects of U.S. aid, see Alan S. Milward, *The Reconstruction of Western Europe, 1945–1951* (Berkeley and Los Angeles: University of California Press, 1984), and "Was the Marshall Plan Necessary?" *Diplomatic History*, 13 (Spring 1989).

54. In 1960, after the global economic regimes had begun to function fully, the OEEC was transformed into the OECD—Organization for Economic Cooperation and Development—of which Japan also became a member.

55. U.S. Congress, *Congressional Record*, 80th Congress, 1st Session, 1947, pp. 2418–2422; and Hogan, *The Marshall Plan*, p. 39.

56. Pollard, *Economic Security*, chaps. 1, 2, and 4.

57. See the discussions in Lawrence S. Kaplan, "An Unequal Triad: The United States, Western Union, and NATO," in Olav Riste, ed., *Western Security: The Formative Years* (Oslo: Universitetsforlaget, 1985); Martin H. Folly, "Breaking the Vicious Circle: Britain, the United States, and the Genesis of the North Atlantic Treaty," *Diplomatic History*, 12 (Winter 1988); and Steve Weber, "Shaping the Postwar Balance of Power: Multilateralism in NATO," in John Gerard Ruggie, ed., *Multilateralism Matters* (New York: Columbia University Press, 1993).

58. Michael Howard, "Introduction," in Riste, *Western Security*, p. 14.

59. The most recent comprehensive study of the nature of that threat is by Melvyn P. Leffler, *A Preponderance of Power: National Security, the Truman Administration, and the Cold War* (Stanford: Stanford University Press, 1992).

60. See Anders Stephanson, *Kennan and the Art of Foreign Policy* (Cambridge: Harvard University Press, 1989), p. 140; David Mayers, *George Kennan and the Dilemmas of US Foreign Policy* (New York: Oxford University Press, 1988), pp. 152–155; and Geir Lundestad, *America, Scandinavia, and the Cold War, 1945–1949* (New York: Columbia University Press, 1980), pp. 172–173, 188–189. In his memoirs, Kennan recalled that he had favored a dumbbell arrangement, but one in which the two sides of the Atlantic would be linked, not by a treaty, but merely by a U.S.-Canadian guarantee of assistance in case of Soviet attack. George F. Kennan, *Memoirs: 1925–1950* (Boston: Little, Brown, 1967), pp. 406–407.

61. Walter Issacson and Evan Thomas, *The Wise Men* (New York: Simon &

Schuster, 1986), pp. 449–450. The authors report that Lovett found Kennan too indecisive, too much of an egghead, and "too damn esoteric."

62. Article 51 had not been drafted with a future NATO in mind. It was a response to extreme agitation by the Latin American countries at San Francisco once they realized that the Security Council veto would enable the United States to block any proposed UN action in response to U.S. intervention in the Western hemisphere. They wanted a charter provision permitting the creation of a hemispheric security organization that was beyond the reach of the U.S. veto. The Latins not only comprised a sizable voting bloc in their own right but also had allies in the Arab world, the British Commonwealth, and among some West European states. To avoid a potentially serious rift, Vandenberg and Gladwyn Jebb of the British delegation drafted the clause that proclaimed the "inherent right of self-defense, either individual or collective," which ultimately became Article 51. See J. Tillapaugh, "Closed Hemisphere and Open World? The Dispute Over Regional Security at the U.N. Conference, 1945," *Diplomatic History*, 2 (Winter 1978).

63. Daryl J. Hudson, "Vandenberg Reconsidered: Senate Resolution 239 and American Foreign Policy," *Diplomatic History*, 1 (Winter 1977), p. 63. Vandenberg, in Kaplan's words, "had been converted to internationalism on the strength of the United Nations providing collective security for all." Lawrence S. Kaplan, *NATO and the United States: The Enduring Alliance* (Boston: Twayne Publishers, 1988), p. 36.

64. Kaplan, "Unequal Triad," p. 112.

65. Folly, "Breaking the Vicious Circle," p. 68.

66. McCullough, *Truman*, p. 735. The Inter-American Treaty of Reciprocal Assistance (Rio Pact), concluded in 1947, in some respects was a forerunner of the North Atlantic Treaty, though both motivation and circumstances were entirely different. The Rio conference was held to take up Latin America's desire for a hemispheric security organization in which the United States could not veto measures the Latin American countries might want to adopt in response to U.S. intervention there (see note 62, above). Under the Rio Pact, a two-thirds majority in the Council of the Organization of American States was empowered to determine collective measures. Roger R. Trask, "The Impact of the Cold War on United States-Latin American Relations, 1945–1949," *Diplomatic History*, 1 (Summer 1977), pp. 277–279.

67. Quoted in Folly, "Breaking the Vicious Circle," p. 67.

68. Howard, "Introduction," p. 16.

69. Article 16 of the covenant made diplomatic and economic sanctions automatic upon a state's being declared an aggressor, but not military action, which remained discretionary. NATO commitments concern only the realm of military responses.

70. Arnold Wolfers, "Collective Defense Versus Collective Security," in Wolfers, *Discord and Collaboration* (Baltimore: Johns Hopkins University Press, 1962).

71. Wolfers's distinction became paradigmatic for the security studies field, treating NATO as a traditional alliance, militarily more integrated than previous alliances but "multilateral" only in the sense of (ultimately) having sixteen members, not by virtue of any principled differences. But Wolfers's analysis was not without problems. While insisting that NATO was simply a multimember alliance Wolfers called the 1945 Act of Chapultepec, which led to the Rio Pact, "not . . . an alliance but . . . a regionally circumscribed system of collective security for the Americas." Ibid., p. 190. Oddly, the core concept of Chapultapec—that an attack on one is an attack against all, calling for a collective response—is identical to the North Atlantic Treaty, but Wolfers did not bother to explain the anomaly. Ernest May intuits the difference between NATO and a traditional alliance but, lacking a vocabulary to describe it, he gropes too far afield for a metaphor. Under the North Atlantic Treaty, May contends, the United States and its major European allies "had become, at least temporarily, part of an organic federal system." Ernest R. May, "The American Commitment to Germany, 1949–55," Diplomatic History, 13 (Fall 1989), p. 459.

72. Kaplan, NATO and the United States, p. 37.

73. Robert A. Taft, A Foreign Policy for Americans (Garden City, N.Y.: Doubleday, 1951), pp. 88–89. Initially, the North Atlantic Treaty was in force for twenty years.

74. Kaplan, NATO and the United States, p. 37.

75. Walter LaFeber, "NATO and the Korean War," Diplomatic History, 13 (Fall 1989), p. 474.

76. Pollard, Economic Security, affords an excellent comparison of U.S. policy in Western Europe and East Asia. See also Marc S. Gallicchio, The Cold War Begins in Asia (New York: Columbia University Press, 1988); Nancy Bernkopf Tucker, Patterns in the Dust: Chinese-American Relations and the Recognition Controversy, 1949–1950 (New York: Columbia University Press, 1983), chap. 1; and Bruce Cumings, ed., Child of Conflict: The Korean-American Relationship, 1943–1953 (Seattle: University of Washington Press, 1983).

77. Cited in Pollard, Economic Security, p. 176.

78. The American classic in this genre was William Appleman Williams, The Tragedy of American Diplomacy (Cleveland: World, 1959). For a full bibliography, see Geir Lundestad, The American "Empire" (Oxford: Oxford University Press, 1990).

79. The essay is included in Lundestad, The American "Empire."

80. George F. Kennan, "Mr. Hippisley and the Open Door," in Kennan, American Foreign Policy, 1900–1950 (Chicago: University of Chicago Press, 1951).

81. Tony Smith, The Pattern of Imperialism: The United States, Great Britain, and the Late-Industrializing World Since 1815 (New York: Cambridge University Press, 1981), pp. 145–146.

82. Fromkin, In the Time of the Americans, p. 540.

83. The terms "diffuse" and "specific" reciprocity are due to Robert O. Keohane, "Reciprocity in International Relations," *International Organization*, 40 (Winter 1985).

84. Ronald Dworkin, *Law's Empire* (Cambridge: Harvard University Press, 1986), p. 413.

3. Competitive Security

1. Theodore H. White, *In Search of History: A Personal Adventure* (New York: Harper, 1978), p. 224.

2. Robert Jervis, "The Military History of the Cold War," *Diplomatic History*, 15 (Winter 1991), p. 112.

3. John Lewis Gaddis, *The Long Peace* (New York: Oxford University Press, 1987).

4. David Fromkin, *In the Time of the Americans: The Generation That Changed America's Role in the World* (New York: Knopf, 1995), p. 372.

5. Unless otherwise noted, this discussion of the conference is based on Robert C. Hilderbrand, *Dumbarton Oaks: The Origins of the United Nations and the Search for Postwar Security* (Chapel Hill: University of North Carolina Press, 1990). Actual negotiations took place among the United States, Britain, and the Soviet Union, followed by consultations with China.

6. Ibid., p. 65.

7. See Perry McCoy Smith, *The Air Force Plans for Peace, 1943–1945* (Baltimore: Johns Hopkins University Press, 1970), esp. pp. 49–51.

8. Hilderbrand, *Dumbarton Oaks*, p. 142.

9. Ibid., pp. 149–151.

10. Hans Kelsen, *The Law of the United Nations* (New York: Praeger, 1951), p. 755.

11. See D. W. Bowett, *United Nations Forces: A Legal Study* (New York: Praeger, 1964), pp. 12–18.

12. See Daryl J. Hudson, "Vandenberg Reconsidered: Senate Resolution 239 and American Foreign Policy," *Diplomatic History*, 1 (Winter 1977), pp. 60–61.

13. Cited in William Stueck, "The Korean War as International History," *Diplomatic History*, 10 (Fall 1986), p. 297.

14. Denis Stairs, "The United Nations and the Politics of the Korean War," *International Journal*, 25 (Winter 1969–70), p. 308.

15. Taft feared, not unreasonably, that the measure at some future time could be used to circumvent the U.S. veto.

16. Stueck, "The Korean War as International History," p. 298; see also Joseph M. Siracusa and Glen St. John Barclay, "Australia, the United States, and the Cold War, 1945–51: From V-J Day to ANZUS," *Diplomatic History*, 5 (Winter 1981).

17. Dean Acheson, *Present at the Creation* (New York: Norton, 1969), p. 699; see also Stairs, "The United Nations and the Politics of the Korean War."

18. Melvyn P. Leffler, *A Preponderance of Power: National Security, the Truman Administration, and the Cold War* (Stanford: Stanford University Press, 1992).

19. Robert E. Osgood, *NATO: The Entangling Alliance* (Chicago: University of Chicago Press, 1962), p. 59.

20. This is the statutory language as quoted in ibid., p. 46, emphasis added.

21. Michael J. Hogan, *The Marshall Plan* (New York: Cambridge University Press, 1987), pp. 311–312.

22. The following discussion draws on Osgood, *NATO*; Lawrence S. Kaplan, *NATO and the United States: The Enduring Alliance* (Boston: Twayne Publishers, 1988); Brian R. Duchin, "The 'Agonizing Reappraisal': Eisenhower, Dulles, and the European Defense Community," *Diplomatic History*, 16 (Spring 1992); Ernest R. May, "The American Commitment to Germany, 1949–55," *Diplomatic History*, 13 (Fall 1989), and, in the same issue of that journal, Walter LaFeber, "NATO and the Korean War," and Geoffrey Warner, "The Anglo-American Special Relationship."

23. Warner, "Anglo-American Special Relationship," p. 495.

24. Cited in Duchin, "Agonizing Reappraisal," p. 202.

25. In an amendment to the Mutual Security Program appropriation for 1953–54, introduced by Representative James Richards of South Carolina. Osgood, *NATO*, p. 95; and Duchin, "Agonizing Reappraisal," p. 207.

26. Osgood, *NATO*, pp. 86, 92.

27. Ibid., pp. 96–97.

28. Ernst B. Haas, *The Uniting of Europe* (Stanford: Stanford University Press, 1958).

29. Jonathan E. Helmreich, "The United States and the Formation of EURATOM," *Diplomatic History*, 15 (Summer 1991), p. 409.

30. Dwight D. Eisenhower, *Waging Peace, 1956–61* (Garden City, NY.: Doubleday, 1965), p. 125.

31. John D. Steinbruner, *The Cybernetic Theory Decision* (Princeton: Princeton University Press, 1974), pp. 153–198.

32. Steve Weber, "Shaping the Postwar Balance of Power: Multilateralism in NATO," in John Gerard Ruggie, ed., *Multilateralism Matters* (New York: Columbia University Press, 1993), p. 258.

33. Quoted in John Lewis Gaddis, *Strategies of Containment* (New York: Oxford University Press, 1982), p. 150.

34. Quoted in Warner, "Anglo-American Special Relationship," p. 491. For a broader discussion of McNamara's strategic innovations, see Robert Jervis, *The Illogic of American Nuclear Strategy* (Ithaca: Cornell University Press, 1984), and Jervis, *The Meaning of the Nuclear Revolution* (Ithaca: Cornell University Press, 1989).

35. This is the story told by Steinbruner, *The Cybernetic Theory Decision*.

36. Fromkin, *In the Time of the Americans*, p. 7.

37. Quoted in Seyom Brown, *The Faces of Power* (New York: Columbia University Press, 1983), p. 81.

38. See Arthur J. Dommen, *Conflict in Laos* (New York: Praeger, 1965), pp. 194–195.

39. This summary draws on Donald Neff, *Warriors at Suez* (New York: Simon and Schuster, 1983), and Keith Kyle, *Suez* (London: Weidenfeld & Nicolson, 1991).

40. Neff, *Warriors at Suez*, p. 87, and *passim*.

41. Michael Graham Fry, "Decline, Sanctions, and the Suez Crisis, 1956–1957," *Diplomatic History*, 17 (Spring 1993), p. 326.

42. Quoted in Neff, *Warriors at Suez*, p. 365.

43. See Diane B. Kunz, *The Economic Diplomacy of the Suez Crisis* (Chapel Hill: University of North Carolina Press, 1991), chap. 6; France had borrowed enough before the crisis to withstand U.S. financial pressure.

44. Quoted in Warner, "Anglo-American Special Relationship," p. 486.

45. Quoted by Louise Richardson, "Avoiding and Incurring Losses: Decision-Making in the Suez Crisis," in Janice Gross Stein and Louis W. Pauly, eds., *Choosing to Cooperate: How States Avoid Loss* (Baltimore: Johns Hopkins University Press, 1993). Eisenhower might have been hard pressed to oppose the covert overthrow of Nasser, having authorized CIA-orchestrated coups in Iran and Guatemala, in 1953 and 1954 respectively.

46. See Lester B. Pearson, *Mike: The Memoirs of the Right Honourable Lester B. Pearson*, vol. 2: 1948–1957 (Toronto: University of Toronto Press, 1973), pp. 244–278. Pearson was awarded the Nobel Peace Prize for his efforts.

47. Thomas Hamilton, "Rift in West Big 3 Emerging at UN," *New York Times*, October 31, 1956, p. 16.

48. George F. Kennan, letter to the editor, *Washington Post*, November 3, 1956, p. A8.

49. Eisenhower exhibited little awareness of the textbook model of collective security that drove the realists to despair. He used the term to mean more generically cooperative, institutionalized approaches to dealing with security problems.

50. Hans J. Morgenthau, letter to the editor, *New York Times*, November 13, 1956, p. 36.

51. Wolfers felt that all was well in the end, however, because "Britain, France, and Israel gave in to the demand for reestablishing the *status quo ante* before any more compelling action than condemnation was recommended or taken." Arnold Wolfers, *Discord and Collaboration* (Baltimore: Johns Hopkins University Press, 1962), p. 198. Wolfers's account is factually wrong in ignoring the punishing economic sanctions the United States imposed on Britain as well as the denial of intelligence data to all three.

52. Brian Urquhart, "Thoughts on the Twentieth Anniversary of Dag Hammarskjold's Death," *Foreign Affairs*, 60 (Fall 1981), p. 6.

53. Quoted in Neff, *Warriors at Suez*, p. 388.

54. For a comprehensive survey of peacekeeping, see William J. Durch, ed., *The Evolution of UN Peacekeeping* (New York: St. Martin's Press, 1993).

55. Eisenhower, *Waging Peace*, p. 574. Unfortunately for the future welfare of the people of Zaire, the CIA also helped engineer the accession to power of Mobutu Sese Seko.

56. Ernst B. Haas, "Collective Conflict Management: Evidence for a New World Order?" in Thomas G. Weiss, ed., *Collective Security in a Changed World* (Boulder: Lynne Rienner, 1993), p. 63. It should be noted that Haas's assessment includes all collective security organizations, including regionals, and all institutional means to manage conflicts, not only peacekeeping.

57. See Richard W. Nelson, "Multinational Peacekeeping in the Middle East and the United Nations Model," *International Affairs*, 61 (Winter 1984/1985).

58. Daniel Patrick Moynihan, *A Dangerous Place* (Boston: Little, Brown, 1975).

59. Ernst B. Haas, *Why We Still Need the United Nations* (University of California, Berkeley: Institute of International Studies, Policy Papers in International Affairs, No. 26, 1986).

60. Haas, *Why We Still Need the United Nations*; also see Mark W. Zacher, *International Conflicts and Collective Security* (New York: Praeger, 1979); and Jonathan Wilkenfeld and Michael Brecher, "International Crises, 1945–1975," *International Studies Quarterly*, 28 (March 1984).

61. Arthur R. Day, "Conclusions: A Mix of Means," in Arthur R. Day and Michael W. Doyle, eds., *Escalation and Intervention: Multilateral Security and Its Alternatives* (Boulder: Westview, 1986), p. 154.

62. In 1985, the last General Assembly session prior to the UN's revival made possible by the tumultuous changes in the Soviet Union initiated by Mikhail Gorbachev, only 15 percent of the Assembly's resolutions on arms control concerned non-nuclear weapons, this despite the fact that some 80 cents of every one of the $1 trillion spent world-wide that year on arms was spent on conventional weapons. Of that fraction, only 6 of 26 resolutions addressed regional issues that most directly involved Third World countries. Calculated from *The United Nations Disarmament Yearbook* (New York: United Nations, 1986).

63. For an overview, see Lawrence Scheinman, *The International Atomic Energy Agency and World Nuclear Order* (Washington, D.C.: Resources for the Future, 1987).

64. The classic account is Barton J. Bernstein, "The Quest for Security: American Foreign Policy and International Control of Atomic Energy, 1942–1946," *Journal of American History*, 60 (March 1974). Also see See Larry G. Gerber, "The Baruch Plan and the Origins of the Cold War," *Diplomatic History*, 6 (Winter 1982); and McGeorge Bundy, *Danger and Survival: Choices About the Bomb in the First Fifty Years* (New York: Random House, 1988), chap. 4.

65. Bernstein, "The Quest for Security," p. 1004. Dean Acheson voiced the most

significant opposition to the Baruch plan within the Truman administration, arguing that the Russians would take it "as an attempt to turn the United Nations into an alliance to support a U.S. threat of war against the USSR unless it ceased its efforts" to develop its own atomic bomb. Quoted in Gerber, "The Baruch Plan," pp. 84–85.

66. Barton J. Bernstein, "Commentary: The Challenge of 'National Security'—A Skeptical View," *Diplomatic History*, 17 (Spring 1993). On the concept of security dilemmas, see Robert Jervis, "Cooperation Under the Security Dilemma," *World Politics*, 30 (January 1978).

67. Rodney W. Jones, Cesare Merlini, Joseph F. Pilat, and William C. Potter, eds., *The Nuclear Suppliers and Nonproliferation* (Lexington, Mass.: Lexington Books, 1985).

68. See John R. Redick, "The Tlatelolco Regime and Nonproliferation in Latin America," in George H. Quester, ed., *Nuclear Proliferation: Breaking the Chain* (Madison: University of Wisconsin Press, 1981).

69. For some serious thinking about what the world might look like without the NPT, see Joseph F. Pilat and Robert E. Pendley, eds., *Beyond 1995: The Future of the NPT Regime* (New York: Plenum, 1990).

70. For a recent rendition of this refrain, see Ted Galen Carpenter, "A New Proliferation Policy," *The National Interest*, 28 (Summer 1992).

71. Quoted in Osgood, *NATO*, p. 220.

72. See Mitchell Reiss, *Without the Bomb: The Politics of Nonproliferation* (New York: Columbia University Press, 1988), chap. 1; and Thomas W. Graham and A. F. Mullins, "Arms Control, Military Strategy, and Nuclear Proliferation," paper presented at the conference on "Nuclear Deterrence and Global Security in Transition," University of California, Institute on Global Conflict and Cooperation, La Jolla, Calif., February 21–23, 1991. Graham is a former official of the U.S. Arms Control and Disarmament Agency, while Mullins is a staff member of the Livermore nuclear laboratory.

73. Graham and Mullins, "Arms Control, Nuclear Strategy, and Nuclear Proliferation," p. 3.

74. The term is due to Leonard S. Spector, *The New Nuclear Nations* (New York: Vintage Books, 1985), chap. 2.

75. Lawrence Scheinman, "Safeguards: New Threats and New Expectations," *Disarmament*, 15 (No. 2, 1992).

76. Much the same type of clandestine activity continues to supply Iran today; see Chris Hedges, "A Vast Smuggling Network Feeds Iran's Arms Program," *New York Times*, March 15, 1995, p. A1.

77. Joseph F. Pilat, "Iraq and the Future of Nuclear Nonproliferation: The Roles of Inspections and Treaties," *Science*, 255 (6 March 1992), p. 1227; see also Ryukichi Imai, "NPT Safeguards Today and Tomorrow," *Disarmament*, 15 (No. 2, 1992).

78. See Pilat, "Iraq and the Future of Nuclear Nonproliferation"; William J.

Broad, "Iraqi Atom Effort Exposes Weakness in World Controls," *New York Times*, July 15, 1991; and Paul Lewis, "U.N.'s Nuclear Inquiry Exposes Treaties' Flaws," *New York Times*, November 10, 1991, p. A1.

79. Recent discussions include a symposium on "The Origins of the Cold War" in *Diplomatic History*, 17 (Spring 1993), and Gaddis, *The Long Peace*.

4. Cooperative Security

1. Adam Clymer, "House Votes Billions in Aid to Ex-Soviet Republics," *New York Times*, August 7, 1992, p. A1.

2. John Lewis Gaddis, *The Long Peace* (New York: Oxford University Press, 1987).

3. Not everyone accepts the standard view. John Mueller, for example, sparked a lively controversy a few years ago by arguing that major-power war has become normatively obsolescent, going the way of dueling in a previous age. John Mueller, *Retreat from Doomsday: The Obsolescence of Major War* (New York: Basic Books, 1988).

4. The concept is due to Karl W. Deutsch, et. al., *Political Community and the North Atlantic Area* (Princeton: Princeton University Press, 1957).

5. "Peace-Keeping Guidelines," *Washington Post*, Editorial, May 8, 1994, p. C6, commenting on Presidential Decision Directive 25, "The Clinton Administration's Policy on Reforming Multilateral Peace Operations."

6. Flora Lewis, "Next Should Come Europe's 21st Century, Not the 19th," *International Herald Tribune*, December 30, 1994, p. 4.

7. Thomas J. Knock, *To End All Wars: Woodrow Wilson and the Quest for a New World Order* (New York: Oxford University Press, 1992), p. 112.

8. The arguments have not changed much since Henry Cabot Lodge's, described briefly in chapter 1. For theoretically sophisticated rejoinders to some of the standard criticisms, particularly their tendency to turn valid concerns into hyperbole, see George W. Downs and Keisuke Iida, "Assessing the Theoretical Case against Collective Security," in George W. Downs, ed., *Collective Security beyond the Cold War* (Ann Arbor: University of Michigan Press, 1994).

9. Richard K. Betts, "Systems for Peace or Causes of War? Collective Security, Arms Control, and the New Europe," *International Security*, 17 (Summer 1992), pp. 8–9.

10. John J. Mearsheimer, "A Realist Reply," *International Security*, 20 (Summer 1995), p. 88, referring to Charles A. Kupchan and Clifford A. Kupchan, "The Promise of Collective Security," in the same source; and to Charles A. Kupchan and Clifford A. Kupchan, "Concerts, Collective Security, and the Future of Europe," *International Security*, 26 (Summer 1991).

11. Thus, as used here the concept of cooperative security includes any cooperative means of attenuating security dilemmas among states. See Robert Jervis,

"Cooperation Under the Security Dilemma," *World Politics*, 30 (January 1978). A recent Brookings study used the term in a more specialized sense to refer to a future security strategy analytically on par with deterrence and containment, which it termed cooperative engagement: "in essence a commitment to regulate the size, technical composition, investment patterns, and operational practices of all military forces by mutual consent for mutual benefit." Ashton B. Carter, William J. Perry, and John D. Steinbruner, "A New Concept of Cooperative Security," *Brookings Occasional Papers* (Washington, D.C.: The Brookings Institution, 1992), p. 6.

12. Deutsch, *Political Community and the North Atlantic Area*, p. 5.

13. Ibid., p. 36.

14. Ibid., pp. 46 and 66.

15. One who challenges the notion is the conservative commentator, Owen Harries, "The Collapse of the West," *Foreign Affairs*, 72 (September/October 1993): "The political 'West' is not a natural construct but a highly artificial one. It took the presence of a life-threatening, overtly hostile "East" to bring it into existence and to maintain its unity. It is extremely doubtful whether it can now survive the disappearance of that enemy" (p. 42). Hyper-realists, such as John J. Mearsheimer, subscribe to a similar view; see his "Back to the Future: Instability in Europe After the Cold War," *International Security*, 15 (September 1990), a version of which was also published as "Why We Will Soon Miss the Cold War," *Atlantic Monthly*, August 1990.

16. For suggestive attempts to fill in some of the gaps and explore the contemporary utility of the concept, see Emanuel Adler, "Imagined (Security) Communities," as well as Emanuel Adler and Michael N. Barnett, "Security Communities," both papers prepared for delivery at the 1994 annual meeting of the American Political Science Association, New York City, September 1–4, 1994. For an earlier appreciation of the literature, see Richard L. Merritt and Bruce M. Russett, eds., *From National Development to Global Community: Essays in Honor of Karl W. Deutsch* (London: George Allen & Unwin, 1981).

17. In an attempt to counter the (correct) perception that this shift was taking place, President Kennedy coined the expression that NATO had a "European pillar." Not impressed by the rhetoric, France withdrew from NATO's military structure in 1966.

18. Charles L. Glaser, "Why NATO is Still Best: Future Security Arrangements for Europe," *International Security*, 18 (Summer 1993), p. 10.

19. By 1995, 26 countries, all former Soviet Republics, satellite states, or neutrals, and including Russia, had joined NATO's so-called Partnership for Peace. It includes joint military exercises, programs to institute civilian control over the military, as well as steps to adapt military forces and equipment to NATO standards. See Robert E. Hunter, "Enlargement: Part of a strategy for projecting stability into Central Europe," *NATO Review* (May 1995). The Partner-

ship does not extend NATO security commitments to these countries; only full membership would do that.

20. To keep this discussion manageable, my summary of this debate is synthetic, making no attempt to review and assess each and every position. In my judgment, the best case for immediate expansion has been made by the RAND team of Ronald D. Asmus, Richard L. Kugler, and F. Stephen Larrabee, "Building a New NATO," *Foreign Affairs*, 72 (September/October 1993), and by the same authors, "NATO Expansion: The Next Steps," *Survival*, 37 (Spring 1995); and the most incisive case against, arguing that possible future expansion should be strictly contingent on future Russian actions, by Michael E. Brown, "The Flawed Logic of NATO Expansion," *Survival*, 37 (Spring 1995), which also contains extensive up-to-date references of diverse views.

21. Henry Kissinger, "Not This Partnership," *Washington Post*, November 24, 1993, p. A17.

22. Asmus, Kugler, and Larrabee, "Building a New NATO," p. 29.

23. Glaser, "Why NATO is Still Best," p. 9.

24. Brown, "The Flawed Logic of NATO Expansion," p. 35.

25. Ibid., p. 37. Brown reports that Poland and Hungary have reduced military conscription, and the Polish as well as Czech armies have reduced mechanized divisions and disbanded others.

26. Ibid., p. 39.

27. For example, in 1990 the late Jozsef Antall proclaimed that he was not simply Prime Minister of Hungary, but "the leader in the hearts of 15 million Hungarians," including the 5 million living in neighboring countries. By 1995, that sort of rhetoric had largely disappeared, and Hungary had signed a treaty with Slovakia, home to 600,000 ethnic Hungarians, accepting established borders and protecting minority rights. Stephen Kinzer, "Learning from Bosnia: We Can Work It Out," *New York Times*, March 26, 1995, p. E4.

28. Dana H. Allin, "Can Containment Work Again?" *Survival*, 37 (Spring 1995), p. 61. Quite apart from the issue of credibility, not stationing forces on the new front lines poses an additional problem: moving troops into a potentially threatened area at the onset of a crisis could worsen it, while not moving them would leave the area vulnerable.

29. Quoted in Asmus, Kugler, and Larrabee, "NATO Expansion," p. 7.

30. The need to devise some special arrangement with Ukraine as well as Russia is part of this new plan. See Strobe Talbott [U.S. Deputy Secretary of State], "Why NATO Should Grow," *New York Review of Books*, August 10, 1995.

31. Václav Havel, "A Call for Sacrifice," *Foreign Affairs*, 73 (March/April 1994), p. 4.

32. Precision is difficult because NATO's Article 5 commitments and integrated military command do not fit neatly into the two-fold typology of Deutsch, et. al., *Political Community and the North Atlantic Area*. NATO goes well beyond the average pluralistic security community though it is neither intended to

nor does it constitute the amalgamated form. Hence I use the term "tightly coupled" pluralistic security community.

33. Ibid., p. 190.
34. François Heisbourg, "The Future of the Atlantic Alliance: Wither NATO, Whether NATO?" *Washington Quarterly*, 15 (Spring 1992), p. 138.
35. Henry Kissinger, "Expand NATO Now," *Washington Post*, December 19, 1994, p. A27.
36. These include, John Duffield enumerates, "satellite surveillance; command, control, communication, and intelligence; logistics; long-range airlift and sealift; all-weather aviation; amphibious capabilities; large-deck aircraft carriers; and missile defenses." John S. Duffield, "NATO's Functions after the Cold War," *Political Science Quarterly*, 109 (Winter 1994–95), p. 781.
37. The original WEU goes back to the 1948 Brussels pact, which was modified in 1954 to accommodate German rearmament; see chap. 3, above.
38. The Eurocorps originated as a Franco-German brigade in 1990; it has since been enlarged and joined by Belgium, Luxembourg, and Spain, holding its first maneuvers in November 1994. (Agence Europe, "Eurocorps Holds First Major Manoeuvres in Germany and France," November 8, 1994.) Also in 1994, France, Italy, Portugal, and Spain agreed to form an air and sea contingent for the Mediterranean, called Euroforce (Agence Europe, no title, December 20, 1994); and Britain and France agreed to establish a joint airborne command. (Andrew Marshall, "Take-off for Franco-British air HQ," *The Independent* [London], November 1, 1994, p. 10.) French President François Mitterand raised the question, but provided no answer, whether it was possible to imagine a European doctrine for a joint nuclear deterrent; see "La force d'Euro-frappe?" *The Economist*, January 18, 1992, p. 48.
39. See Roger H. Palin, "Multinational Military Forces: Problems and Prospects," *Adelphi Paper # 294* (London: Oxford University Press, for the International Institute for Strategic Studies, 1995), pp. 13–14. These task forces would permit European countries, including nonmembers such as Russia, to participate in WEU peacekeeping operations in which one or both of NATO's North American members may have no interest.
40. See Jean-Marie Guéhenno, "France and the WEU," *NATO Review* (October 1994), and Hans van Mierlo, "The WEU and NATO: Prospects for a More Balanced Relationship," *NATO Review* (March 1995).
41. When the Yugoslav crisis broke out in 1991, Germany supported Slovenia and Croatia, France the Yugoslav federation and, thus, Serbia. After Germany's precipitous recognition of Croatia, which led Bosnia-Herzegovina also to seek immediate autonomy and recognition, thereby triggering the Bosnian war, Germany and France, in the words of a Danish observer, "spent half a year talking each other into a joint position, which was not very impressive and not of much help to the Yugoslav peoples, but it had the one big merit of encapsulating the conflict, of preventing it from spreading and pulling in

more powers." Ole Waever, "The European Security Triangle," draft ms. (Copenhagen: Centre for Peace and Conflict Research, 1995), pp. 8–9. In the spring of 1995, Germany reportedly invoked the incentive of EU economic privileges to prevent Croatia from throwing out UN peacekeepers. See Stephen Engelberg, "In Not Curbing Croat Attack U.S. Took a Calculated Risk," *New York Times*, August 13, 1995, p. 8.

42. The relationship between WEU and NATO security commitments will have to be clarified soon: WEU commitments call for an automatic response by all in case of attack on any one, while NATO responses are more discretionary. The WEU has offered "Associate Partner" status to nine Central European and Baltic countries, and with the accession to the EU of Austria, Finland, and Sweden those countries became eligible for WEU membership.

43. See Emanuel Adler, "Europe's New Security Order: A Pluralistic Security Community," in Beverly Crawford, ed., *The Future of European Security* (Berkeley, Calif.: Center for German and European Studies, University of California, Berkeley, Research Series # 84, 1992).

44. See Victor-Yves Ghebali, "After the Budapest Conference: The Organization for Security and Cooperation in Europe," *NATO Review* (March 1995).

45. A NATO-Russia treaty was first proposed by Zbigniew Brzezinski, "A Bigger—and Safer—Europe," *New York Times*, December 1, 1993, p. A23. Its purpose would be to acknowledge the special roles of the United States and Russia in guaranteeing a stable European security order.

46. Among many other sources, see John Mueller, "A New Concert of Europe," *Foreign Policy*, 77 (Winter 1989–90); Kupchan and Kupchan, "Concerts, Collective Security, and the Future of Europe"; and Richard Rosecrance, "A New Concert of Powers," *Foreign Affairs*, 71 (Spring 1992).

47. Henry A. Kissinger, *A World Restored* (New York: Universal Library, 1964), p. 5. Kissinger concentrates on the *Congress* system, a subset of the Concert that ended by about 1823; the present commentary holds for the entire Concert system.

48. The term is used by Gordon A. Craig and Alexander L. George, *Force and Statecraft* (New York: Oxford University Press, 1983), p. 31.

49. For example, they created and guaranteed the neutrality of Belgium and Greece, thereby removing them from the temptations of competition or partition. The "Eastern Question" in general, Albrecht-Carrié notes—the problem of how to secure orderly change and national independence in the wake of a disintegrating Ottoman Empire—"provides many illustrations of an authentic common preference for orderly and peaceful procedure, more than once successfully implemented." René Albrecht-Carrié, *The Concert of Europe* (New York: Walker, 1968), p. 22.

50. Benjamin Miller, "Explaining the Emergence of Great Power Concerts," *Review of International Studies*, 20 (October 1994), p. 331.

51. Robert Jervis, "Security Regimes," in Stephen D. Krasner, ed., *International*

Regimes (Ithaca, N.Y.: Cornell University Press, 1983), p. 178; also see Jervis, "From Balance to Concert: A Study of International Security Cooperation," *World Politics*, 38 (October 1985); Richard B. Elrod, "The Concert of Europe: A Fresh Look at an International System," *World Politics*, 28 (January 1976); Richard Langhorne, "Reflections on the Significance of the Congress of Vienna," *Review of International Studies*, 12 (October 1986); and Paul W. Schroeder, "Did the Vienna Settlement Rest on a Balance of Power?" *American Historical Review*, 97 (June 1992).

52. Kalevi J. Holsti, "Governance Without Government: Modes of Coordinating, Managing and Controlling International Politics in Nineteenth Century Europe," paper presented at the annual meeting of the International Studies Association, Vancouver, Canada, March 1991.

53. Jervis, "Security Regimes," p. 180.

54. Richard A. Falkenrath, Jr., "Soviet Policy at the United Nations: A Summary of Soviet Proposals and Positions from September 1987 to December 1988," United Nations Association of the United States of America, unpublished manuscript, n.d.

55. "Joint U.S.-Soviet Statement: Responsibilities for Peace and Security in a Changing World," released by the United States and the Soviet Union in New York, October 3, 1990. *Foreign Policy Bulletin*, November/December 1990, pp. 68–69.

56. China genuinely views these abstentions to be positive contributions to international cooperation because it has deep-seated objections to the collective use of force, especially in conflicts that can be said to have an internal dimension—as does China's conflict with Taiwan, for example, or the status of Tibet.

57. In the case of the former Yugoslavia, Russia vetoed no concrete UN action. On several occasions, Russia's Serbian connection proved useful in the pursuit of collective aims vis-à-vis the Serbs.

58. Philip Guillot, "France, Peacekeeping and Humanitarian Intervention," *International Peacekeeping*, 1 (Spring 1994), p. 40.

59. For an early proposal to this effect, see John Gerard Ruggie, "Use U.N. to ease into a global role," *Japan Times*, April 10, 1991, p. 19.

60. "For the Bundeswehr overall, it's been a big success for their image," said German Defense Minister Volker Ruehe of their Somalian expedition. "The soldiers have been on television a lot, and they've portrayed themselves very well. They also learned a lot, and it's strengthened their self confidence." Quoted in Rick Atkinson, "Germany Still Debates Role of Its Army," *Washington Post*, February 25, 1994, p. A23. Rudolf Scharping, then leader of the opposition Social Democrats (SDP), opposed sending the Tornadoes to the Balkans, as did the Green Party, but a significant number of SDP members in parliament supported it. "Time to move on, if not in," *The Economist*, July 1, 1995, pp. 39–42. As for Japan, according to one press report defense forces

"recruiters are enjoying a windfall from intense media coverage of Japanese peacekeeping-type operations in Zaire, Cambodia, Mozambique and the Gulf." "New Spirit for Japan's Military," *International Herald Tribune*, December 23, 1994, p. 5.

61. See Pavel K. Baev, "Russia's Experiments and Experience in Conflict Management and Peacemaking," *International Peacekeeping*, 1 (Autumn 1994). The author finds that "[w]hile in 1992 the rhetoric was restrained and the Russian military adopted an interventionist posture, by 1994 the former had become remarkably bellicose and the latter had turned somewhat cautious" (p. 245).

62. "Still on the prowl," *The Economist*, August 28, 1993, p. 11. Also see Steven Erlanger, "An Army in Need of a Role," *New York Times*, May 23, 1994, p. A6.

63. The dilemma is expressed, but not resolved, by James P. Rubin (Director of Communications, U.S. Mission to the United Nations), "The U.N.'s Firm Line on Russia," letter to the editor, *Washington Post*, September 30, 1994, p. A28.

64. "Statement by the President of the Council," UN Document S/PRST/1994/62 (November 4, 1994). The developing countries, led by Malaysia, had sought to establish a subsidiary organ of the Security Council for this purpose.

65. See Colum Lynch, "Weary UN letting powerful keep watch," *Boston Globe*, July 29, 1994, p. 6, which quotes Colin Keating, New Zealand's UN representative: "There is a pattern emerging, which from the standpoint of small and mid-sized countries, has got to be worrying."

66. There has been an explosion of Security Council decisions, from 15 in 1988, to 78 in 1994. See Barbara Crossette, "U.N. Chief Chides Security Council on Military Missions," *New York Times*, January 6, 1995, p. A3. As of the summer of 1995, more than eighty resolutions had been adopted concerning the former Yugoslavia alone, many of which stood little chance of being successfully implemented.

67. "U.N. Bosnia Commander Wants More Troops, Fewer Resolutions," *New York Times*, December 31, 1993, p. A3.

68. Elaine Sciolino, "Dole Offers Foreign Policy Initiatives," *New York Times*, January 5, 1995, p. A3.

69. See Mats R. Berdahl, "Fateful Encounter: The United States and UN Peacekeeping," *Survival*, 36 (Spring 1994); Barton Gellman, "U.S. Rhetoric Changed, but Hunt Persisted," *Washington Post*, October 7, 1993, p. A37; and Michael R. Gordon, with John H. Cushman, Jr., "After Supporting Hunt for Aidid, U.S. Is Blaming U.N. for Losses," *New York Times*, October 18, 1993, p. A1.

70. In September 1992, I observed that "it is a miracle of no small magnitude that disaster has not yet befallen one of these peacekeeping missions." In subsequent operations the UN ran out of miracles. John Gerard Ruggie, "No, The

World Doesn't Need a UN Army," *International Herald Tribune*, September 26–27, 1992, p. 5.

71. *An Agenda for Peace* (New York: United Nations, 1992).

72. "Supplement to an Agenda for Peace: Position Paper of the Secretary-General on the Occasion of the Fiftieth Anniversary of the United Nations," UN Document A/50/60, S/1995/1 (January 3, 1995), p. 3.

73. "Excerpts from a Resolution On Delivering Somalia Aid," *New York Times*, December 4, 1992, p. A14.

74. See Michael R. Gordon, "U.S. Is Sending Large Force as Warning to Somali Clans," *New York Times*, December 5, 1992, p. A5; and Paul Lewis, "U.N. Says Somalis Must Disarm Before Peace," *New York Times*, December 6, 1992, p. 15.

75. Quoted by Alan Cowell, "Italy, in U.N. Rift, Threatens Recall of Somalia Troops," *New York Times*, July 16, 1993, p. A1.

76. John H. Cushman, Jr., "How Powerful U.S. Units Will Work," *New York Times*, October 8, 1993, p. A14; and "Senate Report Scrutinizes Powell's Role in Somalia Raid," *Washington Post*, October 2, 1995, p. A4.

77. Quoted by Donatella Lorch, "Italian Forces Come Under Fire in Tense Somalia," *New York Times*, July 17, 1993, p. A3.

78. A good discussion of the evolution of the all-or-nothing doctrine from Vietnam to the present may be found in Christopher M. Gacek, *The Logic of Force: The Dilemma of Limited War in American Foreign Policy* (New York: Columbia University Press, 1994).

79. *A Doctrinal Statement of Selected Joint Operational Concepts* (Washington, D.C.: Office of the Joint Chiefs of Staff, U.S. Department of Defense, November 23, 1992).

80. Warren Zimmermann, "The Last Ambassador: A Memoir of the Collapse of Yugoslavia," *Foreign Affairs*, 74 (March/April 1995). In 1992, Gen. Colin Powell angrily rejected former British Prime Minister Margaret Thatcher's suggestion that the West launch limited air strikes to deter further Bosnian Serb shelling of Sarajevo: "As soon as they tell me it is limited, it means they do not care whether you achieve a result or not. As soon as they tell me 'surgical,' I head for the bunker." Quoted in Michael R. Gordon, "Powell Delivers a Resounding No on Using Limited Force in Bosnia," *New York Times*, September 28, 1992, p. A1.

81. At the end of 1994, the U.S. Army produced a new field manual for gray-area conflicts. U.S. Department of the Army, *Peace Operations* (Washington, D.C., Field Manual 100–23, December 30, 1994). It distinguished between "peace operations" and "war-fighting," and further differentiated two types of peace operations: peacekeeping and peace enforcement. The major differences between those two were said to involve the consent of the parties, the role of force, and the degree of impartiality in its application. Thus, in peacekeeping "the belligerent parties consent to the presence and operations" of peacekeepers, and "force may only be used in self-defense or defense [of] a man-

date." In peace enforcement "consent is not absolute and force may be used to coerce or compel"—but not to *defeat* any belligerent (pp. 12–13).

82. See Guillot, "France, Peacekeeping and Humanitarian Intervention."

83. Michael R. Gordon, "Allies Seem to Hope Serbs Won't Attack," *New York Times*, May 24, 1993, p. A7; and personal interviews, UN Headquarters.

84. Guillot, "France, Peacekeeping and Humanitarian Intervention," p. 39; and personal interviews with Generals Morillon and Cot in New York.

85. See, for example, John Pomfret, "U.N. to Attempt Sending Convoys Without Bosnian Factions' Permission, *Washington Post*, February 28, 1994, p. A12; and the retrospective assessment by Roger Cohen, "U.N. Commander Set to Leave Bosnia, After a Year of Triumph and Disaster," *New York Times*, January 22, 1995, p. A6.

86. Lt. Col. C.W.G. Dobbie, "Wider Peacekeeping: An Approach to Peacekeeping Post Cold War," paper distributed at United Nations High-Level Meeting on Peacekeeping, Ottawa, Canada, April 29–May 1, 1994, p. 3. The British Army Field Manual, which Col. Dobbie helped draft, coupled the phrase "spurious historically" with the less inflammatory "misleading doctrinally." *Wider Peacekeeping* (third draft, n.d.), p. II–5.

87. Dobbie, "Wider Peacekeeping," p. 3.

88. Quoted in Roger Cohen, "U.N. General Opposes More Bosnia Force," *New York Times*, September 29, 1994, p. A7.

89. Ibid.

90. Col. Allan Mallinson, "Doctrine dilemma has only two horns," (unpublished ms., April 1994), p. 2; at the time, Mallinson was Assistant Director, Land Warfare, British Army's new Headquarters Doctrine and Training, Upavon, Wiltshire, and a member of the "Wider Peacekeeping" team.

91. The UN never formally adopted a doctrine, but statements by the Secretary General and the Undersecretary General for Peacekeeping came to reflect these "wider peacekeeping" notions. The latter used the distinction between operational and tactical consent to explain certain UN actions on the ground in Bosnia as recently as June 19, 1995, in a plenary presentation at the Eighth Annual Meeting, Academic Council on the United Nations System, Graduate Center of the City University of New York.

92. The preliminary agreement provided for a Bosnia-Herzegovina within its existing borders, but consisting of two entities—a Muslim-Croatian federation, and a Serbian republic. Chris Hedges, "3 Enemies Agree to Serbian State as Part of Bosnia," *New York Times*, September 9, 1995, p. A1. A full peace accord was subsequently reached in Dayton, Ohio, and the UN's military mission was handed off to NATO.

93. For a more elaborate discussion, see John Gerard Ruggie, "Wandering in the Void: Charting the U.N.'s New Strategic Role," *Foreign Affairs*, 72 (November/December 1993).

94. Richard K. Betts, "The Delusion of Impartial Intervention," *Foreign Affairs*, 73 (November/December 1994), p. 21.

95. For an assessment of the generic problems, see Palin, "Multinational Military Forces," pp. 15–21. Also see Report of the Secretary General, "Comprehensive review of the whole question of peace-keeping operations in all their aspects: Command and control of United Nations peace-keeping operations," A/49/681 (21 November 1994).

96. Palin, "Multinational Military Forces," p. 19, suggests this model. It draws on the precedent created by Gen. John Shalikashvili as commander of Operation Provide Comfort, protecting the Kurdish population in Northern Iraq in the wake of the Gulf war.

97. Hans J. Morgenthau, *Politics Among Nations*, 6th Ed. (New York: Knopf, 1985). Morgenthau did not use these two terms. He differentiated between balances that had existed "under the common roof of shared values and universal standards of action," and the "new" or "mechanical" balance of power which held between the United States and the Soviet Union after 1945 (pp. 358–359; see also pp. 388–391). The "associative-adversarial" terminology is due to Richard Little, "Deconstructing the Balance of Power: Two Traditions of Thought," *Review of International Studies*, 15 (April 1989).

98. This shift was codified in Kenneth N. Waltz, *Theory of International Politics* (Reading, Mass.: Addison-Wesley, 1979), the basic neorealist text, in which international norms were rendered strictly as epiphenomenal byproducts of "structural" factors, relegated to legitimating roles.

99. See Mearsheimer, "Why We Will Soon Miss the Cold War."

100. See James Goodby, "The Stockholm Conference: Negotiating a Cooperative Security System for Europe," in Alexander George, Philip Farley, and Alexander Dallin, eds., *U.S.-Soviet Security Cooperation* (New York: Oxford University Press, 1988).

101. Little, "Deconstructing the balance of power," p. 95.

102. For recent overviews, see Paul Dibb, "Towards a New Balance of Power in Asia," *Adelphi Paper* # 295 (London: Oxford University Press for the International Institute for Strategic Studies, 1995); as well as Aaron L. Friedberg, "Ripe for Rivalry: Prospects for Peace in a Multipolar Asia," Richard K. Betts, "Wealth, Power, and Instability: East Asia and the United States after the Cold War," and Desmond Ball, "Arms and Affluence: Military Acquisitions in the Asia-Pacific Region," all in *International Security*, 18 (Winter 1993/94).

103. See *Defining a Pacific Community: A Report of the Carnegie Endowment Study Group* (Washington, D.C.: Carnegie Endowment for International Peace, 1994); and Dibb, "Towards a New Balance of Power in Asia."

104. Dibb, "Towards a New Balance of Power in Asia," p. 67.

5. Economic Stabilization

1. Charles S. Maier, "The Two Postwar Eras and the Conditions for Stability in Twentieth-Century Western Europe," *American Historical Review*, 86 (April 1981), p. 327.

2. Karl Polanyi, *The Great Transformation: The Political and Economic Origins of Our Time* (Boston: Beacon Books, [1944] 1957), pp. 253–254, italics in original.

3. The "security externalities" of trade policy within bipolar systems are demonstrated deftly by Joanne Gowa, "Bipolarity, Multipolarity, and Free Trade," *American Political Science Review*, 83 (December 1989); and Joanne Gowa and Edward Mansfield, "Power Politics and International Trade," *American Political Science Review*, 87 (June 1993).

4. See C. Fred Bergsten, "The New Economics and U.S. Foreign Policy," *Foreign Affairs*, 50 (January 1972), pp. 204, 206, assessing the implications of the 1971 Nixon-Connally shifts in U.S. international economic policy (closing the gold window and imposing a temporary import surcharge); Robert E. Hudec, "Retaliation Against 'Unreasonable' Foreign Trade Practices: The New Section 301 and GATT Nullification and Impairment," *Minnesota Law Review*, 59 (No. 3, 1975); and Robert B. Reich, "Beyond Free Trade," *Foreign Affairs*, 61 (Spring 1983).

5. Robert Triffin, "Jamaica: 'Major Revision' or Fiasco," in Edward M. Bernstein et al., "Reflections on Jamaica," *Princeton Essays in International Finance*, 115 (April 1976), p. 47; and Triffin, "IMS: International Monetary System—or Scandal," *Jean Monnet Chair Papers* (Florence: European University Institute, 1992). Also see Susan Strange, *Casino Capitalism* (Oxford: Basil Blackwell, 1986).

6. For the sake of brevity, I am using the appellation "Bretton Woods" generically here, to include both the monetary and trade regimes. Though the latter was not negotiated at Bretton Woods, the two were viewed in tandem and their provisions were intended to be compatible. At the same time, I am ignoring the World Bank for the purposes of this discussion because it ceased immediately to be part of the formula whereby the industrialized countries sought to stabilize international economic relations among themselves, which is my primary concern here. For fuller documentation of the monetary and trade regimes' parameters, see John Gerard Ruggie, "International Regimes, Transactions, and Change: Embedded Liberalism in the Postwar Economic Order," *International Organization*, 36 (Spring 1982).

7. The term "double screen" is Richard N. Cooper's, in "Prolegomena to the Choice of an International Monetary System," *International Organization*, 29 (Winter 1975), p. 85.

8. The United States, led by Secretary of State Cordell Hull, initially had pursued a more orthodox free-trade line. Opposition to it was universal abroad and nearly so among New Dealers at home. The domestic split was resolved by delaying the trade negotiations until the monetary agreement was concluded—and Hull had retired. "After the Treasury group succeeded in reaching an agreement with the British on postwar monetary arrangements, the State Department found its nineteenth-century style trade proposals essentially incompatible with these agreements" and fell into line. G. John Iken-

berry, "A World Economy Restored: Expert Consensus and the Anglo-American Settlement," *International Organization*, 46 (Winter 1992), p. 310.

9. See Robert Pollard, *Economic Security and the Origins of the Cold War* (New York: Columbia University Press, 1985); Alan S. Milward, *The Reconstruction of Western Europe, 1945–1951* (Berkeley and Los Angeles: University of California Press, 1984); Maier, "The Two Postwar Eras"; and Stephen A. Schuker, "Comments on Maier," *American Historical Review*, 86 (April 1981).

10. "Everybody's Business: International Monetary Reform—A Survey," *The Economist*, October 5, 1985; the citations are from p. 11.

11. Strange, *Casino Capitalism*.

12. Richard N. Cooper, "A Monetary System Based on Fixed Exchange Rates, in Colin D. Campbell and William R. Dougan, eds., *Alternative Monetary Regimes* (Baltimore: Johns Hopkins University Press, 1986), p. 88.

13. In the early 1960s, this understanding was formalized in the well-known Fleming-Mundell thesis, which held that capital mobility, domestic autonomy, and fixed exchange rates could not all be achieved simultaneously; at most, only two could. See J. Marcus Fleming, "Domestic Financial Policies under Fixed and Floating Exchange Rates," *IMF Staff Papers*, 9 (1962); Robert Mundell, "The Monetary Dynamics of International Adjustment under Fixed and Flexible Exchange Rates," *Quarterly Journal of Economics*, 74 (May 1960); and Mundell, "Capital Mobility and Stabilization Policy Under Fixed and Flexible Exchange Rates," *Canadian Journal of Economic and Political Science*, 29 (November 1963).

14. Cooper, "A Monetary System Based on Fixed Exchange Rates."

15. For a good account of this shift in policy preferences, see John B. Goodman and Louis W. Pauly, "The Obsolescence of Capital Controls? Economic Management in an Age of Global Markets," *World Politics*, 46 (October 1993).

16. Richard N. Cooper, "A Monetary System for the Future," *Foreign Affairs*, 63 (Fall 1984), p. 170.

17. Rachel McCulloch, "Unexpected Real Consequences of Floating Exchange Rates," in Robert Z. Aliber, ed., *The Reconstruction of International Monetary Arrangements* (London: Macmillan, 1987), p. 25.

18. Before the next year was out, Robert Triffin proclaimed the famous dilemma that bears his name. He argued that if the United States corrected its balance of payments deficit the result would be world deflation, because gold production at $35 an ounce—its monetary value at the time—could not adequately supply world monetary reserves in place of the dollar. But if the United States continued to run the deficit that supplied world liquidity, the result would be the collapse of the monetary standard, because U.S. foreign liabilities would far exceed its ability to convert dollars into gold on demand. Triffin, *Gold and the Dollar Crisis* (New Haven: Yale University Press, 1960).

19. Cooper, "A Monetary System for the Future," p. 171.

20. Cooper, "A Monetary System Based on Fixed Exchange Rates," p. 90.

21. Thomas L. Friedman, "Never Mind Yen. Greenbacks Are the New Gold Standard," *New York Times*, July 3, 1994, p. E5.

22. R. Taggart Murphy, "Power Without Purpose: The Crisis of Japan's Global Financial Dominance," *Harvard Business Review*, 67 (March–April 1989), p. 75.

23. Friedman, "Never Mind Yen."

24. "A Survey of the World Economy: Who's in the driving seat?" *The Economist*, October 7, 1995, p. 10.

25. Robert V. Roosa, *Economic Instability and Flexible Exchange Rates* (Singapore: Institute of Southeast Asian Studies, 1982), p. 4.

26. McCulloch, "Unexpected Real Consequences," p. 25.

27. Allan H. Meltzer, "Some Evidence on the Comparative Uncertainty Experienced Under Different Monetary Regimes," in Campbell and Dougan, *Alternative Monetary Regimes*. According to Meltzer, variability in nominal and real GNP was higher under the classical gold standard than in the post World War II era, though variance in price level is higher now; money growth shows no consistent pattern. What is most interesting, however, is his finding that variation in estimated forecast errors has declined both in absolute value and relative to the variance in actual outcomes (p. 142). A recent OECD study shows that, for the big seven industrialized economies, volatility in bond yields, exchange rates, and stock markets has decreased since the 1980s. Malcolm Edey and Ketil Hviding, "An Assessment of Financial Reform in OECD Countries" (Paris: OECD Working Paper #154).

28. McCulloch, "Unexpected Real Consequences," p. 25.

29. Louis Uchitelle, "U.S. Corporations Expanding Abroad at a Quicker Pace," *New York Times*, July 25, 1994, p. D2.

30. This draws heavily on Michael C. Webb, "International Economic Structures, Government Interests, and International Coordination of Macroeconomic Adjustment Policies," *International Organization*, 45 (Summer 1991).

31. For a useful summary of the evolution of the IMF's surveillance role from Bretton Woods to the present, see Louis W. Pauly, "The Political Foundations of Multilateral Economic Surveillance," *International Journal*, 62 (Spring 1992); also see Richard N. Cooper, "International Policy Coordination," *Journal of International Affairs*, 48 (Summer 1994).

32. The U.S. Treasury promoted an agreement on policy coordination in 1986, including exchange rate target zones as well as interest rates. The hope was that a plan could be announced at the annual IMF-World Bank meetings. A prior meeting of European finance ministers, however, rejected the idea; at the Fund-Bank meetings, the German and Japanese finance ministers turned down a narrower proposal by Treasury Secretary James Baker to coordinate interest rate reductions. Nevertheless, at the Group-of-Seven summit in Paris the following February, an agreement was reached to stabilize exchange rates more or less at going levels together with modest German fiscal and Japanese

monetary stimuli. See William A. Niskanen, *Reaganomics* (New York: Oxford University Press, 1988), pp. 179–181.

33. Georges de Menil, quoted in Peter Passell, "Europe, Too, Contracts a Bad Case of Inflationphobia," *New York Times*, August 21, 1994, p. E5.

34. See Louis W. Pauly, "From Monetary Manager to Crisis Manager: Systemic Change and the International Monetary Fund," in Roger Morgan, et al., eds., *New Diplomacy in the Post-Cold War World* (New York: St. Martin's Press, 1993); and for a more critical account, Zanny Minton-Beddoes, "Why the IMF Needs Reform," *Foreign Affairs*, 74 (May–June 1995).

35. See Joseph S. Nye, Jr., *Bound to Lead* (New York: Basic Books, 1990), pp. 5–7. Webb, "International Economic Structures," p. 341, notes that the U.S. share of the aggregate GDP of OECD countries declined from 50 percent in the mid-1960s to 40 percent in the 1980s, but suggests that little can be attributed to that fact "[i]n the absence of strong theoretical reasons for claiming that a country is hegemonic when it accounts for 50 percent of total OECD economic output but not when it accounts for 40 percent."

36. Because of its common external tariff and its special relations with a group of Asian-Pacific-Caribbean developing countries, this generalization does not hold fully for the European Union. As Martin Wolf points out, the EU "is not only itself a discriminatory trading arrangement, if looked at as a collection of separate countries, but is embedded in concentric circles of discrimination," consisting of a variety of preferences and restraints. Wolf, "The European Community and the Developing Countries in the International Trading System," *Aussenwirtschaft*, 42, no. 1 (1987), pp. 56–57. These exceptions are perfectly acceptable under existing rules of the game, as we shall see below, and they make relatively little practical difference to the overall trading system.

37. For a summary of these provisions, see Bernard M. Hoekman, *Trade Laws and Institutions: Good Practices and the World Trade Organization* (Washington, D.C.: World Bank, Discussion Paper 282, April 1995).

38. See Robert Gilpin, *The Political Economy of International Relations* (Princeton: Princeton University Press, 1987); Jagdish Bhagwati, *Protectionism* (Cambridge: MIT Press, 1988); Jagdish Bhagwati and Hugh T. Patrick, eds., *Aggressive Unilateralism: America's 301 Trade Policy and the World Trading System* (Ann Arbor: University of Michigan Press, 1990); and Bhagwati, *The World Trading System at Risk* (Princeton: Princeton University Press, 1991); as well as "Echoes of the 1930s," *The Economist*, January 5, 1991, and "America, Japan and the Bogeyman," *The Economist*, December 25, 1993.

39. David R. Cameron, "The Expansion of the Public Economy: A Comparative Analysis," *American Political Science Review*, 72, (December 1978), p. 1254, was the first statistical study to demonstrate this relationship.

40. André Blais, "The Political Economy of Public Subsidies," *Comparative Political Studies*, 19 (July 1986), p. 210.

41. The impact of size on state structures as well as on policy tools vis-à-vis the

international economy are spelled out by Peter J. Katzenstein, "The Small European States in the International Economy: Economic Dependence and Corporatist Politics," in John Gerard Ruggie, ed., *The Antinomies of Interdependence* (New York: Columbia University Press, 1983). For a comparative study of nontariff barriers which reaches similar conclusions using 1980s data, see Edward D. Mansfield and Marc L. Busch, "The Political Economy of Nontariff Barriers: A Cross-National Analysis," *International Organization*, 49 (Autumn 1995).

42. Judith Goldstein, "The Political Economy of Trade: Institutions of Protection," *American Political Science Review*, 80 (March 1986), p. 169; also see Goldstein, "Ideas, Institutions, and American Trade Policy," in G. John Ikenberry, David A. Lake, and Michael Mastanduno, eds., *The State and American Foreign Economic Policy* (Ithaca: Cornell University Press, 1988). Goldstein examines all statutory restraints imposed by the United States since the 1950s.

43. Goldstein, "Political Economy of Trade," p. 180.

44. I. M. Destler, *American Trade Politics*, 2nd. ed. (Washington, D.C.: Institute for International Economics, 1992), p. 145.

45. Niskanen, *Reaganomics*, p. 137.

46. Destler, *American Trade Politics*, p. 201.

47. Ibid., p. 200.

48. Niskanen, *Reaganomics*, p. 150. Among them was the "Gephardt amendment" introduced by the Democratic Representative from Missouri whose presidential bid featured neoprotectionism. The amendment would have imposed import quotas on countries running large bilateral surpluses with the United States. It was eventually replaced by "Super 301" (see below).

49. Destler, *American Trade Politics*, p. 95. Congress began to delegate trade-policy powers to the Executive Branch in the 1930s, largely to facilitate liberalization and to protect itself from domestic protectionist pressures.

50. Former International Trade Commission (ITC) chair Paula Stern describes the situation as of the late 1980s: "less than 1 percent of total U.S. imports were actually challenged as unfair under U.S. trade laws. The volume of U.S. imports affected by antidumping and countervailing duty investigations as a percentage of total imports amounted to only 0.2 percent in 1987, 0.4 percent in 1988, and 0.2 percent during the first half of 1989. Even in the cases where the [ITC] and Department of Commerce (DOC) made affirmative determinations, the average dumping duty applied in 1987 on dumped or subsidized goods was 1.2 percent. In 1988, the average was 3.7 percent; in the first half of 1989, the figure was 1.4 percent." Stern, "Commentary," in Bhagwati and Patrick, *Aggressive Unilateralism*, pp. 192–193.

51. Destler, *American Trade Politics*, p. 207.

52. In 1992, legal fees for the steel sector alone were expected to exceed $100 million. See Keith Bradsher, "Trade Gap too High? Export a Few Lawyers," *New*

York Times, July 2, 1992, p. D1. Economists are beginning to model the costs of the deterrent effects—or anticipated rewards—of being bogged down in trade relief procedures; see Michael P. Leidy, "Trade Policy and Indirect Rent Seeking: A Synthesis of Recent Work," *Economics & Politics*, 6 (July 1994).

53. See Hoekman, *Trade Laws and Institutions*.

54. The pace and extent of adjustment was not invariant but had a great deal to do with industry structure, as shown by Vinod K. Aggarwal, Robert O. Keohane, and David B. Yoffie, "The Dynamics of Negotiated Protectionism," *American Political Science Review*, 81 (June 1987).

55. This feature of VERs was pointed out some time ago by Brian Hindley, "Voluntary Export Restraints and GATT's Main Escape Clause," *The World Economy*, 3 (November 1980). Under GATT's Article XIX safeguards provisions all importers face the same tariff or quota restriction, and those who are adversely affected may apply for compensation through GATT.

56. Gary Clyde Hufbauer and Kimberly Ann Elliott, *Measuring the Costs of Protection in the United States* (Washington, D.C.: Institute for International Economics, 1994).

57. David E. Sanger, "U.S. Finds Itself Virtually Alone on Japan Trade," *New York Times*, May 29, 1995, p. A1.

58. "Joint Announcement by Ryutaro Hashimoto, Minister of International Trade and Industry of Japan, and Michael Kantor, United States Trade Representative, Regarding Autos and Auto Parts," Geneva, June 28, 1995; "Joint Announcement on Dealerships"; and "Joint Announcement Regarding the Japanese Auto Companies Plans." Also see "Clinton's Phoney Peace," *The Economist*, July 1, 1995.

59. The term is due to Bhagwati and Patrick, *Aggressive Unilateralism*.

60. See Thomas O. Bayard and Kimberly Ann Elliott, *Reciprocity and Retaliation in U.S. Trade Policy* (Washington, D.C.: Institute for International Economics, 1994).

61. Michael P. Ryan, "USTR's Implementation of 301 in the Pacific," *International Studies Quarterly*, 39 (September 1995). While this study focuses on the Pacific, by and large the generalization holds for Europe as well.

62. Bayard and Elliott, *Reciprocity and Retaliation in U.S. Trade Policy*; for an earlier study of the interaction between unilateral U.S. actions and multilateral developments, see Julia Christine Bliss, "GATT Dispute Settlement Reform in the Uruguay Round: Problems and Prospects," *Stanford Journal of International Law*, 23 (No. 1, 1987).

63. Brazil and India were also named in the initial U.S. review, largely for tactical reasons having to do with positions they took in the Uruguay Round which the United States viewed to be obstructionist, but those cases were quietly resolved.

64. Richard Blackhurst, Nicolas Marian, and Jan Tumlir, "Trade Liberalization, Protectionism and Interdependence," *GATT Studies in International Trade*, 5 (November 1977), p. 11.

65. See Edward J. Lincoln, *Japan's Unequal Trade* (Washington, D.C.: The Brookings Institution, 1990).

66. Louis W. Pauly and Simon Reich, "Convergence in the 1990s? Multinational Corporate Behavior in the Triad," paper presented at the annual meeting of the International Studies Association, Chicago, February 22–25, 1995.

67. Lincoln, *Japan's Unequal Trade*; also see John Ravenhill, "The 'Japan Problem' in Pacific Trade," in Richard Higgott, Richard Leaver, and John Ravenhill, eds., *Pacific Economic Relations in the 1990s: Cooperation or Conflict?* (Sydney: Allen and Unwin, 1993). For a view on these issues more favorable to Japan, see Gary R. Saxonhouse, "Comparative Advantage, Structural Adaptation, and Japanese Performance," in Takashi Inoguchi and Daniel I. Okimoto, eds., *The Political Economy of Japan* (Stanford: Stanford University Press, 1988); and Saxonhouse and Robert M. Stern, "An Analytical Survey of Formal and Informal Barriers to International Trade and Investment in the United States, Canada, and Japan," in Robert M. Stern, ed., *Trade and Investment Relations Among the United States, Canada, and Japan* (Chicago: University of Chicago Press, 1989).

68. "In adversarial trade the seller's goods displace the goods produced by the manufacturers of the buying country without any compensating purchases from that country." Peter Drucker, "Japan and Adversarial Trade," *Wall Street Journal*, April 1, 1986, p. 32. Paul Krugman, in an article explaining why Japan is not the major cause of America's economic woes, nevertheless notes that "Japan is a great economic power that does not play by the same rules as the other great economic powers." Krugman, "Japan Is Not Our Nemesis," *New Perspectives Quarterly*, 7 (Summer 1990), p. 44.

69. "Japan's troublesome imports," *The Economist*, January 11, 1992, p. 61.

70. Lincoln, *Japan's Unequal Trade*, p. 60.

71. In no sector is this challenge perceived to be of greater economic and political importance than in high-technology industries. See Laura D'Andrea Tyson, *Who's Bashing Whom? Trade Conflict in High-Technology Industries* (Washington, D.C.: Institute for International Economics, 1992).

72. As host to the inward flow of investments, Japan accounted for a mere 1 percent of the world's total in 1980—and that same mere 1 percent in 1988. The 1988 figures for the European Community and U.S. were 23 and 31 percent, respectively. United Nations Centre on Transnational Corporations (UNCTC), *World Investment Report, 1991: The Triad in Foreign Direct Investment* (New York: United Nations, 1991); also see Dennis J. Encarnation, *Rivals Beyond Trade: America versus Japan in Global Competition* (Ithaca: Cornell University Press, 1992). Japan differs in its outward investment patterns as well, with Japanese multinationals far more likely to favor home-country sourcing. See Mordechai E. Kreinin, "How Closed Is Japan's Market?" *The World Economy*, 11 (December 1988); and Pauly and Reich, "Convergence in the 1990s?" Because American and European firms also exhibited this pattern at an earlier time, some observers suggest that it may be only temporary for

Japanese firms. But the UNCTC study suggests (p. 42) that Japanese manufacturers abroad recently have been joined by their home-country suppliers, thereby transplanting overseas the relatively closed producer-supplier networks that prevail domestically in Japan.

73. Such an approach was proposed by Stephen D. Krasner in *Asymmetries in Japanese-American Trade: The Case for Specific Reciprocity* (Berkeley: Institute of International Studies, University of California, 1987).

74. Robert E. Hudec, "'Mirror, Mirror, on the Wall': The Concept of Fairness in United States Trade Policy," paper presented at the Roundtable on Fair Trade, Harmonization, Level Playing Fields and the World Trading System: Economic, Political and International Legal Questions for the 1990s, Columbia University, 10 January 1992, p. 1.

75. See Merit E. Janow, "Trading with an Ally: Progress and Discontent in U.S.-Japan Trade Relations," in Gerald C. Curtis, ed., *The United States, Japan, and Asia* (New York: Norton 1994).

76. Robert E. Hudec, "Thinking About the New Section 301: Beyond Good and Evil," in Bhagwati and Patrick, *Aggressive Unilateralism*.

77. James Sterngold, "Japan I s Trying New Approach in Trade Battles," *New York Times*, June 8, 1992, p. A1.

78. "Regionalism and Trade: The Right Direction?" *The Economist*, September 16, 1995, p. 23.

79. For a sophisticated discussion, see Jagdish Bhagwati, "Regionalism and Multilateralism: An Overview," presented at a World Bank Conference, April 2–3, 1992, and summarized in "The Trouble with Regionalism," *The Economist*, June 27, 1992, p. 79.

80. An early realist rendition was Robert Gilpin, *U.S. Power and the Multinational Corporation* (New York: Basic Books, 1975); more recently, see Kenneth N. Waltz, "The Emerging Structure of International Politics," *International Security*, 18 (Fall 1993).

81. Clair Wilcox, *A Charter for World Trade* (New York: Macmillan, 1949), pp. 70–71; also see Andreas F. Lowenfeld, "What the GATT Says (Or Does Not Say)," in William Diebold, Jr., ed., *Bilateralism, Multilateralism and Canada in U.S. Trade Policy* (Cambridge, Mass.: Ballinger, for the Council on Foreign Relations, 1988), pp. 55–68.

82. United Nations Conference on Trade and Development, *Trade and Development Report, 1991* (New York: United Nations, 1991), Table 23, p. 72, covers the period from 1973 to 1988; for more recent years, see World Trade Organization, *Regionalism and the World Trading System* (Geneva: WTO, April 1995).

83. "Regionalism and trade: The right direction?" p. 24.

84. Stephen J. Kobrin, "Regional Integration in a Networked Global Economy" (Philadelphia: Joseph H. Lauder Institute, The Wharton School, University of Pennsylvania, discussion paper, December 1994), p. 6.

85. UNCTC, *World Investment Report, 1991*, p. 36.

86. For a judicious assessment, see Peter A. Petri, "The East Asian Trading Bloc," in Jeffrey A. Frankel and Miles Kahler, eds., *Regionalism and Rivalry* (Chicago: University of Chicago Press, 1993).

87. Jagdish Bhagwati, *Protectionism* (Cambridge: MIT Press, 1988), p. 56.

88. The GATT figure is taken from Dan Kovenock and Marie Thursby, "GATT, Dispute Settlement and Cooperation," *Economics & Politics*, 4 (July 1992); and the U.S. figures from Destler, *American Trade Politics*, Table 6.1, p. 166.

89. This case is made by Robert Wolfe, "Opening Up the Green Box: Why Agriculture Dominated the Uruguay Round," paper prepared for presentation to the International Studies Association, Acapulco, Mexico, March 1993; and by the same author, "Does Embedded Liberalism Endure? Some Evidence from the Uruguay Round Negotiations on Investment" (Kingston, Ontario: Centre for International Relations, Queens University, n.d.).

90. See Stephen D. Krasner, "The Tokyo Round: Particularistic Interests and Prospects for Stability in the Global Trading System," *International Studies Quarterly*, 23 (December 1979).

91. See Helen V. Milner, *Resisting Protectionism: Global Industries and the Politics of International Trade* (Princeton: Princeton University Press, 1988); and Milner and David B. Yoffie, "Between Free Trade and Protectionism: Strategic Trade Policy and a Theory of Corporate Demands," *International Organization*, 41 (Spring 1989).

92. Stanley D. Nollen and Dennis P. Quinn, "Free Trade, Fair Trade, Strategic Trade, and Protectionism in the U.S. Congress, 1987–88," *International Organization*, 48 (Summer 1994).

93. Ibid., p. 518.

94. This phrase is due to Merit E. Janow, former Deputy Assistant United States Trade Representative, personal communication.

95. Robert Z. Aliber, "Fixed Exchange Rates and the Rate of Inflation," in Campbell and Dougan, *Alternative Monetary Regimes*, p. 120.

6. Economic Transformation

1. "Capitalism at Christmas," *Financial Times*, December 24, 1993, p. 6.

2. "In Search of Security," *The Economist*, October 16, 1993, p. 25.

3. Two works that come to mind readily are Edward Chamberlin, *The Theory of Monopolistic Competition* (Cambridge: Harvard University Press, 1929), and Joan Robinson, *The Economics of Imperfect Competition* (London: Macmillan, 1931).

4. Articles 47 through 52, as well as Article 54, further defined the salient terms and specified the remedies available under the ITO. Article 53 made special provisions for handling restrictive practices in what are now known as traded services. The full text is reprinted in Clair Wilcox, *A Charter for World Trade* (New York: Macmillan, 1949), pp. 281–287.

5. These words were taken almost verbatim from the ITO Charter, which the Soviets had a hand in drafting. See Jacob Viner, "Conflicts of Principle in Drafting a Trade Charter," *Foreign Affairs*, 25 (January 1947); and Herbert Feis, "The Conflict Over Trade Ideologies," *Foreign Affairs*, 25 (July 1947). For the corresponding assumptions on the monetary side, see Raymond Mikesell, "The Role of the International Monetary Agreements in a World of Planned Economies," *Journal of Political Economy*, 55 (December 1947).

6. Richard Blackhurst, "The Twilight of Domestic Economic Policies," *The World Economy*, 4 (December 1981).

7. Ibid., p. 363.

8. Patricia Kalla, "The GATT Dispute Settlement Procedure in the 1980s: Where Do We Go from Here," *Dickinson Journal of International Law*, 5 (Fall 1986), p. 95.

9. Sylvia Ostry, "Beyond the Border: The New International Policy Arena," in OECD, *Strategic Industries in a Global Economy* (Paris: Organization for Economic Cooperation and Development, 1991), pp. 83–84.

10. Ibid., p. 84.

11. Merit E. Janow, "Public and Private Restraints that Limit Access to Markets" (Paris: Organization for Economic Cooperation and Development, TD/RD (95)13, 28 April 1995), p. 4.

12. For example, even though the U.S.-Japan Structural Impediments Initiative was intended to be "mutual" and "reciprocal" in scope, the United States challenged Japan's domestic structures and practices while blunting consideration of its own. Merit E. Janow, former Deputy Assistant United States Trade Representative, personal communication.

13. Robert E. Hudec, "'Mirror, Mirror, on the Wall': The Concept of Fairness in United States Trade Policy," paper presented at the Roundtable on Fair Trade, Harmonization, Level Playing Fields and the World Trading System: Economic, Political and International Legal Questions for the 1990s, Columbia University, January 10, 1992, p. 1.

14. The archetype of the so-called revisionist school is Chalmers Johnson. See, for example, "The Japanese Political Economy: A Crisis in Theory," *Ethics & International Affairs*, vol. 2 (1988). More mainstream views on Japan's domestic structure as it relates to international trade, may be found in Daniel I. Okimoto, "Political Inclusivity: The Domestic Structure of Trade," in Takashi Inoguchi and Daniel I. Okimoto, eds., *The Political Economy of Japan*, vol. 2, *The Changing International Context* (Stanford: Stanford University Press, 1988); on Japan's industrial policy, see Daniel I. Okimoto, *Between MITI and the Market: Japanese Industrial Policy for High Technology* (Stanford: Stanford University Press, 1989); on investment policy, Dennis J. Encarnation, *Rivals Beyond Trade: America Versus Japan in Global Competition* (Ithaca: Cornell University Press, 1992); and on the electoral system as it affects multilateral commitments, see Peter F. Cowhey, "Elect Locally—Order Globally: Domes-

tic Politics and Multilateral Cooperation," in John Gerard Ruggie, ed., *Multilateralism Matters* (New York: Columbia University Press, 1993).

15. Blackhurst, "The Twilight," p. 369, emphasis in original.

16. The Clinton administration has favored the OECD over the WTO for these new issues. But OECD recommendations would lack the universality or legal powers of WTO rules. See Alan Riding, "O.E.C.D. Being Pressed to Change Its Mission," *New York Times*, June 5, 1994, p. D2. The OECD's predecessor, the OEEC, it may be remembered from chapter 2, was established to monitor the implementation of the Marshall Plan. Whereas the Soviet Union rejected participation in that program for itself and its satellites, Russia has now signed an association agreement with the OECD, and Hungary, Poland, the Czech Republic, and Slovakia are "partners in transition." Mexico became the first developing country to join.

17. William J. Drake and Kalypso Nicolaidis, "Ideas, Interests, and Institutionalization: 'Trade in Services' and the Uruguay Round," *International Organization*, 46 (Winter 1992), p. 45.

18. For a brief summary, see "Nothing to Lose but Its Chains: A Survey of World Trade," *The Economist*, September 22, 1990.

19. Its provisions are summarized in Bernard M. Hoekman, *Trade Laws and Institutions: Good Practices and the World Trade Organization* (Washington, D.C.: World Bank, Discussion Paper 282, April 1995), pp. 46–50.

20. "A Gatt for Services," *The Economist*, October 12, 1985.

21. For a good conceptual discussion along these lines, see Jagdish Bhagwati, "Trade in Services and the Multilateral Trade Negotiations," *The World Bank Economic Review*, 1 (No. 4, 1987), and by the same author, "International Trade in Services and Its Relevance for Economic Development," in Orio Giarini, ed., *The Emerging Service Economy* (London: Pergamon Press, 1987).

22. William Drozdiak, "Historic Trade Pact Signed, but Global Tensions Persist," *Washington Post*, April 16, 1994, p. A12.

23. Daniel C. Esty's book, *Greening the GATT: Trade, Environment, and the Future* (Washington, D.C.: Institute for International Economics, 1994), is an admirable effort to establish some degree of conceptual order and policy priorities among the many and diverse issues involved. For a detailed study of the relationship between trade agreements and environmental standards, see David Vogel, *Trading Up: Consumer Environmental Regulation in a Global Economy* (Cambridge: Harvard University Press, 1995).

24. See Esty, *Greening the GATT*, chap. 7.

25. U.S. Corporate Average Fuel Economy (CAFE) mileage standards for cars are illustrative. Though technically nondiscriminatory, in practice they discriminate against European upscale imports—in addition to excluding light trucks, which would lower U.S. fleet averages. A model-by-model tax would be truly nondiscriminatory.

26. "The Greening of Protectionism," *The Economist*, February 27, 1993, p. 25.

27. A law suit brought by the Earth Island Institute, a small California environmental group, forced a reluctant U.S. government to impose a ban on the import of Mexican tuna caught using purse seine nets because that process also killed dolphins in excess of limits set by the U.S. Marine Mammal Protection Act. Mexico took the case to GATT, which decided against the United States. The ruling lent itself to the interpretation that trade dominates the environment on principled grounds within GATT, and that unprotected common property resources have no standing in GATT trade law. Indeed, Mexico became so concerned about the adverse impact of the ruling on prospects for NAFTA that it never sought to have it officially adopted by GATT. See Esty, *Greening the GATT*, pp. 29–33.

28. "Exporting Labor Standards," *Washington Post*, April 10, 1994, p. C6.

29. William Drozdiak, "New Global Markets Mean Grim Trade-Offs," *Washington Post*, August 8, 1994, p. A1.

30. This program is described briefly in Terry Collingsworth, J. William Goold, and Pharis J. Harvey, "Time for a Global New Deal," *Foreign Affairs*, 73 (January/February 1994).

31. Philip G. Cerny, "Globalization and the Changing Logic of Collective Action," *International Organization*, 49 (Autumn 1995), p. 621.

32. Milton Friedman, "Internationalization of the U.S. Economy," *Fraser Forum*, February 1989, p. 8.

33. Ibid., p. 10.

34. In a controversial article published more than a quarter century ago, Kenneth Waltz, a leading academic realist, advanced a similar argument, using as his measures (1) the relatively smaller size of the external sector of the major economic powers today as a percentage of their domestic economies, compared to the late nineteenth/early twentieth centuries (also noted by Friedman), and (2) the lower degree of intersectoral specialization in their trade. Kenneth N. Waltz, "The Myth of National Interdependence," in Charles P. Kindleberger, ed., *The International Corporation* (Cambridge: MIT Press, 1970). With intrasectoral flows dominating trade among the major economies today the second part of Waltz's definition has become a truism. The first is far less the case today than when he published his article, but more importantly it is also less relevant, for reasons we discuss below. For a more recent realist rejection of the proposition that the world economy is undergoing fundamental change, see Ethan B. Kapstein, "We are US: The Myth of the Multinational," *The National Interest*, 26 (Winter 1991/92).

35. "A Survey of the World Economy: Who's in the driving seat?" *The Economist*, October 7, 1995, p. 5.

36. The typology is due to Oliver E. Williamson, *Markets and Hierarchies* (New York: Free Press, 1975); and Walter W. Powell, "Neither Market Nor Hierarchy: Network Forms of Organization," *Research in Organization Behavior*, Vol. 12 (Greenwich, CT: JAI Press, 1990).

37. John M. Stopford and Susan Strange, *Rival States, Rival Firms: Competition for World Market Shares* (Cambridge, England: Cambridge University Press, 1991), p. 40.

38. This and the following figures are taken from "A Survey of the World Economy: Who's in the driving seat?"

39. As of 1993, only about 6% of U.S. stocks, for example, were owned by foreigners. Alan S. Blinder, "Remarks Before Community Leaders Breakfast Meeting," San Francisco, California, March 9, 1995, p. 7.

40. Geoffrey Garrett, "Capital Mobility, Trade, and the Domestic Politics of Economic Policy," *International Organization*, 49 (Autumn 1995), Figure 1, p. 661.

41. "A Survey of the World Economy," p. 24.

42. Stephen J. Kobrin, "An Empirical Analysis of the Determinants of Global Integration," *Strategic Management Journal*, 12 (Summer 1991), p. 20.

43. Joseph Grunwald and Kenneth Flamm, *The Global Factory: Foreign Assembly in International Trade* (Washington, D.C.: The Brookings Institution, 1985).

44. Walter B. Wriston, "Bashing Japan With Flawed Figures," *Washington Post*, August 4, 1994, p. A31. Also see Peter F. Cowhey and Jonathan D. Aronson, *Managing the World Economy: The Consequences of Corporate Alliances* (New York: Council on Foreign Relations, 1993), chaps. 5–7, which contain detailed case studies of the automobile, semiconductor, and telecommunications industries.

45. "The Discreet Charm of the Multicultural Multinational," *The Economist*, July 30, 1994, p. 57.

46. Jane Sneddon Little, "Intra-Firm Trade: An Update," *New England Economic Review* (May/June 1987).

47. Stephen Kobrin's work has been helpful to me in conceptualizing this transformation; see "An Empirical Analysis of the Determinants of Global Integration," and "Beyond Geography: Inter-Firm Networks and the Structural Integration of the Global Economy" (William H. Wurster Center for International Management Studies, Wharton School, University of Pennsylvania, WP 93–10, November 1993).

48. Powell, "Neither Market nor Hierarchy," p. 304.

49. Kobrin, "Beyond Geography," stresses this causal factor.

50. "The Discreet Charm of the Multicultural Multinational," p. 58; also see Vanessa Houlder, "Today's Friend, Tomorrow's Foe," *Financial Times*, October 2, 1995, p. 10.

51. Paul McCracken, "Costlier Labor, Fewer Jobs, Unemployment—The Crisis Continues," *Wall Street Journal*, January 7, 1994, p. A10.

52. Reported in Robert D. Hershey, Jr., "U.S. Wages Up 2.7% in Year, A Record Low," *New York Times*, November 1, 1995, p. A1. Inflation for the same period was 2.5%, producing a 0.2% rate of increase in real wages.

53. Anthony B. Atkinson, Lee Rainwater, and Timothy M. Smeeding, *Income Distribution in OECD Countries* (Paris: Organization for Economic Cooperation and Development, 1995).

54. Drozdiak, "New Global Markets Mean Grim Trade-Offs." U.S. unemployment figures of less than 6% are sure to be at least somewhat understated. As the senior economist of the National Association of Manufacturers—not usually closely allied with labor—has stated: "There are large numbers of temporary, part-time and contract workers out there who are counted as employed but are in reality competing for permanent jobs. . . . There are enormous amounts of disguised slack in the labor market." Quoted by Louis Uchitelle, "A Matter of Timing—Debate on the Fed's Latest Rate Increase Focuses on Capacity and Wage Demands," *New York Times*, August 18, 1994, p. D16.

55. Richard T. Curtin, the Director, quoted by Louis Uchitelle, "The Rise of the Losing Class," *New York Times*, November 20, 1994, p. E1.

56. Since 1973, it has barely averaged annual increases of 1 percent. See Angus Maddison, *Dynamic Forces in Capitalist Development* (New York: Oxford University Press, 1991), p. 51.

57. For an accessible account, see Peter F. Drucker, "The Age of Social Transformation," *Atlantic Monthly*, November 1994.

58. Jeff Madrick, "The End of Affluence," *New York Review of Books*, September 21, 1995, p. 14.

59. Some of the U.S. figures are cited in Keith Bradsher, "Skilled Workers Watch their Jobs Migrate Overseas," *New York Times*, August 28, 1995, p. A1.

60. Perhaps the strongest case that imports from low-wage countries adversely affect workers in the industrialized countries is made by Adrian Wood, *North-South Trade, Employment and Equality* (Oxford: Clarendon Press, 1994). For a critical survey of the economics literature, see Richard G. Harris, "Globalization, Trade, and Income," *Canadian Journal of Economics*, 26 (November 1993). Harris notes the confounding factor that the respective employment effects of labor-reducing technologies and globalization have not yet been clearly distinguished in rigorous empirical studies. Nor, Bhagwati adds, have these studies demonstrated the logically necessary intermediating step that the domestic prices of goods using unskilled labor have declined as a result of outsourcing to poor countries, which in turn would put downward pressure on domestic wages. Jagdish Bhagwati, "Trade and Wages: A Malign Relationship?" (Department of Economics, Columbia University, discussion paper # 761, October 1995). Finally, the dynamic gains from trade have not yet been incorporated into most studies.

61. Bhagwati, "Trade and Wages," p. 23; also see Bhagwati and Vivek Dehejia, "Freer Trade and Wages of the Unskilled—Is Marx Striking Again?," in Jagdish Bhagwati and Marvin Kosters, eds., *Trade and Wages* (Washington, D.C.: American Enterprise Institute, 1994).

62. J. Steven Landefeld, Obie G. Whichard, and Jeffrey H. Lowe, "Alternative Frameworks for U.S. International Transactions," *Survey of Current Business*, December 1993.

63. G. John Ikenberry, "Funk de Siècle: Impasses of Western Industrial Society at Century's End," *Millennium: Journal of International Studies*, 24 (Spring 1995).

64. Harris, "Globalization, trade, and income," p. 761.

65. Garrett, "Capital Mobility, Trade, and the Domestic Politics of Economic Policy."

66. Richard N. Cooper, *Economic Policy in an Interdependent World* (Cambridge: MIT Press, 1986), p. 96.

67. As a proportion of GDP, public sector debt increased from 15 percent in 1974 to 40 percent twenty years later. "A Survey of the World Economy," p. 15.

68. David M. Andrews, "Capital Mobility and State Autonomy: Toward a Structural Theory of International Monetary Relations," *International Studies Quarterly*, 38 (June 1994), p. 204.

69. "A Survey of the World Economy," p. 16.

70. In the words of *The Economist*: to "borrow recklessly, run inflationary policies or try to defend unsustainable exchange rates." Ibid., p. 37.

71. Andrews, "Capital Mobility and State Autonomy," p. 201.

72. U.S. regulatory authorities have been particularly worried about this problem. See, for example, E. Gerard Corrigan, "A Perspective on the Globalization of Financial Markets and Institutions," Federal Reserve Bank of New York, *Quarterly Review*, 12 (Spring 1987), p. 2. Corrigan at the time was President of the New York Fed, and did much to push this agenda.

73. George Soros, "Hedge Funds and Dynamic Hedging," an edited version of testimony given to the U.S. House of Representatives Committee on Banking, Finance, and Urban Affairs on April 13, 1994 (New York: Soros Fund Management, May 1994), p. 13. Soros also challenged certain beliefs by economists: "The generally accepted theory is that financial markets tend towards equilibrium and, on the whole, discount the future correctly. I operate using a different theory, according to which financial markets cannot possibly discount the future correctly because they do not merely discount the future; they help to shape it. . . . When that happens, markets enter into a state of dynamic disequilibrium and behave quite differently from what would be considered normal by the theory of efficient markets"(pp. 1–2). In 1992, Soros' Quantum Fund bet on one such "dynamic disequilibrium" in the value of the British pound, winning $1 billion in one week while helping to push the pound out of the European currency arrangement.

74. Little, "Intra-Firm Trade."

75. See Mark Cassons, *Multinationals and World Trade* (London: Allen & Unwin, 1986); and the earlier but still useful study by Gerald C. Helleiner, *Intra-Firm Trade and the Developing Countries* (London: Macmillan, 1981).

76. Robert B. Reich, *The Work of Nations* (New York: Knopf, 1991), chap. 25.

77. The case involved Brothers Industries Ltd. of Japan, and Smith Corona. Adding another element of complexity, Smith Corona is owned 48 percent by Hanson P.L.C., a British group. Robert B. Reich, "Dumpsters," *The New*

Republic, 10 June 1991, p. 9. The Brothers request was subsequently denied, the ITC concluding that the firm was not enough of a domestic producer to claim injury.

78. See Theodore Moran, "The Globalization of America's Defense Industries: Managing the Threat of Foreign Dependence," *International Security*, 15 (Summer 1990).

79. Cowhey and Aronson, *Managing the World Economy*, pp. 16–17.

80. Cerny, "Globalization and the Changing Logic of Collective Action," p. 619.

81. At least, this was true of its post-1938 variant, as Alan Brinkley shows in a recent study, *The End of Reform: New Deal Liberalism in Recession and War* (New York: Knopf, 1995).

82. Mary Ruggie, "The Paradox of Liberal Intervention: Health Policy and the American Welfare State," *American Journal of Sociology*, 97 (January 1992).

83. See Steve Fraser, "The 'Labor Question,' " in Steve Fraser and Gary Gerstle, eds., *The Rise and Fall of the New Deal Order* (Princeton: Princeton University Press, 1989).

84. I. M. Destler, *American Trade Politics*, 2nd Ed. (Washington, D.C.: Institute for International Economics, 1992), p. 23.

85. Ibid., pp. 152–153.

86. See Frank Swoboda, "Reich Targets Several Job Programs," *Washington Post*, January 28, 1994, p. A1

87. See Thomas Janoski, *The Political Economy of Unemployment: Active Labor Market Policy in West Germany and The United States* (Berkeley and Los Angeles: University of California Press, 1990).

88. OECD, *Employment Outlook* (Paris: OECD, 1993), Table 8.19.

89. "Training up America," *The Economist*, January 15, 1994, p. 27.

90. The seminal study of the ill-effects of believing otherwise remains Karl Polanyi, *The Great Transformation: The Political and Economic Origins of Our Time* (Boston: Beacon Books, [1944] 1957); for an equally enduring contemporaneous work, see Edward Hallett Carr, *The Twenty Years' Crisis, 1919–1939* (New York: Harper, [1939] 1964).

91. OECD, *The Future of Social Protection* (Paris: OECD, 1988). Social expenditures average roughly one-third of GDP in the OECD countries today, though they are substantially lower in the United States.

92. Quoted by Frank Swoboda, "Reich Targets Several Job Programs."

93. Quoted by Geoffrey York, "Grits vow radical social reform," *Globe and Mail* (Toronto), February 1, 1994, p. A7.

94. See, for example, Robert E. Lucas, "On the Mechanics of Economic Development," *Journal of Monetary Economics*, 22 (July 1988), and Robert Barro, "Government Spending in a Simple Model of Endogenous Growth," *Journal of Political Economy*, 98 (October 1990).

95. Charles P. Kindleberger, *The World in Depression, 1929–1939* (Berkeley: University of California Press, 1973).

7. Polarity, Plurality, and the Future

1. Charles Krauthammer, "The Unipolar Moment," *Foreign Affairs*, 70 (Winter 1990/91), pp. 24–25.

2. Johanna Neuman, "Christopher: U.S. will lead, but not in Bosnia," *USA Today*, May 28, 1993, p. 6A. Secretary of State Warren Christopher had rushed to "clarify" Tarnoff's remarks, which provoked a flap in Washington and abroad.

3. See USIP, *Peace Watch*, 1 (February 1995), p. 1.

4. Terry Deibel, "Strategies Before Containment: Patterns for the Future," *International Security*, 16 (Spring 1992), p. 79, emphasis added.

5. Quoted in Manfred Jonas, *Isolationism in America* (Ithaca: Cornell University Press, 1966), p. 5.

6. An idealist strain of isolationism that has been present in American political life almost from the start is the "City on the Hill" model: that the United States is, or should strive to be, such an example to the world that others will want to emulate it, as a result of which the United States can shape the international order without significant intervention in it. For a sophisticated post-cold war variant, see Eric A. Nordlinger, *Isolationism Reconfigured: American Foreign Policy for a New Century* (Princeton: Princeton University Press, 1995). Nordlinger urges disengagement in the security realm beyond North America to create the autonomy by which to pursue, more actively, U.S. economic interests and American ideals.

7. Quoted in Jonas, *Isolationism in America*, p. 5.

8. The bills in question are H.R. 7 in the House and S. 5 in the Senate; repeal of the War Powers Act was subsequently withdrawn by the legislation's sponsors, presumably because they did not wish a Democratic president to be so freed from a newly Republican controlled Congress.

9. Deibel, "Strategies Before Containment," p. 89.

10. Quoted in Robert Kuttner, "Look Who Wants to Tinker with Market Forces," *Business Week*, October 2, 1995, p. 26.

11. Deibel, "Strategies Before Containment," p. 85.

12. Krauthammer, "The Unipolar Moment."

13. In a draft of the Defense Planning Guidance for the Fiscal Years 1994–1999, which was leaked to the press. See Patrick E. Tyler, "U.S. Strategy Plan Calls for Insuring No Rivals Develop," *New York Times*, March 9, 1992, p. A1; and "Excerpts From Pentagon's Plan: 'Prevent the Re-Emergence of a New Rival,'" ibid., p. A14.

14. "Excerpts From Pentagon's Plan," emphasis added.

15. See Patrick E. Tyler, "Senior U.S. Officials Assail Lone-Superpower Policy," *New York Times*, March 11, 1992, p. A6; and Tyler, "Pentagon Drops Goal of Blocking New Superpowers," *New York Times*, May 24, 1992, p. A1.

16. Christopher Layne, "The Unipolar Illusion: Why New Great Powers Will Rise," *International Security*, 17 (Spring 1993), p. 7. One exception to the cho-

rus of realist criticism was Samuel P. Huntington, "Why International Primacy Matters," in ibid., arguing that "the welfare and security of Americans and . . . the future of freedom, democracy, open economies, and international order" hinge on continued American primacy (p. 83). Huntington was mostly responding to Robert Jervis, "International Primacy: Is the Game Worth the Candle," in ibid.

17. John Le Carré, *Our Game* (New York: Knopf, 1995), p. 52.

18. Samuel P. Huntington, "The Clash of Civilizations?" *Foreign Affairs*, 72 (Summer 1993).

19. Ibid., p. 48.

20. For a more sophisticated and also more hopeful treatment of these issues, see Mark Juergensmeyer, *The New Cold War? Religious Nationalism Confronts the Secular State* (Berkeley: University of California Press, 1993).

21. Layne, "The Unipolar Illusion"; and Kenneth N. Waltz, "The Emerging Structure of International Politics," *International Security*, 18 (Fall 1993).

22. Layne, "The Unipolar Illusion," p. 37; Waltz concurs that this is likely.

23. Waltz, "The Emerging Structure of International Politics," p. 72.

24. On Japan, see, for example, Peter J. Katzenstein and Nobuo Ikawara, "Japan's National Security: Structures, Norms, and Policies," *International Security*, 17 (Spring 1993), and Thomas U. Berger, "From Sword to Chrysanthemum: Japan's Culture of Anti-militarism," in ibid.; for a compatible discussion of Germany and Europe more generally, see Stephen Van Evera, "Primed for Peace: Europe After the Cold War," *International Security*, 15 (Winter 1990/91).

25. Richard K. Betts, ". . . And What to Do about It," *Washington Quarterly*, 19 (Winter 1996), p. 103, emphasis added—a comment on Don M. Snider, "The Coming Defense Train Wreck . . . ," in ibid. For a discussion of America's considerable "intangible" sources of power, including its adaptable institutions and universalistic culture, see Joseph S. Nye, Jr., *Bound to Lead: The Changing Nature of American Power* (New York: Basic Books, 1990).

26. Waltz hedges his argument by noting that nuclear weapons have changed the strategic game of states, requiring only a secure second strike capability for effective deterrence to hold. But if that is the new definition of what constitutes a "pole," then the international order has been multipolar for more than forty years—throughout most of the era of bipolarity.

27. See, respectively, Layne, "The Unipolar Illusion"; Waltz, "The Emerging Structure of International Politics"; and John J. Mearsheimer, "Back to the Future: Instability in Europe After the Cold War," *International Security*, 15 (September 1990). On Mearsheimer's list of preferred recipients are Germany and Ukraine (on the latter, see his "The Case for a Ukrainian Nuclear Deterrent," *Foreign Affairs*, 72 [Summer 1993]); Germany, as we noted, has shown little interest to date, and Ukraine with some alacrity got rid of the nuclear weapons left on its soil when the Soviet Union broke up.

28 .See Henry Kissinger, "Expand NATO Now," *Washington Post*, December 19, 1994, p. A27; Mearsheimer, "Back to the Future"; and Waltz, "The Emerging Structure of International Politics."

29. Huntington, "Why International Primacy Matters," p. 76.

30. Joseph L. Nogee, "Polarity: An Ambiguous Concept," *Orbis*, 18 (Winter 1975), pp. 1193–1194.

31. Kissinger, *Diplomacy* (New York: Simon & Schuster, 1994), p. 833.

32. This is true not only of the foreign policy and military apparatus of the state, but even of its domestic welfare components. On the latter, see Theda Skocpol, *Protecting Soldiers and Mothers: The Political Origins of Social Policy in the United States* (Cambridge: Harvard University Press, 1992).

33. The phrase was introduced in the late 1940s by the noted Yale sociologist Harold Lasswell. For a good discussion of why it did not materialize in the form feared, see Aaron L. Friedberg, "Why Didn't the United States Become a Garrison State?" *International Security*, 16 (Spring 1992).

34. The influence of Wallace on Republican strategy is the subject of Dan T. Carter, *The Politics of Rage: George Wallace, the Origins of the New Conservatism, and the Transformation of American Politics* (New York: Simon & Schuster, 1995).

35. David E. Sanger, "Seismic Shift in the Parties Reflects View on Business," *New York Times*, September 24, 1995, p. E1. Sanger reports that nearly 60 House Republicans elected in 1994 fall into this category.

36. See Michael Clough, "Grass-Roots Policymaking: Say Good-Bye to the 'Wise Men,'" *Foreign Affairs*, 73 (January/February 1994).

37. See Everett Carll Ladd, "The 1994 Congressional Elections: The Realignment Continues," *Political Science Quarterly*, 110 (Spring 1995), and William F. Connelly, Jr. and John J. Pitney, Jr., "The Future of the House Republicans," *Political Science Quarterly*, 109 (Fall 1994).

38. Ladd, "The 1994 Congressional Elections," pp. 18–19.

39. For a partial yet judicious survey, see Daniel Bell, "The Cultural Wars: American Intellectual Life, 1965–1992," *The Wilson Quarterly*, 16 (Summer 1992).

40. See David A. Hollinger, *Postethnic America: Beyond Multiculturalism* (New York: Basic, 1995).

41. The late teens and early twenties, for example, were far worse; see Robert Dallek, *The American Style of Foreign Policy* (New York: Oxford University Press, 1983), pp. 92–94. For a two-century history of American curricular controversies, consult W. B. Carnochan, *The Battleground of the Curriculum: Liberal Education and American Experience* (Stanford: Stanford University Press, 1993).

42. Hollinger, *Postethnic America*. The quotations are from p. 82 (where Hollinger, in turn, approvingly cites Gary B. Nash's phrase) and p. 113.

43. Ibid., p. 85.

44. Ibid., p. 84.

45. Ibid., p. 14 and p. 134.

46. See Jack Citrin, Ernst B. Haas, Christopher Muste, and Beth Reingold, "Is American Nationalism Changing? Implications for Foreign Policy," *International Studies Quarterly*, 38 (March 1994). Their analysis was primarily based on data from a 1991 California poll, and the 1992 American National Election Study survey conducted by the University of Michigan.

47. Ibid., p. 11.

48. Ibid., pp. 13–15.

49. Ibid., p. 20; see also Table 5, p. 21.

50. Ibid., pp. 26–27. Liberalism here refers not to partisan-political orientation but to a belief in the validity of such principles as liberty, individualism, popular sovereignty, and the like.

51. David Fromkin, *In the Time of the Americans* (New York: Knopf, 1995), p. 7.

52. See "U.S. Public Support for U.N. Unexpectedly Grows, New Poll Shows," press release, United Nations Association of the United States of America, December 7, 1995, summarizing a nation-wide survey conducted by the Wirthlin Group.

Index

Acheson, Dean, 39, 57, 191n65
Act of Chapultepec (1945), 187n71
Adams, John Quincy, 8
Adenauer government, 62
Afghanistan, 90
Africa, 64, 66
African Americans, 168
An Agenda for Peace (Boutros-Ghali), 95
Aidid, Mohammed Farah, 96, 177n5
Albania, 55
Albrecht-Carrié, René, 197n49
Aldrich, Winthrop, 35
Algeria, 64
Aliber, Robert, 134
Allin, Dana, 84
Ambrosius, Lloyd E., 178n34
American Federation of Labor, 112
American Foreign Policy (Kennan), 47
Angola, 90, 95
Antall, Jozsef, 195n27
ANZUS Pact, 56, 63
Arab countries: Baghdad Pact and, 63;
    General Assembly and, 57; Israeli rela-
    tions with, 55, 65, 66; UN Charter
    Article 51 and, 186n62; *see also* Islam;
    Muslims
Argentina, 73, 74, 129
Aronson, Jonathan D., 152, 215n44
Asia, 30, 57, 63, 66; *see also* East Asia;
    South Asia

Asia-Pacific Economic Cooperation Forum,
    105, 130
Asmus, Ronald D., 195n20
Aspin, Les, 96
Association of Southeast Asian Nations
    (ASEAN), 105, 130; ASEAN Regional
    Forum, 105
Aswan Dam, 64, 65
Atlantic Alliance, *see* North Atlantic
    Treaty Organization
Atlantic Charter, 32
Atomic Energy Commission (UN), 71
Australia, 56, 63
Austria, 16, 88, 129, 197n42
Austro-Hungarian Empire, 81
Axis countries, 31
Axworthy, Lloyd, 155
Azerbaijan, 91

Baghdad Pact, 63, 64
Baker, James, 205n32
Balkan countries, 198n60
Baltic countries, 83, 84, 197n42
Bank for International Settlements, 151
Baruch Plan, 71–72, 191–92n65
Belarus, 84
Belgian Congo, 68, 95; *see also* Zaire
Belgium, 68, 73, 74, 196n38, 197n49
Benelux countries, 59
Bergsten, Fred, 108

Berlin airlift, 1
Bernstein, Barton, 71–72
Betts, Richard, 101, 164
Beveridge, Albert J., 178n35
Bevin, Ernest, 44
Bhagwati, Jagdish, 132, 149, 216n60
Bismarck, Otto von, 20
Blackhurst, Richard, 137–38, 139
"Black Monday" on Wall Street (1987), 123
Bolshevik Revolution, 181n73
Bolsheviks, see Comintern (Communist International); Communism; Soviet Union
Borah, William E., 15, 16, 17, 159, 179n46; and "Battalion of Death," 179n46
Bosnia: British intervention in, 98–99, 100; Dayton accord for, 201n92; European response to, 171; former Soviet republics and, 84; French-German relations and, 196–97n41; NATO air strikes on, 93, 96, 98, 100, 102; Tarnoff on, 157; Thatcher on, 200n80; UN intervention in, 78, 90, 91, 92, 99–100, 204n91; U.S. intervention in, 93, 97–98; vital interest debate on, 159
Boutros-Ghali, Boutros, 95
Brazil, 73, 74, 129, 208n63
Bretton Woods Conference (1944), 28, 203n6; British-U.S. Joint Statement of Principles, 109; "double screen" component of, 37–38; Polanyi anticipation of, 108; regime established by, 109–12, 113, 114, 115, 118–19; Soviet participation in, 29, 36, 184n39
Briquemont, Francis, 92
Britain: Bosnian crisis and, 98–99, 100; currency of, 113, 217n73; Cyprus crisis and, 68; 1950s defense responsibilities of, 59; Dumbarton Oaks Conference and, 188n5; Dunkirk Treaty and, 41–42; Eastern Mediterranean instability and, 39; EURATOM and, 61; French Security Council membership and, 32; GATT and, 111, 184n48; Hong Kong and, 46; hypothetical dominance of, 23–24; IMF and, 110, 118; joint airborne command of, 196n38; Korean War and, 56; "lift-and-strike" proposal and, 93; Monroe Doctrine and, 9; Nazi trade with, 183n36; neoliberal economics and, 119; 19th-century balance of power and, 88; North Atlantic security system and, 44;

nuclear capabilities of, 72; Nuclear Suppliers Group and, 73; Palestine mandate of, 55; peacekeeping by, 90; post-World War II economic negotiations and, 36, 109, 203n8; Suez crisis and, 64, 65, 66, 190n51; UN Military Staff Committee proposal of, 52–53; Wilson and, 26
British Commonwealth, 56, 186n62
British Special Forces, 99
British-U.S. Combined Chiefs of Staff, 52
Brothers Industries Ltd., 152, 217n77
Brown, Michael E., 84, 195nn20, 25
Brussels Pact (1948), 42, 43, 60, 196n37
Brzezinski, Zbigniew, 197n45
Buchanan, Pat, 3, 155, 161
Bulgaria, 55, 83
Bundeswehr (Germany), 197–98n60
Busch, Marc L., 206–7n41
Bush, George, 2, 129–30
Bush, Vannevar, 71
Bush administration, 2, 90, 97, 162

California, 168
California Poll (1991), 221n46
California Proposition 187: 3
Cambodia, 90, 91, 95, 197–98n60
Cameron, David R., 206n39
Camp David Accords, 68
Canada: NAFTA and, 2, 129; North Atlantic security and, 44; Nuclear Suppliers Group and, 73; UN peacekeeping and, 172; wage trends in, 150; welfare reform in, 155; Western European security and, 42, 185n60
Canadian Confederation, 81
Carr, E. H., 179n46, 183n33
Carter, Dan T., 221n34
Carter administration, 122
Caucasus, 95
Central America, 9
Central Europe: aid to, 87; peaceful change possibilities in, 103; post-cold war NATO and, 2, 82, 85, 106, 171; Russian threat to, 83; WEU and, 197n42
Central Treaty Organization (Baghdad Pact), 63, 64
Chapultepec Act (1945), 187n71
Chesterton, G. K., 25
Chile, 129
China: post-war U.N. forces and, 54; civil war in, 46; domestic instability in, 92; Dumbarton Oaks Conference and,

188n5; East Asian security and, 105; "four policemen" scheme and, 30; Japanese invasion of, 16; McKinley policy on, 10, 35, 47; nuclear capabilities of, 72, 73; Security Council membership of, 32, 90, 198n56; Soviet-U.S. relations and, 165; in 21st century, 163; UN representation of, 56; U.S. interests and, 57

"Christian" right, 167

Christopher, Warren, 219n2

Churchill, Winston: on EDC, 59; Eden report to, 182n12; European council proposed by, 30; relations of with Stalin and and FDR, 29; UN vision of, 31

Ciampi, Carlo Azeglio, 96

Clayton, William L., 35

Clinton, Bill, 2, 7, 85, 176n7, 177n5

Clinton administration: Bosnian crisis and, 97–98; economic policy of, 135; foreign policy of, 2, 22, 93, 157; Haiti operation of, 92; "isolationism" charges of, 8; Japanese automotive sector and, 129; NAFTA and, 142, 143–44; OECD and, 213n16; Somali crisis and, 96; trade adjustment assistance and, 154; UN policy of, 2, 7, 22, 78, 93

Cold War, see Soviet Union: U.S. relations with

Combined Chiefs of Staff (U.K.-U.S.), 52

Combined Joint Task Forces (NATO), 87

Comintern (Communist International), 23, 26

Committee on European Economic Cooperation (Organization for European Economic Cooperation), 41, 61, 184n54, 213n16

Common Foreign and Security Policy (EU), 87

Common Market (European Economic Community), 61, 81, 86, 111

Communism, 112; East Asian, 46; Eastern European, 85, 108; Southeast Asian, 63; Western European, 39

Conant, James B., 71

Concert of Europe, 88–89, 182n21, 197n47

Conference on Security and Cooperation in Europe, 87; see also Organization for Security and Cooperation in Europe

Congress of Europe, 197n47

Connally, John B., Jr., 202n4

Conservative Party (U.K.), 36

"Contract with America," 7, 8, 159, 183n30

Cooper, John Milton, 10, 14

Cooper, Richard N., 37, 114, 115, 150, 203n7

Corporate Average Fuel Economy standards, 213n25

Corrigan, E. Gerard, 216n72

Cot, Jean, 98

Council for Security Cooperation in Asia-Pacific, 105

Council on Foreign Relations, 16

Cowhey, Peter F., 152, 215n44

Crimean War, 88

Croatia, 100, 196–97n41, 201n92

Crossette, Barbara, 175–76n6

Cruise missiles, 58

Cuba, 9, 90

Cuban missile crisis (1962), 50

Cyprus, 68

Czechoslovakia, 64; see also Slovakia

Czech Republic, 83, 84, 195n25, 213n16

Dallek, Robert, 9–10, 15, 17, 29, 39

Dayton Accord, 201n92

Deibel, Terry, 158, 160, 162

Democratic Party: fourth FDR nomination of, 28; League of Nations membership issue and, 14–15, 178–79n34, 179n35; organized labor and, 3; Reagan trade policy and, 123; Southern states and, 166; State Department leadership and, 182n22

Denmark, 81

Desert Storm (military operation), 56, 90, 94, 157

Destler, I. M., 122, 123

Deutsch, Karl W., 85, 195–96n32

Dewey, Thomas E., 19, 28

Dibb, Paul, 105

Dienbienphu, Battle of, 63

Dobbie, C. W. G., 201n86

Dole, Robert, 93

Donovan, William, 182n22

Drake, William J., 140, 141

Drucker, Peter, 209n68

Dubrovnik (Croatia), 97

Duffield, John, 195n36

Dulles, John Foster: "collective security" discourse and, 22, 63; on EDC, 60; on IAEA, 74; multilateralism and, 28; Nasser and, 65

Dumbarton Oaks Conference (1944): convening of, 28; enforcement issue and, 52; Kennan on, 34; League of Nations

Dumbarton Oaks...(*Continued*)
    failures and, 29; participants in, 189n5;
    U.S. war powers issue and, 53
Dunkirk Treaty (1947), 41–42
Dworkin, Ronald, 49

Earth Island Institute, 214n27
East Asia: cooperative balance in, 80; eco-
    nomic regionalism in, 130, 131; future
    U.S. role in, 171–72; Japanese trade
    with, 35–36; Section 301 and, 125; secu-
    rity context of, 104–5; Soviet-Chinese
    relations and, 32; U.S. defense of, 46,
    47, 79; *see also* Pacific region
East Asian Co-Prosperity Sphere, 35–36
Eastern Europe: aid to, 87; OECD and,
    213n16; peaceful change possibilities in,
    103; post-cold war NATO and, 2, 82,
    85, 106, 171; Russian threat to, 83; *see
    also* Warsaw Pact
Eastern Mediterranean, 39
Economic and Social Council (UN), 32
The Economist: on Bretton Woods system,
    112; on budget deficits, 151; on eco-
    nomic security, 135–36; on fiscal irre-
    sponsibility, 217n70; on German Torna-
    does, 201n60; on international capital,
    116; on Japanese trade, 128; on "Mon-
    roesky Doctrine," 91; on services, 141
Eden, Anthony, 19, 60, 182n12
Edey, Malcolm, 205n27
Egypt, 63, 64–66
Eisenhower, Dwight D.: on Asia, 63;
    "Atoms for Peace," 61, 72; on collective
    security, 190n49; coups authorized by,
    190n45; EDC and, 60, 61, 76, 82, 165;
    European defense policy of, 40, 62, 165;
    SHAPE and, 57; Suez crisis and, 65–66,
    67, 69; UN and, 19, 68, 71, 76, 78; men-
    tioned, 158
Eisenhower administration: "collective secu-
    rity" discourse in, 22, 63; EDC and, 45,
    60; FDR and, 51; multilateral initiatives
    of, 46; Suez crisis and, 65, 66–67; UN
    security roles and, 64
Eliot, T. S., 168
El Salvador, 90, 95
England, *see* Britain
Esty, Daniel C., 213n23
Ethiopia, 16, 17–18
Eurocorps, 86, 87, 196n37
Eurodollar market, 114

Euroforce, 195n38
Europe: automotive exports of, 213n25; bal-
    ance of power in, 10- 11, 22, 25, 88–89,
    104, 182n21, 197n47; capital flow
    through, 131; colonialism of, 32,
    182n18; currency arrangement of,
    217n73; economic resurgence of, 114,
    119, 133; hypothetical German/Soviet
    integration of, 24; "invitational" U.S.
    involvement with, 47; Japanese trade
    imbalance and, 126; labor conditions in,
    144; "lift-and-strike" proposal and, 93;
    Monroe Doctrine on, 9; North Ameri-
    can relations with, 86; post-cold war
    security prospects for, 80, 82, 88; post-
    World War II stabilization of, 30; pro-
    posed NATO-Russian treaty and,
    197n45; reconstruction of, 15, 26, 59,
    85–86; social democracy in, 153; social
    market economy of, 138; unification of,
    1, 41, 58, 60–61, 86, 163; *see also* Cen-
    tral Europe; Eastern Europe; Western
    Europe
European Atomic Energy Community,
    61–62, 76, 82, 165
European Bank for Reconstruction and
    Development, 87
European Coal and Steel Community, 61
European Communities, 61
European Defense Community, 45, 59–61,
    76, 82, 165
European Economic Community (Common
    Market), 61, 81, 86, 111
European Monetary Union, 115
European Payments Union, 41
European Recovery Program, *see* Marshall
    Plan
European Union: capital flow through, 131,
    209n72; Central/Eastern Europe and,
    103; Croatia and, 196n41; ecodumping
    rules and, 142; former Soviet republics
    and, 84; German dominance and, 164;
    lobbying by, 145; monetary integration
    and, 117; multilateralism in, 48; NATO
    and, 86, 87, 88; North American trade
    with, 130; recent members of, 129; secu-
    rity role of, 171; Export-Import Bank of
    the United States, 65

Far East, *see* East Asia
Federal Republic of Germany, *see* West
    Germany

Federal Reserve Bank of New York, 217n72
Ferguson, Homer, 55
Financial Times, 135–36
Finland, 81, 129, 197n42
Fleming-Mundell thesis, 204n13
Fourteen Points (Woodrow Wilson), 11, 12, 13, 14, 181n73
Fox, William, 29
France: AFL and, 112; Bosnian crisis and, 100; Dunkirk Treaty and, 41–42; economic conditions in, 118; EDC and, 59, 60; EURATOM and, 61–62; Eurocorps and, 86, 87, 196n38; German relations with, 60, 61, 87; Indochina operations of, 46, 59, 63; Iraqi trade with, 74; Katanga secession and, 68; "lift-and-strike" proposal and, 93; NATO and, 87, 164, 194n17; 19th-century balance of power and, 88; nuclear capabilities of, 61, 62, 72, 73; Rhineland occupied by, 12; Security Council membership of, 32; Serbia and, 196–97n41; Suez crisis and, 64, 65, 66, 190n43, 191n51; UN peacekeeping and, 90–91, 98
French National Assembly on EDC, 60
French Revolution, 180n69
Friedman, Milton, 145
Friedman, Thomas, 115
Fromkin, David: on Eisenhower/Kennedy administrations, 62–63; on FDR foreign policy team, 182n22; on global economy, 48; on mid-20th century presidents, 5; on Nazi Germany, 51; on trade issue, 13; on TR imperialism, 9; on U.S. global role, 169
Fry, Michael, 65
Fuchs, Klaus, 71
Fulbright, J. William, 183n23

Gaddis, John Lewis, 31, 50
Garrett, Geoffrey, 150
Gaza, 64
Gelfand, Lawrence, 12
General Agreement on Tariffs and Trade, 37, 111; dispute settlement by, 132; environmental issues and, 142, 143; establishment of, 29; free-trade areas and, 131; intra-industry trade and, 127; ITO and, 38, 137; Japan and, 112, 129; Mexican tuna case and, 214–19n27; policy networks and, 145; regionalism/multilaterism tension and, 130; safeguards

of, 208n55; Section 301 on, 126; structural asymmetries and, 128; Western European bilateralism and, 41; WTO and, 21, 120; *see also* Kennedy Round (GATT); Tokyo Round (GATT); Uruguay Round (GATT)
General Agreement on Trade in Services, 140–42
Generalized System of Preferences Act, 144
Georgian Republic, 91
Gephardt, Richard, 142, 160, 207n48
Germany: Dunkirk Treaty and, 41; Eurocorps and, 195n38; exchange rate negotiations of, 205–6n32; French relations with, 60, 61, 87; French Security Council membership and, 32; global security role of, 91, 92; industrial apprenticeships in, 154; NATO expansion issue and, 84; nuclear weapons and, 220n27; occupation authorities in, 112; post-World War II stabilization and, 30; Russian relations with, 83; Security Council membership prospects of, 91, 92; Somali crisis and, 198–99n60; in 21st century, 163-64; Versailles Treaty on, 12; world economy and, 48; in World War I, 11, 178n25; Yugoslav crisis and, 196n41; *see also* Nazi Germany; West Germany
Goldstein, Judith, 121–22
Gorbachev, Mikhail, 27, 70, 89, 191n62
Gore, Al, 142, 143
Gowa, Joanne, 203n3
Graham, Thomas W., 192n72
Gramm, Phil, 7
Great Britain, *see* Britain
Great Depression: international prices and, 145; isolationism and, 16; labor market and, 148; postwar reconstruction and, 107; Reagan trade policy and, 122; U.S. response to, 145
Great Society programs, 115, 153
Greece: Acheson on, 39; Concert of Europe and, 197n49; leftist insurrection in, 55; NATO membership of, 56; Turkey vs., 68, 81, 84; U.S. aid to, 77
"Green 301" provision, 142
Green Party (Germany), 198–99n60
Greenspan, Alan, 115
Gromyko, Andrei, 71
Group-of-Seven summits, 205–6n32
Gruenther, Alfred, 60

Guatemala, 190n45
Gulf War, see Persian Gulf War

Haas, Ernst B., 68, 190n56
Haggard, Stephan, 37
Haiti, 7–8, 92
Hammarskjold, Dag, 67, 69
Harding, Warren G., 15
Harries, Owen, 194n15
Harris, Richard G., 150, 216n60
Havana trade negotiations, 36
Havel, Václav, 85
Hawaii, 9
Heisbourg, François, 86
Helsinki summit, 87
Hilderbrand, Robert C., 188n5
Hiroshima bombing (1945), 50, 71
Hispanic Americans, 168
Hitler, Adolf, 18, 51, 164
Hogan, Michael J., 59, 184n45
Holland, 54, 73, 172
Hollinger, David A., 167–68, 221n42
Holmes, John, 55
Holsti, Kalevi, 89
Hong Kong, 46
Hoover administration, 122
House, Edward, 11, 178n34
Howard, Michael, 44
Hudec, Robert, 128, 129
Hudson, G. F., 180
Hull, Cordell: bilateral trade agreements of,
    20; Clayton and, 35; Congressional
    Republicans and, 34; embargo proposal
    of, 18; Pasvolsky and, 32; Reciprocal
    Trade Agreement Act and, 37; retire-
    ment of, 184n43, 203–4n8; Vandenberg
    and, 53; Wilsonianism of, 182n22
Hungary, 66, 83, 84, 194nn25, 27, 213n16
Huntington, Samuel P., 163, 164, 219–
    20n16
Hviding, Ketil, 205n27

Ikenberry, G. John, 150
India, 68, 73, 208n63
Indochina, 46, 59, 63
Indonesia, 54, 152
Inter-American Treaty of Reciprocal Assis-
    tance (1947), 186nn66, 71
International Atomic Energy Agency, 72,
    73, 74, 75
International Labor Organization, 181n73
International Monetary Fund: Britain and,

65; "double screen" of, 37; exchange
    rates and, 116; in late 1950s, 111–12;
    lending capacity of, 77; liquidity sup-
    plied by, 115; planning for, 109–10; pol-
    icy coordination by, 117, 118; U.S. Trea-
    sury proposal to, 205–6n32; voting in,
    21; Western European bilateralism and,
    41
International Trade Commission (U.S.),
    152, 207n50, 216n77
International Trade Organization (pro-
    posed), 28, 38, 137, 211n4, 212n5
Iran, 39, 190n45, 192n76
Iraq, 74–75, 89–90, 157, 202n96
Islam, 163; see also Arab countries; Muslims
Isolationism: "City on the Hill model,"
    219n6; Clinton administration on, 8;
    Borah on, 159; components of, 15–18;
    electoral politics and, 166; entrench-
    ment of, 25; FDR rejection of, 19, 29;
    misrepresentation of, 14; persistence of,
    4, 158; post-FDR presidents and, 5;
    prospects for, 169; of Taft, 45; see also
    Neo-isolationism
Israel: Baghdad Pact and, 63; Beirut with-
    drawal of, 68; establishment of, 55; Suez
    crisis and, 64, 65, 66, 190n51
Italy: AFL and, 112; Ethiopia vs., 16, 17–18;
    Euroforce and, 195n38; IMF and, 118;
    Nuclear Suppliers Group and, 73;
    Somali crisis and, 96; Versailles Treaty
    and, 12; WEU and, 60

Jamaica Accords (1976), 108
James, Harold, 184n39
James, Marzenna, 184n39
Janow, Merit E., 211n94, 212n12
Japan: atomic bombing of, 50, 71; capital
    flow through, 131, 209n72; corporatist
    market economy of, 138, 139; currency
    of, 113, 116; economic resurgence of,
    48, 114, 119, 164; exchange rate negoti-
    ations of, 205–6n32; global security role
    of, 91, 92, 198–99n60; imperialist eco-
    nomic regime of, 35–36; labor policy in,
    154; Manchuria invaded by, 16; Nuclear
    Suppliers Group and, 73; occupation
    authorities in, 112; OECD and, 185n54;
    Pearl Harbor attacked by, 1, 17; Philip-
    pines freed from, 32; post-World War II
    reforms in, 46; "protectorate" status of,
    105, 172; reconstruction of, 1; Russian

Empire vs., 10; Security Council membership prospects of, 91, 92; trade of, 120, 124, 125, 126–29, 130, 133, 208n68; in 21st century, 163; Versailles Treaty and, 12

Japan-U.S. Structural Impediments Initiative, 128–29, 139, 212n12

Japanese Ministry of International Trade and Industry, 129

Javits, Jacob K., 46

Jebb, Gladwyn, 186n62

Jervis, Robert, 50, 88–89, 219–20n16

Johnson, Hiram W., 15, 34

Johnson, Samuel, 34

Johnson administration (LBJ), 115, 119

Joint Statement of Principles (U.K.-U.S.), 109

Jonas, Manfred, 15

Kaplan, Lawrence S., 186n63

Kashmir, 68

Katanga (Congo), 68

Katzenstein, Peter J., 207n41

Keating, Colin, 199n65

Kellogg-Briand Pact (1929), 17

Kelsen, Hans, 53

Kennan, George: *American Foreign Policy*, 47; on American idealism, 22, 23; on bipolarity, 39; on Dumbarton Oaks proposals, 34; on Eisenhower administration, 66–67; Lovett on, 187n61; on NATO, 43, 45; on trans-Atlantic security, 185n60; Western European bilateralism and, 42

Kennedy, John F., 154, 194n17

Kennedy administration, 62–63, 82, 119

Kennedy Round (GATT), 121

Keohane, Robert O., 8, 188n83

Kerry, John, 176n8

Keynes, John Maynard, 109, 110

Keynesianism, 118, 153, 155

Kimball, Warren F., 20, 182n21

Kindleberger, Charles, 156

Kissinger, Henry: on American idealism, 22, 23, 165; on European-American relations, 86; on NATO, 164; on 19th-century Europe, 88, 197n47; policies reconsidered by, 4, 6; realism of, 3; security vacuum argument of, 83, 84; on TR/Wilson administrations, 14, 178n31

Knock, Thomas J., 178n25, 178n35, 181n73

Kobrin, Stephen, 131, 215n47

Korea, 46, 47, 105; *see also* North Korea; South Korea

Korean War: ANZUS and, 56, 63; NATO command structure and, 44; UN role in, 50, 55–57, 94; U.S. policy and, 47

Krajina (Croatia), 100

Krauthammer, Charles, 162

Krugman, Paul, 209n68

Kugler, Richard L., 195n20

Ku Klux Klan, 15

Kuomintang, 46

Kurds, 202n96

Kuwait, 89

Labour Party (U.K.), 36

Ladd, Everett, 166–67

Lake, Anthony, 177n6

Langhorne, Richard, 182n21

Larabee, F. Stephen, 195n20

Lasswell, Harold, 221n33

Latin America: AFL and, 112; nuclear weapons ban in, 73; Rio Pact and, 187–88n66; trade in, 129; UN Charter Article 51 and, 186n62; *see also* Central America

Layne, Christopher, 162, 163

League of Nations: failure of, 29, 30; Italian-Ethiopian conflict and, 18; mandates of, 32; proposed U.S. membership in, 1, 12–13, 14–15, 178nn34, 35; Wilsonian vision for, 11- 12, 21, 79–80, 82; mentioned, 16

League of Nations Covenant: Borah and, 179n46; on disarmament, 70; drafting of, 26; Mayer on, 181n73; North Atlantic Treaty and, 44; Wilson on, 11–12

League of the Three Emperors, 20

League to Enforce Peace, 12

Lebanon, 68

Le Carré, John, 163

Leftism, 181n73; *see also* Communism

Lenin, Vladimir Ilich, 26

Lewis, Flora, 79

Limited Test-Ban Treaty (1963), 70

Lincoln, Edward, 127, 128

Lippmann, Walter, 34

List, Friedrich, 164

Little, Richard, 202n97

Lodge, Henry Cabot: interwar unilateralism and, 16; Knock on, 178n35; on League covenant, 44; "reservations" of, 14; unilateralism of, 15, 22

London Foreign Ministers Conference (1947), 41
Lovett, Robert, 43, 186n61
Lucas, Robert, 155–56
Lundestad, Geir, 47
Luxembourg, 196n38

Maastricht Treaty (1991), 86
MacArthur, Douglas, 46, 50, 57
Macmillan, Harold, 62, 65
Maier, Charles, 107
Maistre, Joseph de, 180n69
Mallinson, Allan, 201n90
Manchuria, 16
Mansfield, Edward D., 207n41
Mao Zedong, 63
Marine Mammal Protection Act, 214n27
Marshall Plan, 1, 29, 165; dual role of, 45; ethnic politics and, 26; NATO and, 59, 85–86; OEEC and, 41, 213n16; Truman on, 44; Wilsonianism and, 19
Marshall, George C., 39
May, Ernest R., 187n71
Mayer, Arno J., 181n73
McCracken, Paul, 148
McCulloch, Rachel, 114, 117
McKinley administration, 10, 22, 35, 47
McKinley, William, 9, 15
McNamara, Robert, 62
Mearsheimer, John J., 164, 226n27
Mediterranean region, 39
Meltzer, Allan H., 117, 205n27
Menon, Krishna, 57
Mercosur, 129
Metternichian coalitions, 20
Mexico: domestic instability in, 118; NAFTA and, 2, 129, 142, 144, 214n27; OECD and, 213n16; tuna-dolphin case and, 143, 214n27
Miami Summit of the Americas (1994), 129
Middle East, 61, 66, 68, 69; see also Arab countries
Military Staff Committee (UN), see United Nations Military Staff Committee
Mitterand, François, 196–97n38
Mobutu Sese Seko, 191n55
Mogadishu (Somalia), 93, 96, 97, 177n5
Mohammed Farah Aidid, 96, 177n5
Moldova, 84
Molotov, Vyacheslav, 30
Monroe Doctrine, 9, 42, 45
Morgenthau, Hans J., 34, 67, 104, 202n97

Morillon, Philippe, 98
Moynihan, Daniel Patrick, 69
Mozambique, 90, 91, 198–99n60
Mueller, John, 193n3
Mullins, A. F., 192n72
Multiculturalism, 25, 26, 167–69; and English language, 168
Multifibre Arrangement, 124
Multilateralism, 4–5, 6, 18–27, 158; Asian security and, 46–47, 63, 107–34; of Clinton administration, 2; "diffuse reciprocity" in, 48; economic dimensions of, 35–38, 40–41, 45–46, 107–56, 160–61, 172–73; "inclusive integrity" in, 49; international organizations and, 172; limited options of, 63–64; McKinley open door policy and, 47; milieu goals and, 173; NATO and, 43, 44, 59, 60, 62, 63, 76; post-FDR presidents and, 51; realist opposition to, 34, 40; Republican support for, 28; unilateralism vs., 8; U.S. national identity and, 169, 170; West European security and, 42, 45; Wilsonianism and, 29–30
Mundell, Robert, 204n13
Muslims, 93, 201n92; see also Islam
Mussolini, Benito, 18

Nagasaki bombing (1945), 50, 71
Nagorno-Karabakh, 91
Namibia, 90, 91, 95
Napoleonic wars, 88, 182n21
Nasser, Gamal Abdel, 64, 190n45
National Association of Manufacturers, 216n54
Nationalist Chinese, 46
National Origins Act (1924), 17
Nazi Germany: economic order of, 20, 23, 35, 36, 183n36; empowerment of, 51; hypothetical victory of, 23, 24; Rhineland reoccupied by, 16; USSR vs., 52
Near East, see Middle East
Neo-isolationism, 3, 158–61
Netherlands, 54, 73, 172
Netherlands East Indies, 54
New Deal: free trade issue and, 37, 107, 203n8; international initiatives and, 24; labor market policies and, 154; post-cold war alternatives to, 136, 153; social protections of, 29, 155
New International Economic Order, 69

New International Information Order, 69
New York Federal Reserve Bank, 222n72
New Zealand, 56, 63
Nicaragua, 90
Nicolaidis, Kalypso, 140, 141
Niebuhr, Reinhold, 34
Niskanen, William, 122, 123
Nixon, Richard, 148, 203n4
Nogee, Joseph, 165
Nordic countries, 81, 172
Nordlinger, Eric A., 219n6
North Africa, 64
North America, 81, 86, 130, 131, 219n6
North American Free Trade Agreement:
    Bush negotiations for, 2; Chile and, 129;
    The Economist on, 135; environmental
    issues and, 142; labor issues and, 142,
    143–44, 148; tuna-dolphin case and,
    214n27
North Atlantic Council, 58, 60, 87
North Atlantic Treaty, 42, 44, 45, 186n66,
    186nn69, 71, 73
North Atlantic Treaty Organization
    (NATO): Asian defense contrasted
    with, 46, 47; Bosnian air strikes by, 93,
    96, 98, 100, 102; Bosnian crisis and, 90,
    91, 93, 97, 201n92; collective basis of,
    27; Council of Ministers, 58; Cyprus cri-
    sis and, 68; early strategy of, 59; Eisen-
    hower administration and, 63; establish-
    ment of, 19; ethnic politics and, 26;
    founding members of, 56, 81; France
    and, 87, 164, 194n17; military reorgani-
    zation of, 57; multilateralism in, 43–45,
    76, 187n71; post-cold war prospects for,
    48, 78, 79, 82–88, 106, 172; proposed
    Russian treaty with, 197n45; structure
    of, 21, 195–96n32; Suez crisis and, 66;
    UN charter and, 55, 186n62; U.S.
    nuclear capability and, 58, 62; WEU
    and, 60, 86–87, 88, 171, 196nn39,
    197n42; Wilsonianism and, 19; men-
    tioned, 1, 29, 165
—Combined Joint Task Forces, 87
—Partnership for Peace, 2, 88, 171, 194–
    95n19
North China, 16
Northern Iraq, 202n96
North Korea, 55, 57, 74
North-South relations, 69, 70, 144
Norway, 81, 143
Nuclear Nonproliferation Act (1978), 73

Nuclear Nonproliferation Treaty (1968), 70,
    72–73, 75
Nuclear Suppliers Group, 73

Omnibus Trade and Competitiveness Act
    (1988), 123
One World (Willkie), 28
Operation Desert Storm, 56, 90, 94, 157
Operation Provide Comfort, 202n96
Organization for Economic Cooperation
    and Development: economic openness
    in, 121; financial volatility in, 205n27;
    globalization and, 149, 150, 154; IMF
    and, 118; Japan and, 185n54; on ser-
    vices, 140; social expenditures in,
    218n91; trade-GDP ratio in, 146; U.S.
    and, 206n35; WTO and, 213n16
Organization for European Economic Coop-
    eration, 41, 61, 185n54, 213n16
Organization for Security and Cooperation
    in Europe, 84, 87–88, 91, 171
Organization of American States, 186n66
Osgood, Robert, 58, 60
Ostry, Sylvia, 138
Ottoman Empire, 197n49; *see also* Turkey

Pacific region, 32, 79, 131, 208n61; *see also*
    East Asia
Pakistan, 68, 96
Palestine Liberation Organization, 68
Palestine mandate, 55
Palestine Truce Supervisory Organization
    (UN), 68
Panama, 9
Paraguay, 129
Paris Peace Conference (1919–1920), 12,
    26; *see also* Versailles Treaty (1919)
Partnership for Peace (NATO), 2, 88, 171,
    197n19
Pasvolsky, Leo, 32
Pauly, Louis, 127
Pearl Harbor attack (1941), 1, 17
Pearson, Lester B., 67, 190n46
Perot, Ross, 3, 155, 161
Pershing II missiles, 58
Persian Gulf, 198–99n60
Persian Gulf War: Bush role in, 2; Iraqi
    nuclear program and, 75; Kurds and,
    202n96; Soviet-U.S. relations and,
    89–90; UN role in, 94; *see also* Opera-
    tion Desert Storm
Philippines, 9, 32

Pleven plan, 59
Poland, 83, 84, 195n25, 213n16
Polanyi, Karl, 108
Pollard, Robert A., 41
Portugal, 196n38
Potsdam Conference (1945), 71
Powell, Colin L., 96, 160, 200n80
Progressive Party, 182n22
Proposition 187 (Calif.), 3
Prussia, 88

Quantum Fund, 217n73
Quick Reaction Force (U.S.), 96

Rapid Reaction Force (UN), 91, 100
Reagan, Ronald, 4
Reagan administration, 70, 122–23, 132,
    154
Reciprocal Trade Agreement Act (1934),
    37
Reich, Robert, 152, 155
Reich, Simon, 127
Republican Party: "Contract with America,"
    7, 8, 159, 183n30; FDR courting of, 29;
    free-trade issue and, 133; Hull role for,
    34; on hybrid economic regimes, 37;
    interwar isolationism and, 15; League of
    Nations membership issue and, 13, 14,
    178n35; multilateralism and, 28; "new
    isolationism" and, 3, 7; in 1942 elec-
    tions, 183n25; small-business attitudes
    in, 221n35; on Somali operation, 177n5;
    Southern vote and, 166; Clinton for-
    eign-policy "subcontracting" charges by,
    22, 93; UN and, 19, 175–76n6; Vanden-
    berg Resolution and, 42; War Depart-
    ment and, 182n22; War Powers Act and,
    219n8
Rhineland, 12, 16
Richards, James, 189n25
Rieff, David, 25
Rio Pact (1947), 185n66, 187n71
Romania, 83
Roosa, Robert, 116
Roosevelt, Franklin D., 158, 165; foreign
    policy team of, 182n22; "four police-
    men" scheme and, 19, 24, 30, 82; fourth
    nomination of, 28; liberal internation-
    ists and, 183n25; multilateralism of, 20,
    25, 27, 51, 57, 75–76; on Pearl Harbor
    attack, 1, 17; on perfectionism, 34, 173;
    post-cold war environment and, 88;

Reciprocal Trade Agreement Act and,
    37; TR-Wilson conflict and, 18–19, 33;
    UN forces "joint action" preference of,
    52; UN Security Council enlarged by,
    32; Wilson and, 24–25, 27, 29, 30, 33,
    38
Roosevelt, Theodore: FDR War Department
    and, 182n22; on international interde-
    pendence, 9; interwar unilateralism and,
    16; isolationist heirs of, 15; league pro-
    posal of, 10, 33; Lodge and, 15; wins
    Nobel Peace Prize, 10, 190n46; public
    influence of, 4, 24–25; realism of, 3;
    Wilson vs., 10, 12, 13–14, 19; men-
    tioned, 22
Roosevelt administration (FDR): atomic
    energy and, 71; hybrid economic regimes
    and, 37; international conferences con-
    vened by, 28; Italian-Ethiopian conflict
    and, 17–18; multilateral initiatives of,
    38; peace plans of, 34; see also New Deal
Rooseveltian UN concept, 30, 31, 32–33,
    51; Bosnian crisis and, 93; Bretton
    Woods agreement and, 37; cold war and,
    78; concert of power arrangements and,
    89; NPT and, 73; three-tiered version of,
    182n12; Wilsonian collective security
    and, 80
Rose, Michael, 99
Rosenberg, Emily, 40
Rough Riders, 182n22
Ruehe, Volker, 198n60
Ruggie, John Gerard, 179n 51, 184n45,
    198n59, 199–200n70, 201n93, 203n6
Ruggie, Mary, 153–54
Russian Empire, 88
Russian Federation: domestic instability in,
    105; future of, 103, 163; Georgian opera-
    tion of, 91, 92; militarism in, 199n61;
    NATO and, 88, 195n20, 195n30,
    197n45; "near abroad" of, 91; OECD
    and, 213n16; OSCE and, 87; Serbian
    relations with, 90, 198n57; threat posed
    by, 6, 83–84, 85; U.S. aid to, 77; WEU
    and, 196n39
Russian Revolution (1917), 181n73
Russo-Japanese War, 10
Rwanda, 91, 92, 97
Ryan, Michael P., 208n61

Salter, Arthur, 21
Salvador, see El Salvador

Sanger, David E., 221n35
Sarajevo (Bosnia-Herzegovina), 99, 200n80
Schacht, Hjalmar, 20
Scharping, Rudolf, 198n60
Schuman, Robert, 61
Section 301 (U.S. trade code), 125–26, 129, 208n61
Serbs: Clinton proposal on, 93; French relations with, 196n41; JNA and, 97; in Krajina, 100; peace accord with, 200n92; Russian relations with, 90, 198n57; Sarajevo shelled by, 200n80; UN troops vs., 98
Shalikashvili, John, 202n96
Sinai (Egypt), 65
Singapore, 147, 152
Slovakia, 213n16, 195n27; see also Czechoslovakia
Slovenia, 196n41
Smith, Tony, 34, 48, 183n18
Smoot-Hawley Tariff Act (1930), 17, 35, 122, 161
Social Democratic Party (Germany), 198n60
Somalia, 2; German intervention in, 198n60; UN intervention in, 78, 90, 91, 92, 95, 102; U.S. intervention in, 96–97, 102, 177n5
Soros, George, 151, 217n73
South Africa, 73, 74, 90
South Asia, 135
Southeast Asia Collective Defense Treaty, 63
Southeast Asia Treaty Organization, 63
Southern U.S., 166, 167
South Korea, 1, 55, 142, 147
South-North relations, 69, 70, 144
Soviet Union:
—alleged U.S. similarity to, 47
—Bretton Woods conference and, 29, 36, 183n39
—Chinese Security Council membership and, 32
—collapse of, 8, 157, 163, 220n27
—containment of, 5–6, 22, 31, 40, 48
—Dumbarton Oaks Conference and, 188n5
—Eastern European relations with, 48
—Finnish relations with, 81
—former states of, 2, 77, 84, 91, 194n19; see also Russian Federation
—GATT and, 137
—hypothetical global dominance of, 23, 24
—ITO Charter and, 212n5
—Katanga secession and, 68
—League of Nations and, 12, 26
—Marshall Plan and, 213n16
—NATO and, 58
—nuclear capabilities of, 57, 72, 192n65
—Nuclear Suppliers Group and, 73
—post-World War II multilateralism and, 29, 45–46
—Suez crisis and, 64, 65, 66
—threat posed by: to Eastern Mediterranean, 39; passing of, 4, 158, 162, 169, 173; Truman and, 2, 19; U.S. unawareness of, 38; to Western Europe (see Soviet Union: Western European vulnerability to)
—UN and: air force issue and, 52; Chinese representation issue and, 56; Gorbachev and, 89, 191n62; Security Council membership and, 51; veto power in, 21, 43, 44, 55, 57
—U.S. relations with, 161; atomic weapons and, 71–72; China and, 165; FDR objectives for, 30, 31, 38; ideological aspects of, 26–27; Morgenthau on, 104, 202n97; Persian Gulf crisis and, 89–90; post-cold war adaption of, 78; UN and, 54, 56, 57, 69, 70
—Western European vulnerability to: cheson on, 39; East Asian security and, 46, 105; economic aspects of, 41, 48; Eisenhower and, 40, 62; proposed Canadian-U.S. agreement and, 185n60; SHAPE and, 57; Truman and, 19, 40, 42; U.S. and, 27, 58; West Germany and, 43, 59, 60
Spaak, Paul-Henri, 42
Spain, 86, 196n38
Spanish-American War, 9
Spanish Civil War, 18
Srebenica (Bosnia), 98
Stairs, Denis, 55
Stalin, Joseph: Bretton Woods conference and, 36, 184n39; European council proposed by, 30; on France, 32; relations with Churchill and FDR, 29; Truman and, 71; UN vision of, 31
Steinbruner, John, 62
Stern, Paula, 207n50
Stettinius, Edward, 33
Stockholm Agreement (1986), 104
Strange, Susan, 113
Strauss, Franz-Josef, 62

Strong, Tracy, 25
Structural Impediments Initiative (U.S.-Japan), 128–29, 139, 212n12
Sudetenland, 16
Suez crisis (1956), 61, 64–66, 67, 69, 94
Summit of the Americas (1994), 129
Super 301 (U.S. trade code), 125, 126, 128, 129, 207n48
Supreme Headquarters Allied Powers Europe, 57
Sweden, 73, 81, 129, 197n42
Switzerland, 73, 81
Syria, 68

Taft, Robert A., 45, 56, 188n15
Taft, William Howard, 12
Taiwan, 105, 198n56
Tajikistan, 91
Tarnoff, Peter, 157, 219n2
Taussig, Frank, 13
Thatcher, Margaret, 200n80
Tibet, 198n56
Tlatelolco Treaty (1967), 73
Tocqueville, Alexis de, 168
Tokyo Round (GATT), 122, 132, 140
Tornado squadrons, 91, 198–99n60
Tory Party (U.K.), 36
Trask, Roger R., 186n66
Treaty of Maastricht (1991), 86
Treaty of Versailles, see Versailles Treaty (1919)
Treaty on the Prohibition of Nuclear Weapons in Latin America (1967), 73
Triffin, Robert, 108, 204n18
Truman, Harry S, 158, 165; Brussels Pact and, 42; European defense policy of, 40, 76, 82; farewell address of, 2, 28; FDR and, 39, 40, 51; MacArthur and, 57; on North Atlantic Treaty, 44; postwar plans of, 1; Stalin and, 71; Wilsonianism and, 19
Truman administration: atomic control issue and, 71; FDR and, 51; Kuomintang and, 46; multilateral European defense and, 45; UN permanent-member veto issue and, 43, 55; Vandenberg Resolution and, 42
Truman Doctrine, 1, 29, 39, 40, 55; financial aspects of, 77; "la grande peur" and, 42; Newsweek on, 27
Turkey, 56, 68, 77, 81, 84; see also Ottoman Empire

Ukraine, 83, 84, 195n30, 220n27
Underwood-Simmons bill (1913), 13
Unilateralism: aggressive, 125–29; Brussels treaty and, 42, 43; commercial, 13, 139; isolationism and, 5, 8, 14, 15, 16; Italo-Ethiopian conflict and, 18; multiple conflicts and, 170–71; possible recrudescence of, 6; Republican manifestations of, 159; in Somali conflict, 93; vital-interest test and, 159, 160
Union of Soviet Socialist Republics, see Soviet Union
United Kingdom, see Britain
United Nations: Baruch Plan and, 191n65; Clinton administration and, 22, 78, 93; concert-based role for, 89–93; Dutch-Indonesian conflict and, 54; early plans for, 1, 19; Eisenhower administration and, 64, 76, 78; Gulf War and, 2, 75; Korean War and, 50, 55–57; NATO and, 43, 201n92; OSCE and, 87; post-cold war prospects for, 172; recent U.S. attitudes towards, 3; Serbian-Russian relations and, 198n57; Truman and, 39; unrealized potential of, 79; "wider peacekeeping" and, 201n86, 201n91; see also Rooseveltian UN concept
United Nations Atomic Energy Commission, 71
United Nations Charter: Article 43: 52, 54, 56; Article 45: 52; Article 47: 52; Article 51: 42, 43–44, 55, 186n62; Article 106: 31; on disarmament, 70, 71; on dispute resolution, 32; drafting of, 19, 28, 29; on enforcement, 52, 54, 96, 101; fiftieth anniversary of, 175n6; Gorbachev on, 89; multilateralism and, 45; peacekeeping and, 67, 94; proposed amendments to, 43, 55; on regional arrangements, 87; U.S. Senate and, 10, 33–34, 53, 183n23
United Nations Conference on Trade and Development, 120
United Nations Economic and Social Council, 32
United Nations Educational, Scientific and Cultural Organization, 69
United Nations Emergency Force, 66, 67
United Nations General Assembly: arms control and, 70–71, 191n62; Eisenhower's "Atoms for Peace" address to, 72; Korean War and, 56, 57; Suez crisis

and, 65; "Zionism is racism" resolution
of, 69
United Nations General Assembly Committee on Disarmament, 70
United Nations Military Staff Committee:
arms regulation and, 70; early plans of,
31, 54; establishment of, 52–53; inactiv-
ity of, 56; inadequacies of, 102; responsibilities of, 101
United Nations Monetary and Financial
Conference, see Bretton Woods Confer-
ence (1944)
United Nations Palestine Truce Supervisory
Organization, 68
United Nations Participation Act (1945),
53, 183n30
United Nations Peacekeeping Forces, 67; in
cold war era, 68–70; in Haiti, 7–8; high-
level meeting in post-cold war era, 78,
90–103, 172, 196–97n41, 199–200n70;
Republican opposition to, 7, 159; U.S.
Congressional opposition to, 172; U.S.
Special Operations Command and,
177n5
United Nations Rapid Reaction Force, 91,
100
United Nations Secretary General, 101, 102
United Nations Security Council: additions
to, 32, 91, 92; arms regulation and, 70;
Bosnian crisis and, 98; China and, 56,
90, 198n56; enforcement powers of, 52;
FDR conception of, 89; "four policemen" concept and, 30; heads of state
meeting of, 95; integrating role of, 31;
Iraqi nuclear program and, 75; major
developing countries and, 172; Military
Staff Committee and, 53, 54, 101–2;
proliferating decisions of, 199n66; proposed subsidiary of, 103, 199n64; Resolution 678: 94; Somali crisis and, 96;
Soviet membership in, 51; Suez crisis
and, 65; UN Participation Act on, 53;
veto power in, 21, 31, 55, 57, 69, 71,
186n62
United States Army, 200n81
United States Army Rangers, 93, 96, 97,
176n5
United States Atomic Energy Commission,
61
United States-British Combined Chiefs of
Staff, 52
United States Central Intelligence Agency,

64, 190n45, 191n55; see also United
States Office of Strategic Services
United States Commerce Department,
149–50, 207n50
United States Congress: Boggs-Fulbright
resolutions and, 41; EDC and, 60; hedge
fund hearings of, 151; isolationist legislation of, 17; Japanese MITI and, 129;
McKinley policy and, 47; NAFTA and,
142; NATO and, 59; 1944 elections and,
33–34; on peacekeeping operations, 7,
172, 176n7; post-World War II stabilization and, 30; Reciprocal Trade Agreement Act and, 37; Republican control
of, 3, 219n8; Security Council veto issue
and, 43, 55; Southern Democrats in,
166; trade policy and, 13, 122, 123, 125,
128, 132, 133; in TR era, 9; UN financing and, 93, 172, 176n7; war powers of,
53; Western European bilateralism and,
42; World War I and, 11
—House, 77, 133, 159, 183n25, 221n35
—House Budget Committee, 7
—Joint Committee on Atomic Energy, 62
—Senate: IAEA and, 74; ITO and, 38, 137;
Kellogg-Briand Pact and, 17; League of
Nations membership issue and, 1, 13,
14–15, 178nn34, 35; North Atlantic
Treaty and, 45; "Peace without Victory"
address to, 11, 26, 27, 79; in Reagan era,
123; State Department retrenchment
and, 176n8; UN Charter and, 28, 33–34,
53, 183n23; Vandenberg Resolution
and, 42
—Senate Foreign Relations Committee, 19,
34, 53
United States Constitution and UN forces,
53
United States Defense Department, 59, 162;
see also United States War Department
United States Export-Import Bank, 65
United States Institute of Peace, 157
United States International Trade Commis-
sion, 152, 207n50, 217n77
United States-Japan Structural Impedi-
ments Initiative, 128–29, 139, 212n12
United States Joint Chiefs of Staff, 60, 97
United States Department of Labor, 148
United States Marines, 68
United States Mutual Security Program,
189n25
United States Office of Strategic Services,

United States Office...(*Continued*)
182n22; *see also* United States Central
Intelligence Agency
United States Quick Reaction Force, 96
United States Special Operations Command, 177n5
United States State Department: budget for,
176n8; Korean War and, 57; retrenchments by, 3; trade proposals of, 203–4n8;
on UN charter, 55; UN origins and, 1,
30, 32, 33; Vandenberg Resolution and,
43; Western European bilateralism and,
42; Wilsonian Democrats in, 182n22
United States Tariff Commission, 13
United States Treasury, 1, 146, 203–4n8,
205–6n32
United States War Department, 182n22; *see
also* United States Defense Department
Urquhart, Brian, 67
Uruguay, 129
Uruguay Round (GATT), 125; Brazilian-
Indian positions in, 208n63; Bush
administration and, 2; disciplinary provisions of, 123; nontariff barrier provisions of, 132; signing of, 142; traded services issue and, 140; U.S. Congress and,
122; VERs and, 124; WTO and, 120

Vandenberg, Arthur H.: Kaplan on, 186n63;
NATO and, 19; Truman and, 39–40;
UN charter and, 19, 43–44, 186n62; on
presidential war powers, 53
Vandenberg Resolution (1948), 42, 43
Versailles Treaty (1919), 12–13; *see also*
Paris Peace Conference (1919–1920)
Vietnam, 47
Vietnam War: "all-or-nothing" doctrine
and, 97; expenditures for, 115; termination of, 165; UN and, 69; War Powers
Act and, 8, 159
Viner, Jacob, 37
Vukovar (Croatia), 97

Wallace, George, 166, 221n34
Wallace, Henry A., 182n22
Waltz, Kenneth N., 202n98; on future multipolarity, 163; on NATO, 164; on
nuclear weapons, 220n26; on world
powers, 23, 214n34
War Powers Act (1973), 8, 159, 219n8
Warsaw Pact, 48
Washington, George, 9

Webb, Michael C., 206n35
Weber, Max, 23, 27
Weber, Steve, 62
Welles, Sumner, 183n22
Western countries: as artificial construct,
194n15; Asian interventions of, 63;
Bosnian crisis and, 97, 200n80; economic compromises of, 108; formerly
communist countries and, 85; Iraqi trade
with, 74; Islam and, 163; post-cold war
NATO and, 82, 83; Russian relations
with, 91, 103; south Asian competition
with, 135; UN peacekeeping and, 70;
unraveling domestic-foreign pact and,
136
Western Europe: commercial concessions
to, 111, 112, 184n48; Communist parties in, 39; U.S. "economic security" policy for, 85; European unification and, 86;
exchange fluctuations and, 115; labor
conditions in, 148; Polish independence
and, 84; post-World War II economic
conditions in, 40–41; regional multilateralism in, 45; Section 301 and, 125; as
security community, 64, 78, 81, 82, 103;
Soviet threat to (*see* Soviet Union:
Western European vulnerability to); UN
Charter Article 51 and, 186n62; welfarism in, 154
Western European Union: NATO and, 60,
86–87, 88, 171, 196n39, 197n42; origins
of, 60, 196n37
Western Sahara, 90
Western Union, 60
West Germany: EURATOM and, 62;
exchange rates of, 113; French reconciliation with, 60, 61; Iraqi trade with, 74;
non-nuclear status of, 72; Nuclear Suppliers Group and, 73; nuclear technology and, 73; rearming of, 59, 196n37;
West European fear of, 43
White, Harry Dexter, 37, 109, 110
White, Theodore H., 50
Whitten, Jamie L., 77
Widenor, William, 31
Wilcox, Clair, 130
Willkie, Wendell, 28
Wilson, Pete, 175–76n6
Wilson, Woodrow: on alliances, 181n76;
Ambrosius on, 178n34; conservative
internationalists and, 178n25; on European War, 10–11; FDR and, 24–25, 27,

29, 30, 33, 38; foreign interventions by, 4; Fourteen Points, 11, 12, 13, 14, 180n73; Knock on, 178n35; mid-20th century presidents and, 5, 19; motivation of, 82; multilateralism of, 21, 25; North Atlantic Treaty and, 44; pacifist isolationists and, 15; "Peace without Victory," 11, 26, 27, 79; realist disdain for, 34, 80; TR vs., 10, 12, 13–14, 19

Wilsonianism: failure of, 22; in FDR State Department, 182n22; of Gorbachev, 27; of late 20th-century presidents, 2; post-cold war cooperative security and, 80, 105; post-World War II multilateralism and, 29–30, 40, 49; realist criticism of, 183n33

Wolf, Martin, 206n36

Wolfers, Arnold, 44, 67, 187n71, 190n51

Wolfowitz, Paul, 162

Wood, Adrian, 216n60

Woods, Randall Bennett, 182n23

World Bank, 21, 203–7n6, 204–5n32

World Court, 32

World League for the Peace of Righteousness (proposed), 10

World Trade Organization: dispute-settlement procedures in, 123, 126, 132; environmental issues and, 142, 143; GATT and, 21, 120; Japanese-U.S. trade and, 125; OECD and, 213n16; policy networks and, 145; structural asymmetries and, 128; traded services and, 140; U.S. support for, 2, 172; VERs and, 124

World War I, 10–11, 34, 49, 82

World War II: atomic bombing in, 50; economic aspects of, 107, 153; hypothetical victors of, 23; opinion polls in, 33; origins of, 30; Soviet losses in, 52; victors of, 91–92

Yugoslav Army, 97

Yugoslavia, 55

Yugoslav successor states, 91, 95, 97, 196–97n41, 199n66; see also Bosnia; Croatia; Serbs

Zaire, 91, 191n55, 198–99n60; see also Belgian Congo

Zimmermann, Warren, 97

Zionism, 69